W q Hachten

**National Sovereignty and
International Communication**

COMMUNICATION AND INFORMATION SCIENCE

A series of monographs, treatises, and texts

Edited by
MELVIN J. VOIGT
University of California, San Diego

In preparation

VINCENT MOSCO ● Broadcasting in the United States: Innovative Challenge and Organizational Control

RHONDA J. CRANE ● International Communication Standards and National Politics

STACEY B. DAY ● Communication in Health Care Delivery

MICHEL GUITÉ ● Telecommunications Policy: The Canadian Model

JOHN S. LAWRENCE AND BERNARD M. TIMBERG ● Copyright Law, Fair Use, and the New Media

ROBERT G. MEADOW ● Politics as Communication

ITHIEL DE SOLA POOL ● Retrospective Technology Assessment of the Telephone

CLAIRE K. SCHULTZ ● Computer History and Information Access

National Sovereignty and International Communication

Edited by

Kaarle Nordenstreng
University of Tampere

and

Herbert I. Schiller
University of California, San Diego

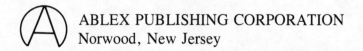

ABLEX PUBLISHING CORPORATION
Norwood, New Jersey

Ablex Publishing Corporation
355 Chestnut Street
Norwood, New Jersey 07648

Library of Congress Cataloging in Publication Data

Main entry under title:

National sovereignty and international communication.

  Includes bibliographies and index.
  1. International broadcasting—Addresses,
essays, lectures. 2. Sovereignty—Addresses,
essays, lectures. 3. Mass media—Addresses,
essays, lectures. I. Nordenstreng, Kaarle.
II. Schiller, Herbert I., 1919-
HE8689.6.N37   301.16′1   78-16046
ISBN 0-89391-008-2

Printed in the United States of America

About the Editors

Kaarle Nordenstreng is Professor of Communications and Chair, Department of Journalism and Mass Communication, University of Tampere. Formerly, he was head of research for the Finnish Broadcasting System (YLE). He is Vice-President of the International Association for Mass Communication Research and President of the International Organization of Journalists (IOJ). He received his Ph.D. in Psychology from the University of Helsinki. His many articles and books include: *Informational Mass Communication* (Editor); and *Television Traffic—A One-Way Street?* (co-author).

Herbert I. Schiller is Professor of Communications at the University of California, San Diego. He is Vice-President of the International Association for Mass Communication Research. He received his undergraduate degree from C.C.N.Y., his Master's degree from Columbia University, and his Ph.D. from New York University. Prior to his present appointment, he was Professor of Economics and Communications at the University of Illinois. Preceding that he was Chair, Department of Social Studies, The Pratt Institute, Brooklyn. He is the author of many articles and books, including: *Mass Communications and American Empire; The Mind Managers; Communication and Cultural Domination;* and *Superstate: Readings in the Military-Industrial Complex* (co-editor).

Contents

Preface

It has been only in the last generation that almost one hundred nations have emerged out of the detritus of Western colonialism. This constitutes roughtly a trebling of the number of countries that participated in the founding of the United Nations in 1945. Though many of these new states were the beneficiaries of "negotiated" independence, a good number fought bitterly and tenaciously for their political freedom.

Yet while new flags and frontiers have proliferated in the last thirty years, less visible but powerful forces have been trespassing over national boundaries on an unprecedented scale. The central organizer of this border-crossing has been the business system, operating globally. In doing so it has relied more on investment flows than armed forces to achieve its ends, although it has not dispensed, by any means, with the instruments of force and violence.

The world business system today is centered on the American economy. It ties together in a loosely constituted core (however divided by contradictions) the market economies of Western Europe, Japan, Canada, and a few other industrial complexes as well. The unit of decision-making that organizes a large part of the flows of capital, goods, technology, managers, workers, and information is the transnational (sometimes called multinational) corporation (TNC)—the privately-owned company with facilities and operations in more than one country.

Most of the TNCs are only indirectly related to the mass media, but still they have a decisive role in determining—largely through advertising—the content of media flows and, consequently, the social consciousness prevailing in society, propagating the system's values and reinforcing its authority as the ultimate definer of issues. There are also TNCs operating directly in the field of (mass) communications and making an important contribution to the revenues and profits of the TNCs. (See Guback and Varis, 1978.) The president of the American Motion Picture Export Association. the U.S. film cartel, offered this information:

> American motion pictures occupy perhaps half of the screen time of theaters of the world. . . Nearly half the theatrical revenues of MPEAA members is derived from foreign showings. . . In 1976, the gross foreign billings of our members from theatrical films and televis.on programming came to approximately $700,000,000, with theatrical movies accounting for a little more than two-thirds. The foreign theatrical market represented 49.5 percent of total film rental grosses. For television the foreign market accounted for 23.4 percent of grosses.*

While the system administered by the TNCs and supported by the power of the State—for the most part, but not exclusively, the U.S. Government—continues to integrate a good part of the world to its needs and designs, it does not have the globe entirely at its disposal. A socialist sector, that originated with the outcome of the Russian Revolution sixty years ago, has continued its growth throughout the twentieth century. It has broken the centuries-old market model of development and held out the prospect for alternate forms of social organization. Perhaps equally important, it has provided assistance to nations and people seeking socioeconomic arrangements different from those prevailing in the still dominant world capitalist order.

The experiences of some socialist states have been particularly instructive to those who presently contest the authority of the dominant system and who seek new courses for their social development. For example, the American-imposed isolation of China for twenty years after the Chinese Revolution, and the U.S. blockade of Cuba after its political transformation, reveal sharply the benefits as well as the disadvantages of (enforced) isolation from the dominant world system. Indicative is the view of a former head of the United States Information Service concerning the possible lifting of the U.S. blockade against Cuba:

> . . . if I were Castro, I would lie back laughing about how years of enforced isolation from the United States and most of Latin America had enabled me to brainwash a whole generation of Cubans. . . To invite insiders in, especially American diplomats and tourists, carries for Castro the grave risk of inviting in assassins, subversives, every enemy of "the revolution" that is imaginable. . . . (Rowan, 1977)

The author, considering his vantage point, should know something about the "risks" he prophesizes will accompany increased United States intercourse with Cuba. But perhaps Canadians are better qualified to speak about the effects of American media exposure. They are in the "front lines" so to speak, hourly and daily. It is reported that in some of the major Canadian cities the people view American TV programming far more heavily than Cana-

---

*Statement of Jack Valenti, President, Motion Picture Export Association of America, before the Subcommittee on Government Operations, U.S. Senate Foreign Relations Committee. *Congressional Record,* 95th Congress, First Session, Vol. 123, No. 103, June 15th, 1977.

dian. In Vancouver, for example, "only about 20 percent of the total programming available is Canadian." In Calgary the figure is less than 23 percent, and in prime time, between 8:00 and 11:00 P.M., the proportion is "as low as 12 percent." In Ottawa, the capital of Canada, "the proportion of Canadian programming available reaches 35 percent." These grim figures make the president of the Canadian Broadcasting Corporation describe Canada's "American media connection" as the "relentless American cultural penetration"; the "American electronic rape of Canada"; "U.S. cultural colonization"; Canada as "an American cultural colony," and finally, "a system (Canadian) savaged by an overabundance of American programming." (All quotations and statistics are from Johnson, 1977a, b).

Full disengagement, however, may not be feasible for every nation. But stricter requirements for national determination in the economy and in the culture, implemented with a socialist policy, create major dilemmas for the world market system. Accordingly, the hostility of the controllers of that system to genuine socialist measures is not misplaced. Furthermore, the growth of the socialist world sector—however diverse—is not slowing down.

Closely associated with this growth is the broadening of the national liberation movement in the Third (formerly colonial) World. While almost one hundred nations have achieved political independence since the second World War, the overwhelming majority of these states remain economically and culturally dependent on a few developed capitalist countries. The intensifying efforts to break the fetters of dependency, though subject to varying internal social control situations in each society, contribute further to the overall pressure on the dominant world system. The latter's space for maneuver and control are diminished, however gradually.

This general condition explains the current prominence of the issue of national sovereignty. It also suggests the vital importance of communication in the struggle to achieve meaningful national autonomy.

It is misleading, however, to describe the current situation in the international informational sphere as entirely a question of competing national interests of dominating and dominated nations and of rival sectors comprised of a unified capitalist orbit, a homogeneous Third World component, and a monolithic socialist sphere. In reality these three categories are far less neatly arranged and much more complicated.

National boundaries *do* exist—though they are often disputed. But *inside* these physical markers reside social classes whose material and nonmaterial interests differ and usually are incompatible with each other. This has been referred to as the "nonhomogeneity of the national state." (See, e.g., Nordenstreng and Varis, 1973.) The present-day informational condition, locally and globally, can only be appreciated in terms of these conflictual interests. The information that moves practically instantaneously across the globe, into public places, private homes, and individual receivers, is most often the expression of the social relations that exist between the dominating stratum and the other social classes in the advanced industrial market societies.

Briefly, the informational facilities and the flows that circulate, locally and internationally, are, with few and generally trifling exceptions, responsive to, if not at the disposal of, the power centers in the dominant national states. These centers, and the groups who own and manage them, constitute the corporate propertied-stratum of the Western world.

The cultural agendas of the world, a nation, and a local community are determined by the informational system, itself organized on the same basis as the worldwide business system's hierarchy of power and values. Also, it is remarkable but true that relatively little of this vast enterprise of cultural production and distribution occurs according to some minutely calculated central control apparatus. The institutional conditions determining the global and local ownership, availabilities and distribution of plant and equipment, raw materials, labor, education, technology, and communications also work inevitably to advance the interests of the ownership class. At the same time they create the appropriate social environment in which these interests can prosper and their values be internalized in the rest of the population.

Thus, the fact that the world is divided into rich and poor, into developed and developing societies, in no way diminishes the reality that classes and ideologies are present in *all* the nations that are caught up in the world business system. The dependency factor makes it appear that domination and control are exclusively foreign and extraterritorial. To a certain but only limited extent is this true. Actually, in countries connected to and accepting the general principles of the international market system, the social patterns prevailing in the power centers of the system are replicated or created afresh peripherally, though modified by local conditions. The values, goals, social relationships, to say nothing of the basic production relations specific to capitalism, are reproduced, however much they may be filtered first through unique local experiences of history and geography. It is not a surprise, therefore, when "local" media owners in Latin America, for example, are as vociferous as their North American counterparts and mentors in opposing national efforts to make communication systems more responsive to the social needs of the Latin populations.

In this historical period, then, the preservation of national sovereignty may be understood best as a step in the still larger struggle to break the domination of the world business system. In this ongoing effort, international communication has been an extremely effective and direct agent of the market system. All the time this has been so, the overseers of the system have insisted that communications are not only neutral but that they are beneficial to receiver societies and individuals everywhere. This, in brief, is the rationale of those who have pressed the free flow of information doctrine on the world community since the early 1940s. (For the genesis of the free flow doctrine, see, Chapter 2 in Schiller, 1976.)

In arguing for the free flow principle, a considerable vocabulary has been adopted to present as attractively and as humanistically as possible an economic system and a media component thereof which, at best, disregard human and social needs. Since World War II, the rhetoric of freedom has been the preferred usage of American corporate monopolies, press and other, to describe the mechanisms of the system that favors their operation. Attention has been directed only rarely to the contradiction between the language of freedom and the practice of monopoly. When in fact this has been pointed out, as in the issuance of the Hutchins Commission's Report *A Free and Responsible Press* in 1947, indignation erupts in media management circles. Wilbur Forrest, assistant editor of the *New York Herald Tribune* and president of the American Society of Newspaper Editors (ASNE), at the time the report was made public, declared: "I, for one, further deplore any attempt from any quarter to tear down our prestige at a time we seek by our leadership to establish world freedom of information." And again, ". . . the American press is in the position of leadership . . . (to) bring about world freedom of information. I am afraid that it (the report) has hurt. . ." (Blanchard, 1977). No comparable critique of the information process in the United States, carrying the same authority, has been made since.

In recent years, new key words and expressions have been added to the terminology employed by the publicists of domination. "Interdependence" and "internationalism," for example, have become heavily utilized favorites while "national sovereignty" is regarded suspiciously. The semantic arsenal has been raided to provide language which historically has had a progressive meaning insofar as it represented the hopes and aspirations of people toward economic and social equality. The words are given either new meaning or are applied to contexts that provide conclusions that the words do not themselves suggest. "Internationalism," following this practice, offers a semantic vehicle for viewing with equanimity the activities of marauding TNCs. "Interdependence" becomes a word used to describe benignly the web of unequal relationships that the modern world business system wraps around its adherents.

Correspondingly, resistance to freedom to dominate is characterized as reactionary and backward. Preserving national sovereignty as the most effective means of resistance finds itself labeled as a concept out-of-step with modernity, or worse yet, a subversive construct: "The Soviets, with their passion for promoting the concept of state sovereignty as superseding all else. . . ."*

The control of the information system allows these deliberate semantic confusions to be widely circulated and accepted as fitting descriptions of reality. Issues themselves are being framed and defined by the controllers of the in-

---

*Statement of William G. Harley, former Vice-Chairman of the U.S. Commission for UNESCO and President Emeritus of the National Association of Educational Broadcasters before the Subcommittee on International Operations of the U.S. Senate Foreign Relations Committee. *Congressional Record*, 95th Congress, First Session, Vol. 123, No. 101, June 13, 1977.

formation process. In such a situation, it becomes difficult to identify what actually is the problem and, of course, this is precisely the objective of the systemic control. This makes it imperative that, along with the economic infrastructure, the semantic terrain be recaptured from those who currently sit astride the system of world power.

The present volume is an attempt to help all those interested and concerned with communications to orient themselves on this slippery semantic terrain. We have sought to do this by pooling some recent contributions by authors representing different sociopolitical and national outlooks. However, work from the socialist countries has been omitted. This decision has been made, not for the sake of exclusion or minimization of work done in these countries, but rather because of a recognition that to adequately present socialist thinking requires at least a separate volume.

The book is addressed largely to a Western audience which—despite the vaunted (media) pluralism that it is said to enjoy—is quite uninformed about contemporary fundamental global social currents. The overall aim of this book, then, is to reduce this sphere of ignorance and offer presentations that discuss and analyze the issues noted above. A wide range of perspectives is included so that the reader may review a spectrum of expert opinion. If the emphasis is tilted to the "critical" side, this may be justified by the near absence of such opinions in the general and even academic discussion.

It seems to us that the concept of national sovereignty will increasingly emerge as a point of reflection for the most fundamental issues of international communication and related national questions. Like "domination" and "dependence," this concept has become an integral part of the debate around the so-called "new international information order" which is ultimately aiming at the "decolonization" of information conditions in the developing countries, and in general advocating respect for the cultural and political sovereignty of all nations.

However, sovereignty as such has so far received hardly any attention in the scholarly work in this field. Thus the present collection of papers may only indirectly contribute to its comprehensive analysis—mainly by suggesting that this concept be placed high on the agenda of further research.

Consequently, this book concerns itself with the basic contemporary issues of international communication, with the concept of national sovereignty as the springboard for a unifying perspective. We have not aimed at an extensive volume to cover all aspects of international communications but rather at helping to organize, at a theoretical level, the rapidly accumulating material—data and debate—related to this rapidly developing field of academic as well as political concern. Still, our ambitions naturally cannot surpass the limits set by an ecclectic method of compiling such an anthology: our effort is not ultimately a theoretically unified study. Rather, it is a collection of relevant ideas for further analysis and deeper understanding.

KAARLE NORDENSTRENG
La Jolla, California   HERBERT I. SCHILLER

REFERENCES

Blanchard, M.A. (1977). "The Hutchins Commission, the Press, and the Responsibility Concept." *Journalism Monographs* No. 49.

Guback, T., and Varis, T. (1978). "Transnational Communication: Film and Television." UNESCO, Paris. (Reports and Papers on Mass Communication.)

Johnson, A.W. (1977a). "Touchstone for the CBC." Canadian Broadcasting Corporation, Ottawa, Ontario, Canada.

Johnson, A.W. (1977b). "We're All in This Together." (Talk delivered to the Harvard Club of Toronto, May 24, 1977.)

Nordenstreng, K., and Varis, T. (1973). The nonhomogeneity of the national state and the international flow of communications. *In* "Communication Technology and Social Policy" (G. Gerbner, L.P. Gross, and W.H. Melody, eds.), pp. 393-412. Wiley, New York.

Rowan, C.R. (1977). Proposed trade with Cuba not irrational, *San Diego Union,* May 18.

Schiller, H.I. (1976). "Communication and Cultural Domination." International Arts & Sciences, White Plains, New York.

National Sovereignty and
International Communication

Part 1

Communication and National Development:
Changing Perspectives

Introduction

Kaarle Nordenstreng
Herbert I. Schiller

The concept of the nation and related problems of national sovereignty and national development were long thought of in the Western hemisphere as predominantly domestic issues or, at most, issues concerning only the established (that is, primarily European–North American) world. It has been only in the past two decades that this ethnocentric world view of the industrialized West has been replaced by a more global appreciation of other peoples and different socioeconomic systems, including formerly colonized parts of the world.

It is important to recognize that this new appreciation arises not from voluntary Western reappraisals, but from the continuing struggle for social change by disadvantaged peoples around the world. A natural outcome of this upheaval is that the concept of the nation—along with such inseparable issues as national sovereignty and national development—now encompasses ideas heavily influenced by the Third World and underdeveloped countries.

Accompanying this shift in Western perception was the emergence of the development theme on the agenda of Anglo-American communications research. Daniel Lerner's classic study, *The Passing of Traditional Society*, was published in 1958; Lucian Pye's collection *Communications and Political Development* came to the market in 1963; and Wilbur Schramm's *Mass Media and National Development* (an indication of UNESCO's commitment to the question—then from an American point of view) captured attention in 1964. Elaboration of this theme followed rapidly, due in part to the semigovernmental stimulation of such institutions as the East–West Center in Hawaii ("East" here denoting the developing world of Asia). "The East–West Center has become an important institution and has added strength to our national policy which calls for an alliance of free men based on a common interest in mankind's well-being," declared Lyndon B. Johnson in his foreword to Lerner and Schramm's 1967 volume, *Communication and Change in Developing Countries*.

We shall not attempt here to summarize this first generation of communication and development studies; a concise review of the ideas contained by it are to be found, for example, in Merrill (1974, Chapter 2; also reprinted in Fischer and Merrill, 1976). Let us note only that this changing focus in communication research was evidently an integral part of an overall new orientation with which the Western market system reacted to the far-reaching shifts in the global relation of forces—changes running against the interests of those in command of this system. (If the motivation had been a genuine desire to contribute to "a common interest in mankind's well-being," research attention certainly would have turned to these problems well before the time when the Third World began to accuse the capitalist world order of being responsible for its underdevelopment, and to challenge the long-prevailing rules of the world market system.)

It is important to note here that, typical of this generation of studies, there is an uncritically-accepted concept of development; a more or less direct derivative of the Western model was taken for granted. It is also typical of these studies that problems were viewed predominantly on a national scale without considering the history or the continuing interaction of the world market system, which naturally conditions each society, however traditional. No wonder, then, that the notion of national sovereignty is hardly visible in the conceptual–theoretical overview, or paradigm, of these studies.

The first generation of research into problems of communication and development was soon challenged—again in parallel with a more fundamental reappraisal of the general issues of development, noticeable since the end of the 1960s in political and other expert circles.

Among the first signs of a new critical orientation were the meetings of experts sponsored by UNESCO (in 1970 and 1971). As recently noted by Everett M. Rogers, himself a member of the first generation, "by the mid-1970s it seemed safe to conclude that the dominant paradigm had 'passed,' at least as the main model for development in Latin America, Africa, and Asia" (Rogers, 1976, p. 131). Research evidence stemming from the first generation paradigm had itself led scholars to question their points of departure, as indicated in another collection of Schramm and Lerner (1976).

This situation has recently given rise to a new generation of studies (or, thus far, outlines of studies) on communication and development, based on a less Western ethnocentric, and a more socially comprehensive, understanding of the concept of development. A landmark of this second generation is the study *Communication and Development: Critical Perspectives*, compiled in 1976 by Rogers. He notes that a wider role for communication is implied by the newer conceptions of development:

. . . The mobilization of a mass audience through its social organization at the local level depends heavily on communication and in a quite different way than the industrialization approach to development.

In the past, communication research has dealt very incompletely with various aspects of development. Much of such investigation has been concerned with the diffusion of innovations in agriculture, health, and family planning. Other communication research focused on the role of the media in formal and in informal schooling. More generally and less directly, mass media contributions to raising expectations and creating an attitudinal climate for modernization have been studied.

But little attention has been given to how the mass media can foster mass mobilization for development purposes, to how the audience can control the media institutions through feedback, or to the role of the media in narrowing (or at least in not further widening) the gap between the socioeconomically advantaged and disadvantaged segments of the total audience. The last issue points to greater consideration by communication researchers of the distribution of information within an audience. (pp. 8–9)

This new tradition, however, does not completely abandon the old paradigm of the 1960s; what remains virtually untouched is the notion of a relatively isolated nation that is being developed or underdeveloped by conditions determined mainly within the society, although many of these conditions may be imported from outside influence. It is symptomatic that whereas Rogers (1976) lists "external causes of underdevelopment" (p. 132) as one of the emerging alternatives to the dominant paradigm and he even refers to the "dependency theory" advocated by scholars whom he calls "radical economists" (pp. 128–129), such aspects do not significantly carry over into his own "newer conceptions of development communication: self-development, the communications effects gap, and new communication technology" (p. 138).

Rogers, representing a second wave of communication research, continues to regard development as something that takes place within the (more or less) "black box" of a nation state—though considering, it is true, some of the internal social contradictions. But the analytical connections of this paradigm to the global (market) system are limited to indications of alien influence in the developing society in question, its mass media system, and finally its communication research tradition. Convincing evidence of all this influence, in the case of Latin America, is provided by Beltrán and Fox de Cardona in their chapter to follow in this volume, and that included in Rogers (1976). Hence, external causes are taken to mean various forms of transfer (technology, ideology, etc.) from an abstract sphere of outside international influence into the national arena, which is, de facto, understood to be the only real sphere of organic sociopolitico-economic processes. Given such an approach, it is again only logical that the concept of national sovereignty has not found its way to the forefront of this paradigm.

But another new paradigm is emerging, leading to what may be called the third generation of communication and development research. Characteristic of this new perspective is an emphasis on global structure, whereby it is precisely the international sociopolitico-economic system that decisively determines the course of development within the sphere of each nation. In this approach, the national conditions—including class contradictions—serve as more or less intervening variables on influences emanating from a historically determined global design. (As the reader may appreciate, the Preface to this volume has been written from this perspective, in which the TNCs have a central role).

Consequently, the second generation paradigm broke the myth of a single Western model of development *within* the society. The third generation paradigm is breaking the myth of an international system of sovereign nation-states, operating without a basic structure to determine relations *between* societies. Indeed, the most comprehensive version of the latest paradigm amounts to a synthesis of the analytical elements of both national and international structures. This is the thrust of Osvaldo Sunkel's (1976) analysis:

> . . . Development thought, therefore, quite simply, had to start addressing itself to the understanding of the contemporary dynamics of capitalism, both in its core and in its peripheries, in the relationship between them, and—last but not least—in its relations with socialism.
>
> In other words, it became evident that the unit of analysis of development could not be the nation-state. Even if we obviously must concentrate on the particular country we are interested in, its historically peculiar national development process must be put into the context of the evolution of capitalism globally, and its local, internal manifestations . . .
>
> Even if not very satisfying, the analytical frameworks of classical political economy, and particularly of Marxism, do at least go in the directions required to analyse development: globalism and wholism. But at the same time—as indicated before—they require historical specificity, that is, the analysis of the structural characteristics of a society at a particular time and place, since these are the determinants of the functioning and development of that society. In other words, the mode of operation of a capitalist economy, even if we assume that the basic laws of capitalist development are unchanged, vary under different institutional arrangements and cultural traditions . . .
>
> The failure to perceive development as capitalist development, the ignorance of the history of capitalist development both in the centre and in the peripheries, the lack of recognition of the peculiar characteristics of contemporary capitalism, and the ideology of modernization are some of the fundamental reasons for the surprise of development specialists with the results of development: economic growth with increased unemployment, growing polarization and inequality, new forms of dependence, and authoritarian regimes. The ideological blinkers of the modernization paradigm put all the emphasis on the positive and *ex-post* aspects of capitalist development, treating its *end products*—high living standards, moderate inequality, urban-industrial life styles, political democracy—as the *means* of development; the real history of capitalist development standing on its head. Capitalist development, as Schumpeter so aptly put it a very long time ago, is a process of "creative-destruction" . . . (Pp. 16–20)

The third generation paradigm is based not only on the observation of the realities of the contemporary world scene by radical economists. Another significant source of its inspiration is to be found directly in the centers of world capitalism—in, for example, American foreign policy-oriented foundations and research organizations, and in the United States Congress itself. For example, Senator George McGovern, in his chairman's introduction to a recent report to the Subcommittee on International Operations of the Senate Committee on Foreign Relations (U.S. Senate, 1977), concerning "the role and control of international communications and information," writes:

> We think it can fairly be said that the public, the Congress and the Administration do not yet understand the impact of:
> —increasing dependence on the communication of information by nations, people, business, and other international institutions.
> —the control of information and the technology to transmit it, in a world where satellites connect sophisticated "crisis centers" with towns which have no paved roads;
> —changes in the economic system, where international financial transactions which might affect millions of people are accomplished in a fraction of a second;
> —the potential for breakdowns in worldwide communications systems which could lead to serious international conflicts. (p. III)

Thus, the latest generation of development thinking is being constructed on a firm and solid basis—both intellectually and politically—but also with serious ideological contradictions. And this time the concept of national sovereignty has become the center of attention.

The contributions to follow in this section may be seen to represent the transition from the second to the third generation paradigm. Closest to the second generation is perhaps the chapter by Elihu Katz, whereas the chapter by Raquel Salinas and Leena Paldán, in its efforts to summarize dependency theory, moves considerably toward the third generation.

The first three chapters, by Sauvant, Schiller, and Beltrán and Fox de Cardona, complement each other by displaying essential features of the international economico-informational structures, pointing to the need for a genuinely theoretical and holistic analysis of the global determinants of national development. Dallas Smythe's chapter offers a historical and cultural-philosophical perspective, thus casting some humanistic light on considerations that too often are missing in mechanistic and ahistorical approaches.

As noted in the Preface, we shall not be able to offer in this volume a comprehensive theory, or even an advanced framework for the construction of one. But we are convinced that the third generation paradigm is rapidly taking shape, and that substantive theoretical works will soon follow.

REFERENCES

Fischer, H.-D., and Merrill, J. C., eds. (1976). "International and Intercultural Communication." Hastings House, New York.

Lerner, D. (1958). "The Passing of Traditional Society." New York: Collier-Macmillan, 1958.

Lerner, D., and Schramm, W., eds. (1967). "Communication and Change in Developing Countries." East-West Center Press, Honolulu, Hawaii.

Merrill, J. C. (1974). "The Imperative of Freedom." Hastings House, New York.

Pye, L. W., ed. (1963). "Communications and Political Development." Princeton University Press, Princeton, New Jersey.

Rogers, E. M. (1976). "Communication and Development: Critical Perspectives." Sage Publications, Beverly Hills, California.

Schramm, W. (1964). "Mass Media and National Development." Stanford University Press, Stanford, California.

Schramm, W., and Lerner, D., eds. (1976). "Communication and Change: Ten Years After." University of Hawaii/East-West Center Press, Honolulu, Hawaii.

Sunkel, O. (1976). "The Development of Development Thinking." Institute of Development Studies, University of Sussex, Sussex, England. (Occasional paper)

UNESCO. (1970). "Mass Media in Society: The Need of Research." UNESCO, Paris. (Reports and Papers on Mass Communication No. 59.)

UNESCO. (1971). "Proposals for an International Programme of Communication Research." UNESCO, Paris. (COM/MD/20.)

U.S. Senate. Committee on Foreign Relations. (1977). "The Role and Control of International Communications and Information. Report to the Subcommittee on International Operations of the Committee on Foreign Relations, United States Senate. 95th Congress, 1st Session." U.S. Government Printing Office, Washington, D.C.

1

Sociocultural Emancipation

Karl P. Sauvant
United Nations

Karl P. Sauvant is Transnational Corporations Affairs Officer, Centre on Transnational Corporations, United Nations, New York. A citizen of the Federal Republic of Germany, he has studied at Freie Universität, Berlin, and The Institute for Social Research, University of Michigan, and he has received a PhD in International Relations from the University of Pennsylvania. Dr. Sauvant was project director of the Foreign Policy Research Institute study, "Multinational Corporations in the International System." He is the author of many articles in the field of international economics and is joint editor of *The New International Economic Order: Changing Priorities on the International Agenda; Controlling Multinational Enterprises: Problems, Strategies, Counterstrategies; The New International Order: Confrontation or Cooperation between North and South*; and *The Third World without Superpowers: The Collected Documents of the Non-Aligned Countries*.

This contribution is a slightly revised reprint of "His Master's Voice," an article that appeared in *CERES*, the FAO Review on Development, Vol. 9 (Sept.–Oct. 1976), pp. 27–32. Published by permission of Karl P. Sauvant.

POLITICAL AND ECONOMIC EMANCIPATION

In the 1950s and 1960s, it was widely believed that the problems of the developing countries were largely a function of the political status of these states. After independence from formal or informal colonialism, and after some transitional difficulties (to be resolved by such international development efforts as those represented by the United Nations First Development Decade, the Alliance for Progress, and association conventions like that of Yaoundé), it was expected that they would become full and equal members of the inter-

The author gratefully acknowledges helpful comments by Edmundo Fuenzalida Faivovich, Herbert I. Schiller, Osvaldo Sunkel, and Tapio Varis on an earlier draft. The views expressed in this article do not necessarily reflect those of the institution with which the author is currently affiliated.

national community. By the end of the 1960s, however, these hopes had been shattered. The international development efforts did not deliver what they had seemed to promise. If anything, the gap between North and South had increased. At the same time, it became obvious that political independence is a mere chimera unless based on economic independence. Economic decolonization and development thus came to be viewed with new urgency.

In their search for solutions to their problems, the developing countries embraced the concept of individual and collective self reliance. This concept was enunciated by the Non-Aligned Countries—the political organization of the Third World—at their summit of heads of state or government in Lusaka (1970), further elaborated at their foreign ministers' conference in Georgetown (1972), and since then has been included in most major international economic documents. Self-reliance became all the more important since industrialization had often turned into dependent industrialization, especially through transnational enterprises and their foreign affiliates, thereby reinforcing already existing structures and extending them into other areas.

Self-reliance is a program. It requires that the political, economic, and sociocultural structures created to link colonies to metropolitan countries (in a status of dependence) be altered to link developing countries to one another (in a status of interdependence). In the political sphere, this process had commenced in the 1960s when the developing countries emancipated themselves from the political tutelage of their former rulers and organized themselves in the nonaligned movement. The Lusaka summit marked the beginning of increased efforts to achieve economic decolonization. However, it soon became apparent that these efforts needed a broader and more comprehensive economic program in the framework of which self-reliance could be pursued and economic development could take place. Quite naturally, this framework had to deal with the external conditions of development and, more specifically, with the structure of the international economic system. The nonaligned movement formulated such a program, drawing on work done by the group of 77, by UNCTAD and by the United Nations (especially in connection with the development decades). As a result, the Non-Aligned Countries adopted,* at their summit in Algiers in September 1973, an "Economic Declaration" and an "Action Programme for Economic Cooperation," which, in turn, constituted one of the primary foundations (at times verbatim) of the resolutions adopted eight months later at the United Nations Sixth Special Session.†

---

*For an analysis of the economic program of the nonaligned movement and the evolution of this movement into an international economic pressure group for the restructuring of the international economic system, see Jankowitsch and Sauvant (1978).

†See, Fourth Conference of Heads of State or Government on Non-Aligned Countries, "Economic Declaration" and "Action Programme for Economic Cooperation," (included in Jankowitsch and Sauvant, 1977); and United Nations, General Assembly resolution 3201(S-VI) "Declaration on the Establishment of a New International Economic Order" and General Assembly resolution 3202(S-VI) "Programme of Action on the Establishment of a New International Economic Order," adopted May 1, 1974.

The major importance of the Algiers and the Sixth Special Session resolutions does not lie only in the adoption of a comprehensive international economic program—in fact, such comprehensiveness had already been approached elsewhere, especially in the United Nations Action Programme for the Second Development Decade. Rather, the importance of these resolutions is that they represent the recognition by the developing countries that their problems are not only a function of their political, but also their economic, status and that, consequently, economic decolonization is a matter of the utmost importance. This awareness made economic decolonization and development highly politicized issues.* During the 1960s—and even at UNCTAD III (1972)—questions of economic development were essentially regarded as "low politics," left to the economics, financial, and planning ministries. Attempts at politicizing these issues, e.g., the Group of 77's Charter of Algiers (1967), therefore failed. With the beginning of the 1970s, however, this attitude changed, and economic decolonization and development became "high politics" issues: they were elevated from the level of heads of departments to the level of heads of state or government. This change found its first full expression when the Algiers summit of the Non-Aligned Countries—which was attended by more heads of state or government than any other previous international conference—embraced these issues, for the first time at so high a level, as major themes of its deliberations and actions.

The key importance of the Algiers summit is, therefore, that it politicized the economic decolonization and development issues at the highest level. Furthermore, this occurred at a time when the Non-Aligned Countries had mobilized most of the Third World into their movement, had succeeded in establishing closer lines of communication among themselves, and had given themselves a highly structured organizational framework. Finally, with the growing awareness of the importance of economic matters, developing countries also became cognizant of one of their main assets—natural resources—and began to use them as effectively as they could. OPEC's success was, in fact, instrumental in elevating the development issue from a priority item on the agenda of the Non-Aligned Countries to a priority item on the agenda of the international community (Jankowitsch and Sauvant, 1978). As a result, most international conferences since Algiers and the Sixth Special Session have dealt with aspects related to the establishment of the New International Economic Order.†

---

*In Latin America, where most countries had become formally independent in the earlier nineteenth century, this process had already begun in the 1950s: Latin American countries, therefore, were also the most important leaders in the Group of 77 (formed 1964).

†For a discussion of the main issue areas of the New International Order, the dimensions and structures of economic dependence, and strategies of change, see Sauvant and Hasenpflug (1977) and Erb and Kallab (1975).

SOCIOCULTURAL EMANCIPATION

The self-reliance discussion led to a realization by top-level decision makers in the Third World that emancipation from colonial dependence is a multidimensional process. It showed that political independence had to be complemented by economic independence. A third dimension of this process, however, has so far largely been ignored. During the colonial period, or, in the case of Latin American countries, the period of quasi-suzerainty, the countries of the Third World were not only subjected to political and economic but also to sociocultural colonization. The values and behavioral patterns of important segments of the Third World societies had gradually been transformed to reflect those of the metropolitan countries. After independence hardly any change took place, although the attempt to explore self-reliance as an alternative development model, itself, constitutes a first step toward sociocultural emancipation.

In general, however, the infused patterns have been maintained and reinforced through a variety of mechanisms.* Education has traditionally played an important role. Members of the elite and the middle class were—and are—frequently educated in the major developed countries, where, of course, they were (are) also exposed to the life-styles of the host societies. Similarly, domestic education in many Third World countries is based on material imported from former metropolises. Old sociocultural ties are also strengthened by foreign-language broadcasts, newspapers, and extensive cultural programs of major developed countries. In addition, local broadcasting frequently draws on whole series of programs acquired from developed countries, and popular music programs in particular are strongly foreign (and especially U.S.) dominated. An even higher degree of import-dependence is characteristic for the film industry, a dependence that is virtually total for news films (including for news occurring within the country). Newspapers and magazines, in many of which syndicated U.S. comics have become fixtures, have to rely for their global news (including news about other developing countries) almost entirely on two or three international news agencies (UPI, AP, and Reuters) and their selection of what is newsworthy. (To break this pattern, in 1976 a number of developing countries decided to establish, within the framework of the nonaligned movement, a pool of nonaligned news agencies. See Somavía, 1976.†)

The most important development in this area has, however, been the spread

---

*For a more detailed discussion of these mechanisms, see Varis (1975) and O'Brien (1975).

†For a more detailed conceptualization of (and some data on) the role of TNEs in the diffusion of (business) culture, see Sauvant (1976). See also Sunkel and Faivovich (1975) and Schiller (1973). A number of the papers presented at a Meeting of Experts on the Study of the Impact of Transnational Corporations on the Development and International Relations within the Fields of Competence of UNESCO, held in Paris in June 1976, are also relevant in this context.

of television since the end of the 1950s and the beginning of the 1960s. TV may be reaching already approximately one-quarter of the world population. A high percentage (between one-third and two-thirds) of the television programs in developing countries—especially during prime time—is imported from a few countries, mainly the U.S., the United Kingdom, and France (Nordenstreng and Varis, 1974; for a brief summary, see Varis, 1974). Through television, therefore, an increasing number of persons is exposed, on a daily basis, to the way of life of the main developed countries, to their pre-' conceptions and ideals. Together, all these mechanisms (whose control is usually also highly concentrated) disseminate the values and behavioral patterns of a few major developed countries, which thus keep—intentionally or not—the developing countries within the sociocultural orbit of these countries.

TRANSNATIONAL ENTERPRISES

A new and important mechanism has been added to those discussed above through the growth of transnational enterprises (TNEs).† The critical point is that foreign direct investment does not involve only capital and technology, but is usually also accompanied by sociocultural investments. In the traditional raw material ventures this was not a major factor, since many of them were capital intensive and frequently located in enclaves not linked to the rest of the country. But with the expansion of manufacturing foreign direct investment in the 1950s and especially during the 1960s, foreign affiliates became closely integrated into their host countries. In this process, they began to shape the production apparatus of the host economy and increasingly determined what was to be produced by it, i.e., for what type of production the resources of the host country would be utilized.

Beyond this direct impact, TNEs introduced into their foreign affiliates novel business practices, modes of operation, values, and behavioral patterns—all sociocultural investments. These, in turn, are disseminated in the host country through forward and backward linkages as well as the foreign-affiliate experience of employees. In the first case, foreign affiliates may, for instance, insist on the introduction of new standards, different production methods, etc., on the part of their domestic suppliers. In the second case, the employees of foreign affiliates—who are constantly being exposed to the foreign-affiliate environment and for whom the frequently foreign-trained or expatriate top management may constitute a model—are potentially very effective transmitters (in a multiplying manner) of the values and patterns of behavior represented by the foreign affiliate to other spheres of the host society.

---

*Veblen made this distinction in the early 1920s, at a time when American enterprises had just begun to shift towards "salesmanship;" see Veblen (1923).

The importance of the role of TNEs, as discussed so far, is therefore twofold: They directly contribute to the shaping of the production apparatus of the host economy, and they can be expected to have a significant impact on the shaping of a host country's business culture and, through it, the sociocultural orientation of the society as a whole. On the face of it, the changes thus introduced may be beneficial in that they contribute to the industrialization and modernization of developing host countries. TNEs would then play the role of dynamic agents of change, expediting socioeconomic development and bringing to this task the vast resources of their global networks and their ability to combine various factors of production in an economically efficient way. Before such a conclusion can be drawn, however, a closer look has to be taken at the kind of change that is being introduced, promoted, and disseminated. This, in turn, requires a brief examination of the nature of the linkages between foreign affiliates and their headquarters, their choice of production, and the content of the transmitted values and behavioral patterns.

The linkages between foreign affiliates and their headquarters are characterized by the former's very high responsiveness to headquarters' policies, a responsiveness that is based on a variety of formal and informal control mechanisms. Most significant among these are majority ownership of foreign affiliates by the parent enterprise, prerogatives of headquarters in key decision-making areas of their affiliates, and the presence of expatriate personnel in top managerial positions of the affiliate. Such personnel not only exercise a valuable control function, but also fulfill, as noted above, an important social model function vis-à-vis members of the indigenous society. The unidirectionality and asymmetry of this relationship, already inherent in a hierarchical business organization, is further accentuated by the absence of any representation of the interests of foreign affiliates (or host countries) in parent enterprises. Parent enterprises are almost exclusively owned and managed by home-country nationals and in no way reflect the international involvement of the enterprise system as a whole.

Thus, central to the nature of the relationship between headquarters and foreign affiliates is the fact that the linkage between them is not only strong but clearly unidirectional and consequently asymmetrical. In this situation, headquarters are free, within the boundaries of global economic rationality, to determine the production of their foreign affiliates. Naturally, this choice will take into account two important factors. The first one (and excluding export-platform operations) is the nature of the local market—or, more precisely, the part of the market that has purchasing power. This means the small elite and middle class, i.e., groups that can be expected to have most thoroughly internalized the values and wants of developed countries. The second factor concerns product development by and production processes of TNEs. Both are based on R & D conducted almost entirely in home countries, R & D that reflects the factor endowments of the same countries; and both are geared primarily to the satisfaction of the wants of consumers in developed countries. Naturally, TNEs prefer to utilize these experiences when establishing themselves in developing countries.

The choice of production for affiliates in developing countries is therefore largely a combination of the production and R & D experiences of the parent enterprise, on the one hand, and the wants of the small elites and middle classes in host countries, on the other. The problem is that both factors reflect the relative abundance of developed countries and not the absolute poverty of developing ones, the wants of consumers in developed countries and not the needs of large proportions of the population in developing countries. For instance, TNEs in developing countries tend to use high-skill, capital-, and energy-intensive production processes, and not low-skill, labor-intensive ones. They tend to concentrate on luxury and advanced consumption industries and not on basic foodstuff. They tend to serve the individual wants of some, and not the collective needs for essential goods and services of most. Consequently, the direct impact of TNEs (and of domestic enterprises imitating their methods) on the production apparatus of developing host economies tends to lead to a misallocation of scarce resources and, in a larger perspective, tends to keep the host economy on an inappropriate development path. Furthermore, these patterns of production tend to keep the host economy dependent on inputs from abroad because both demand and supply orient themselves at markets and capabilities at a higher level of development.

Closely linked to the question of choice of production is the question of the content of the transmitted values and behavioral patterns. As suggested above, they influence local managers in foreign affiliates and in the operations attached to them through forward and backward linkages, and they shape the foreign-affiliate experience of employees in general. Again, given the nature of the linkage between foreign affiliates and headquarters, they are home-country values and behavioral patterns, reflecting, in other words, the possibilities of economies and societies at a different level of development and endowed with different factors of production. More concretely, they include, especially in their American variation (see Canada, 1972), a strong preference for a free enterprise system and, therefore, opposition to state intervention; exploitation of resources as soon as discovered; planned obsolescence; product innovation and differentiation; emphasis on packaging and branding; and increased consumption through mass-marketing techniques, including want–creation, style changes, and hard-sell advertising.

Among these characteristics, those pertaining to and resulting from advertising are of special interest because they concern differences that at least until recently (and to a limited degree even still today) distinguished American from non-American business philosophies. The differences revolve around "product orientation" and "market orientation" and the implications of these two approaches for the production process. Product orientation—still typical for some non-American enterprises—ideally places the major emphasis on cost consciousness and on the production of relatively durable goods with long life cycles, designed to satisfy recognized consumer needs. Research and development, product development, and so forth, are geared to this objective. The resulting product is then put on the market where it finds its customers. Thus, to use Thorstein Veblen's terminology, emphasis is on "workmanship" and not on "salesmanship."*

In the United States, these priorities have come to be reversed in the time since World War II. Emphasis is placed on salability and consumption, as opposed to conservation; and sales, marketing, and advertising considerations tend to determine research and development, product development, and production. "Product management" plays a key role in this approach. Often, product management is aimed at limiting the lifespan of a product, for instance through frequent changes in the design and appearance of a product (but not in its function or purpose). Built-in or planned obsolescence, as well as the deliberate creation of wants and needs, is the logical culmination of this policy; and advertising, obviously, is one of its most important tools.

The content of the values and behavioral patterns transmitted by TNEs—especially as pertaining to business culture—therefore further supplements and supports the observations made at the end of the preceding section. In fact, these observations can be further amended to read that the business philosophy on which the production patterns in question are based is being internalized by local management and local employees. Thus, not only the products and the production methods of TNEs, but also the business philosophy underlying them tend to be inappropriate for developing countries.

ADVERTISING

As already noted, advertising plays a crucial role in the process of want–creation. It appeals directly to a society's value orientations, manipulating especially its consumer values. But the function of advertising, especially if accompanied also by public-relations activities, is not merely to sell products but to sell ideas. And these ideas are promoted, of course, in the interest of the client—in particular the (advertising) budget-strong TNE client. Advertising, therefore, is an important mechanism to maintain and further develop the want-oriented demand patterns in developing countries, thereby supporting corresponding production patterns.

The acceleration in the transnationalization of production in the 1960s made

---

*For a more detailed discussion of the international advertising industry, including the dates presented below, see Sauvant (1976). See also Schiller (1971), Weinstein (1974), and Chevalier (1974).

it imperative for the advertising industry—as a service industry—to follow its globally expanding clients. This move was greatly facilitated by the parallel spread of television to developing countries. Frequently, agencies established abroad started out with a few major clients already served by the parent agency at home. Given the dominant position of the U.S.-based TNEs in international direct investment, their special preference for the usage of advertising, and the superior know-how and experience of U.S. advertising agencies, it is not surprising that U.S. shops acquired a prominent position in international advertising.

In fact, international advertising—an industry whose volume was estimated at $33.1 billion in 1970—is almost entirely a U.S. industry: twenty-one of the twenty-five largest agencies in the world are United States agencies (or strongly linked with them), and most of them generate about half of their billings abroad.* Moreover, while U.S. agencies (or agencies with a strong U.S. partner) are omnipresent, major non-U.S. shops are either entirely domestic (Japan) or of only regional significance (Western Europe). The dominant U.S. position becomes apparent from data concerning the presence, in 1973, of foreign affiliates among the five largest shops of forty-six developing countries for which information could be obtained. In all countries, and for each of the one hundred and thirty-five agencies on which data were available, foreign ownership—whether majority or minority—means (with only one exception) that the parent agency is either entirely North American or has strong U.S. participation. More specifically, in twenty-nine of these forty-six countries, the largest advertising agency is foreign majority owned, and in an additional four countries foreigners have acquired an often substantial minority interest. In all, in only thirteen (or 28%) of the forty-six countries is the biggest agency entirely owned by nationals. A similar pattern prevails for the other rankings. Of the total one hundred and thirty-five agencies, nearly two-thirds are foreign majority owned, 9% have foreign minority participation, and less than 30% are entirely in national hands. Furthermore, only a very limited number of agencies account for most foreign shops. The Interpublic Group of Companies (with McCann–Erickson as the predominant partner) alone controls about one-fifth of all foreign majority-owned shops. If SSC & B. Inc., J. Walter Thompson Co., I.M.A.A., and Grant Advertising are added, this share increases to close to two-thirds; and if five further parent agencies are added, nearly 90% of all foreign shops are accounted for. (It should be noted that a similar pattern prevails in developed countries. See Sauvant, 1976.)

The pattern-setting potential of foreign affiliates of TNEs in their various linkages with host countries thus receives powerful additional support from

*The author is grateful to Edmundo Fuenzalida Faivovich and Osvaldo Sunkel for drawing attention to this dialectic which may be the basis for a movement away from the prevailing patterns.

advertising, with the converging effect of creating, maintaining, or further reinforcing home-country values in developing countries.

CONCLUSIONS

Just as it has been realized that political independence cannot be achieved without economic emancipation, it also has to be realized that economic independence is, to a certain extent, a function of sociocultural emancipation. The values and patterns of behavior acquired during the colonial era, and especially the consumption patterns created, maintained, or reinforced by TNEs and transnational advertising agencies, do not reflect the conditions of developing countries. Rather, they reflect the wants and the abundance of developed countries. At least for the time being, these wants can only be satisfied through continued inputs from abroad. Consequently, economic dependence on countries and institutions that can help to fulfill these foreign-oriented wants continues and is reinforced. At the same time, scarce domestic resources are siphoned off and squandered for production and in production processes that do not provide for basic goods and services for the great majority of the population.

As long as TNEs can simply transfer their production and production-process experiences to developing countries, and as long as a ready market awaits them or is allowed to be created, it can not be expected that this pattern will be broken. After all, the purpose of TNEs is to make profits, not to promote development. It also cannot be expected that all of the values and behavioral and consumption patterns under discussion can be avoided altogether; some of them may be unavoidable concomitants of industrialization. In fact, and to go one step further, they may be unavoidable concomitants of production carried out by profit-seeking institutions. To the extent that this is the case, it is not so much (or not only) the foreign or domestic status of an enterprise that is responsible for its nonsocial production, but rather the profit-seeking character of the institution itself. However, given that TNEs are most advanced in this area, they can be expected to introduce, magnify, and/or cultivate such patterns.

Nevertheless, what can be expected is that foreign affiliates adapt themselves to meet specific demands of developing countries, be it for sociocultural identity or for the appropriate use of scarce economic resources in the interests of meeting basic minimum needs of the entire population. The initiative for breaking the pattern of dependence, however, has to be taken by host countries. In particular, they have to reorient their consumption patterns toward local conditions, persuade TNEs—which will continue to play an important role in the socioeconomic development of the Third World—to reorient their production and production processes in a similar manner, and they have to prevent that domestic entrepreneurs imitate their foreign models.

To take such an initiative, however, is not easy. Not only does it have to deal with the prevailing practices of TNEs, but also with the existing preferences of large parts of the leading social groups, the middle class, and the professional elites, which themselves are adhering to the values and behavioral patterns of the main metropolitan countries. These latter groups are, in other words, self-colonized, willing victims of sociocultural colonization. The impetus, therefore, has to come from those parts of host societies that are relatively independent—especially the intelligentsia and popular movements not wedded to established structures. In fact, the very intensity of sociocultural colonization (and self-colonization) and the resulting disintegration of the preexisting sociocultural value and behavioral systems create, in a dialectical manner, reintegrative reactions in the societies concerned, however weak these reactions still may be.*

Self-reliance (and the related concentration on fulfilling basic needs) constitutes such a reaction, even if the concept has been used so far mainly to denote an economic program. But economic self-reliance, to be effective, requires sociocultural emancipation. If such emancipation does not take place in the developing countries, if industrialization continues to orient itself toward and at the demand and supply situation of the developed countries, the economic development of the Third World may well remain development-dependent. And this, in the final analysis, will hinder the achievement of political independence. What is needed, then, is an Algiers declaration for sociocultural emancipation, a declaration that could serve as the basis of national action programs in the developing countries.

REFERENCES

Canada, Government of, (1972). Foreign direct investment in Canada. *Information Canada,* p. 294.
Chevalier, M. (1974). Which international strategy for advertising agencies? *European Business 41* (Summer), 26–34.
Erb, G. F., and Kallab, V., eds. (1975). "Beyond Dependency: The Developing World Speaks Out." Praeger, New York.
Jankowitsch, O., and Sauvant, K. P. (1977). "The Third World without Superpowers: The Collected Documents of the Non-Aligned Countries." Oceana, Dobbs Ferry, New York.
Jankowitsch, O., and Sauvant, K. P. (1978). The evolution of the non-aligned movement into a pressure group for the establishment of the new international economic order. *In* "The New International Economic Order: Changing Priorities on the International Agenda" (K. P. Sauvant and O. Jankowitsch, eds.). Pergamon, Oxford, England.
Nordenstreng, K., and Varis, T. (1974). "Television Traffic—A One-Way Street?" UNESCO, Paris. (Reports and Papers on Mass Communication, No. 70.)
O'Brien, R. C. (1975). Domination and dependence in mass communications: Implications for

*The documents pertaining to the news agencies pool of the Non-Aligned Countries are included in Jankowitsch and Sauvant (1977).

the use of broadcasting in developing countries. University of Sussex. *Institute of Development Studies Bulletin 6* (Mar.), 85–99.

Sauvant, K. P. (1976). The potential of multinational enterprises as vehicles for the transmission of business culture. *In* "Controlling Multinational Enterprises: Problems, Strategies, Counterstrategies" (K. P. Sauvant and F. G. Lavipour, eds.), pp. 39–78. Westview Press, Boulder, Colorado.

Sauvant, K. P., and Hasenpflug, H., eds. (1977). "The New International Economic Order: Confrontation or Cooperation between North and South?" Westview Press, Boulder, Colorado.

Schiller, H. I. (1971). Madison Avenue imperialism. *Transaction 8* (Mar.–Apr.), 52–58.

Schiller, H. I. (1973). Authentic national development versus the free flow of information and the new communications technology. *In* "Communications Technology and Social Policy" (G. Gerbner, L. R. Gross, and W. H. Melody, eds.), pp. 467–480. John Wiley, New York.

Somavía, J. (1976). "The Transnational Power Structure and International Information: Elements for Determining Policy with Respect to Transnational News Agencies." (Paper presented at a seminar on "The Role of Information in the New International Order," Mexico City, May, 1976.)

Sunkel, O., and Faivovich, E. F. (1975). "The Effects of Transnational Corporations on Culture." Institute of Development Studies, University of Sussex, Brighton, England. (Mimeograph copy.)

Varis, T. (1974). Global traffic in television. *Journal of Communication 24* (Winter), 102–109.

Varis, T. (1975). "The Impact of Transnational Corporations on Communication." Tampere Peace Research Institute, Tampere, Finland. (Tampere Peace Research Institute. Research Reports, No. 10.)

Veblen, T. (1923). "Absentee Ownership and Business Enterprise in Recent Times." Viking, New York.

Weinstein, A. K. (1974). The international expansion of U.S. multinational advertising agencies. *MSU Business Topics 22* (Summer), 29–35.

2

Transnational Media and National Development

Herbert I. Schiller
University of California, San Diego

Paper presented at the Conference on the Fair Communication Policy for the International Exchange of Information, The East–West Center, Honolulu, Hawaii, March 28–April 3, 1976, and originally published in the Report on the Conference, *New Perspectives in International Communication*, edited by Jim Richstad, East–West Communication Institute, East–West Center, Honolulu, Hawaii, 1977.

How national is the national development that (sometimes) occurs in the poorer parts of the world? Domestic and international economic activities today, outside the state-planned societies, are organized according to the explicit and implicit rules of what Wallerstein (1974) calls the "modern world-system." What this amounts to, in fact, is a global market economy, presiding with varying flexibility over the allocation of resources, human and natural. Within this near-world orbit, each nation-state seeks, as a minimum, to provide its governing stratum protection and support in the system's overall operation. At the same time, the international division of labor and the allocation of resources are largely influenced, if not determined, by, and in, the advanced, industrialized centers of the global structure.

Consequently, it is somewhat fanciful to term the development of unindustrialized states, attached to the system, if and when it occurs, *national*. The decisions affecting their economies are made by forces largely outside national boundaries. In this process, transnational media occupy an important position. Though profitability is their main concern, they comprise, at the same time, the ideologically supportive informational infrastructure of the modern world system's core—the multinational corporations (MNCs).

21

THE INFORMATIONAL INFRASTRUCTURE OF THE
MULTINATIONAL CORPORATION

Transnational media are engaged directly in the generation and transmission of messages inside and across state boundaries. They are film companies, publishing firms, TV producing businesses, and many other image-producing activities that will be considered later in this chapter. The powerful media corporations that finance and control the varied enterprises of message-making are still only a subset of the international informational system. At the system's center are the multinational corporations (some of which are themselves transnational media companies), engaged in manufacturing, industrial, financial, and administrative operations. The MNC, as Mowlana (1975) observes, "has become one of the chief organizers and manufacturers of the international flow of communications" (pp. 89–90).

The generalized informational activities of *all* MNCs, at least their more visible arrangements, include: generation and transmission of business transactions data, utilizing thereby an enormous share of the international media facilities; the export of management techniques; training programs for executives and workers; promotion of a common language, English (Sauvant, 1977); and direct, personal associations with the leading echelons of host governments.

Additionally, three vital informational service activities directly assist the MNC's specific sales operations. First in importance is the international advertising agency, in practically all instances, a United States firm with global subsidiaries. The ad agency is the message-creating facility of the MNC, assembling the world's creative talent to produce an effective sales message.

Then there are the market survey and opinion polling services, sometimes part of the advertising agency, sometimes separate corporate entities. These heavily utilized services seek to discover the best means of audience penetration and the ways to evaluate the extent of the penetration that may have occurred.

Finally, there are the public relations firms whose practices are not always easily distinguishable from those of the advertising and market research companies. More will be said about the operational behavior of these different informational services.

The MNC's own informational activities, along with those of the services just mentioned, constitute the core of the MNC message-producing and processing system. There are also the *channels* through which these messages flow; these include the conventional media circuits: radio, television, the press, publishing, film, and periodicals. In addition, there are the less acknowledged channels of international image and message circulation. In part, these are represented by governmental information creation and dissemination services. With respect to the United States there are the publicly acknowledged activities (U.S.I.A. and the Armed Forces Radio and Television) and, until fairly recently, the unacknowledged ones (Radio Free Europe, Radio Liberty, etc.).

Tourism and the export of technology and technological systems are major message transmission channels, though not always identified as such.

Most of the messagery utilizes the hardware of international communications: cables, satellites, broadcasting facilities, and publishing equipment.

The objectives of this diverse and multifaceted media mix, besides the immediate one of profitability, are the promotion, protection, and extension of the modern world system and its leading component, the MNC, in particular.

A BRIEF REVIEW OF UNITED STATES EXPERIENCE

To understand transnational media dynamics, a brief review of media functioning in the center of the modern world system in the last half-century, i.e., recent United States historical experience, is certainly instructive and may be essential.

The utilization of public information channels for the objectives of the corporate business system occurs in its most direct and pure form in the United States. Here, the last fifty-five years have seen the near-total application of the new informational technologies and processes to the needs of corporate marketing. Radio and television, along with the traditional print media, have been integrated fully into the marketing system. Harold Geneen (1974), former chairman and chief executive officer of ITT, puts it nicely:

> The introduction of the household radio in the 1920s brought into being another primary medium for the dissemination of product information, and with the advent of television in the 1940s and 1950s, yet another powerful medium was launched. . . . Some would argue that the buyers, trade and consumer, in the United States and abroad, are being overwhelmed by the vast amount of advertising material now directed at them.
>
> We at ITT disagree. As a multinational company with corporate responsibilities in countries at every level of industrial development and technology, we feel that the need for responsible advertising is far greater than ever before. (pp. 7–8)

The apparent effect of saturation, through every medium of the advertising message, has been to create packaged audiences whose loyalties are tied to brand-named products and whose understanding of social reality is mediated through a scale of commodity satisfaction. People are consumers and participants in a system whose social dilemmas are experienced as individual problems (Smythe, 1977).

These social phenomena are most observable in the United States. Their appearance has been more and more noticeable since the end of World War II throughout the world.

THE INTERNATIONALIZATION OF CAPITAL AND THE
EXPORT OF CONSUMERISM

The generative force behind the consumer culture has been the worldwide expansion of American corporate enterprise through the vehicle of what has come to be called the multinational corporation. From 1953 to 1973, the *book* value of United States direct foreign private investment ballooned from $16.3 to $107.3 billion. "The *market* value of these investments, furthermore, is of the order of $160 billion and the average annual increase over the past three years (1971–1973) has been $10 billion."

These investments represent a gigantic global buildup in plant and structure "of a few giant corporations with concentration more pronounced than for domestic corporations. Thus, nearly 90% of foreign tax credits were claimed by corporations with assets above $250 million, a group of corporations comprising only 1% of the total but obtaining 50% of U.S. corporate income."

These investments embrace all kinds of economic activity but they are concentrated most heavily in manufacturing, especially consumer durable goods, with automobile manufacture very prominent. The sales of these overseas branches of U.S. companies now exceed U.S. exports, hitherto the most important indicator of the country's foreign economic activity. "By 1968," states a recent governmental report, "total sales of manufacturing affiliates abroad had reached 10 percent of total manufacturing sales in the U.S. Manufacturing sales abroad by (U.S.) foreign affiliates were more than twice that of U.S. manufactured exports. Foreign sales of affiliates in the motor vehicle industry were from four to five times the level of such exports" (Musgrave, 1975, pp. xi–xii).

Accompanying the massive expansion of U.S. private business abroad has been the internationalization of American advertising. "By 1972," reports one study, "only three of the world's top thirty agencies were not U.S.-owned (two Japanese and one British). In each European country about half of the top ten billing agencies are U.S.-owned; for example, in Belgium it is six, Britain eight, Netherlands five, Sweden three, Switzerland two, and West Germany six" (Masson and Thorburn, 1975, p. 101). Seen from the American side, the proportion of international business in the accounts of the top U.S. ad agencies is now predominant (O'Gara, 1976).

One immediate consequence of the huge, American-owned productive complex now operating internationally is the pressure it generates to obtain access to and domination of the local media. Only in this way can it attract and process indigenous audiences into consumerism.

Here the American experience in marketing is relevant. As observed in an annual report of the Harvard University Program on Information Technologies and Public Policy (Harvard University, 1975), "the pattern of information resource development in the United States differs sharply from that of the rest of the world. Nowhere else is the private sector so predominant.'' This may be conflict-producing, as the Harvard study further indicates. ''. . . the American mode of communication through private capitalist enterprise seeking markets is at . . . variance with the communications mode of the rest of the world with its consensus-minded government monopolies'' (Vol. 2, p. 13).

Accordingly, in the modern world system, as it has evolved in recent years under American pressure, commercialization of the mass media is an almost universally observed tendency. Even in the most advanced capitalist countries, longstanding public (State) administration of communications facilities (postal systems, telegraph, and broadcasting) is being eroded. In Europe today, with the exception (temporary?) of Belgium, Denmark, Norway, and Sweden, television is relying heavily on advertising revenue. And the pressure for increased commercialization intensifies as the multinationals extend their economic activity. Locally, this is sometimes expressed as ''decentralization,'' with its implication of extending audience choice. Actually, it provides the means for the extension of advertising and commercialism.

Europe, with four hundred years of commercial and industrial development behind it, increasingly is unable to maintain autonomous national communications systems. Less developed and newly independent nations are even less capable of resisting the pressure of the modern world system.

The manufacture of culture in the advanced capitalist countries, and especially in the United States, has developed along with the general capacity to increase physical output and improve worker productivity. In the United States, the largest share of the annual cultural production is accounted for by a relatively small number of cultural conglomerates—much as automobile or steel or chemical output is concentrated in half a dozen or so giant industrial corporations. Three television networks, a handful of major film companies, the almost complete disappearance of the independent publishing house, the one-newspaper city, are the indicators of contemporary cultural production and concentration.

It is only after careful editorial consideration, for example, that some of the big culture-producers (Disney, CBS, RCA, Gulf & Western, Warner Communications, ABC, etc.) appear in the annual *Fortune* listing of the 500 largest *manufacturing* corporations in the United States.

The production of movies, television programs, games, records, magazines, and books is consolidated in a few corporate superstructures and made part of multiproduct lines of profit-maximizing combines. These culture-producing business aggregations, with the acquiescence of the judiciary, confer on themselves the legal status of individuals and take for granted their protection under the U.S. Constitution's Bill of Rights. They cover their expansionist drives for markets under the principle of the ''free flow of information,'' and, more recently, ''the right to communicate'' (Schiller, 1976, pp. 24–45).

The transformation of national media structures into conduits of the corporate business system, and the heavy international traffic of commercial media products flowing from the center to the periphery, are the most prominent means by which weaker societies are absorbed culturally into the modern world system. Yet other powerful forces are also operating.

PUBLIC RELATIONS AND MARKET SURVEYS

There are, for example, the organization and dissemination of messages of utility to the dominant power structure through what appear to be neutral or nonpartisan channels. Nonattributable information which flows, seemingly independently, into public organs of transmission is the stuff of public relations, a shadowy activity that merits more scrutiny than it receives. It is difficult to determine to what extent any community is being processed by public relations techniques. The practice, to be effective, requires concealment or at least discretion. To measure the public relations activity of MNCs and their agents in foreign locales presents great problems, for obvious reasons.

One estimate of the size of the public relations business in the United States is $3 billion annually, with $1 billion of that amount accounted for by the forty leading companies. It is noted that the leading U.S. public relations firm, Hill & Knowlton, has "developed international expertise. About 30% of its business last year (1975) was done outside the United States with foreign companies or with multinational companies of American origin" (Bender, 1976).

It is enlightening to note what a public relations firm promises, though does not necessarily deliver, to its client. In a recent exposure, a contract with the Government of Iran and Iran National Airlines and the American public relations firm, Ruder & Finn, the latter contractually offered to act as intermediary to "professional men and women" and "top businessmen" . . . "while making approaches to such publications as the *New York Times, Time* magazine, *Harper's* and the *Washington Post,* with a goal toward the publicizing of articles on key areas of interest to Iran." The contract also said that Ruder & Finn would seek to set up "small, elite meetings, some of which would be held under the cosponsorship of such prestigious organizations as the Aspen Institute or the Brookings Institute (sic) and others who would be willing to cooperate with us" (Lyons, 1976).

These, it must be remembered, are public relations activities undertaken in the United States, the center of the modern world market system. Countervailing forces negating such efforts might well be anticipated. The situation is very different in smaller, weaker societies, where such influences can well overpower the less heterogeneous local scene.

Alongside the advertising agencies, the public relations firms, and sometimes the direct efforts of the MNCs, exist the market research and opinion polling enterprises. I have written elsewhere of their operations (Schiller, 1973, pp. 104–123). Utilizing advanced statistical sampling techniques, survey research offers its sponsors—ordinarily the MNCs and government—detailed fill-ins on respondents' beliefs, hopes, aspirations, and intentions. Clearly of great potential utility to marketeers of products or ideas, the relationship, as generally structured, contributes to further social control and manipulation. The surveyor assists the power-wielder, while persuading the respondent of having participated in an expression of choice or preference.

Most surveys do not divulge their sponsors or their affiliations. In fact, often the surveyed population is unaware that it is being used and observed and questioned for reactions/answers that will permit still more effective control of its behavior.

The U.S. market research industry, like the advertising industry, has extended its activities and services globally and is itself, as one report puts it, "becoming big business." In 1975, the top ten research organizations, five of which are subsidiaries of larger, nonresearch corporations, had a net research activity volume of $313.8 million, of which $116.4 million, more than 37%, was "done outside the U.S.; a reflection of the fact that six of the ten are doing business through subsidiaries in foreign countries. *Research, then, is an export industry for the U.S.*" The largest market research company in the United States, the A. C. Nielsen Co., reports that three-quarters of its revenue "comes from what is clearly earmarked as marketing and advertising research; (and) an estimated 50% of this research volume comes from abroad" (Honomichl, 1976).

DIRECT INTERVENTION IN LOCAL MEDIA BY MNCS AND/OR THE U.S. GOVERNMENT

The processes that have been described thus far originate in the workings of a worldwide market economy in which certain centers dominate for a variety of economic and socio-historical reasons.

The normal operation of the system presupposes that capital is exported to places where the return is attractive, industrial facilities are created in new locations, workers are recruited, and production is expanded (or contracted) according to market demand. New social classes emerge, and old social formations are absorbed or decay. All of these developments, and many more, occur without central direction or political intentionality once the underlying model of capitalistic enterprise has been established and set on its course. And, as we have observed, transnational (and local) media participate vigorously in the process, both as profit-making businesses with products to sell and as promotional and marketing agents in the system overall.

However, if the basic patterns of capitalistic enterprise in a country seem threatened, a development that occurs with increasing frequency, intentionality replaces the less deliberate processes of conventional system maintenance. When this in fact does occur, the role assigned to the media is large indeed. For it is to be expected that the transnational media will do everything they can to rally support for the political "climate" that they find hospitable. Examples abound, but the case of Chile provides the paradigm.

In Chile, intervention was massive and successful. There, the short-lived efforts to restructure the society more equitably during the brief presidency of Salvador Allende, 1971–1973, occasioned a torrent of hostility in both the local antigovernmental and the transnational media (Morris et al., 1974).

Thus, where the power of the MNC and its allies in the media and intelligence services can be introduced effectively—which is not always the case, as Cuba, Vietnam, Mozambique, and Angola demonstrate—development that attempts to take a direction contrary to MNC criteria is thwarted and overturned.

Coups generally are a last resort and are undertaken only when the situation has gotten out of hand. Ordinarily, the "locals" remain quiet while the political machinery and the elites are integrated into the world system. Recent disclosures have revealed that many of the most well-known U.S. multinational corporations have systematically engaged in multiple forms of payoffs and bribes in the countries in which they do their business (Shabecoff, 1976 a, b). The pervasiveness of corruption may offer the most up-to-date refinement of the two-step flow theory of influence and opinion-making—in this version, from MNC to local elite.

In developed as well as undeveloped nations, the ruling elites are the administrators, representatives, and "bag men" of the international corporations. Parliaments and parties are bought and sold. In Italy, for example, the governing party for thirty years, it is now acknowledged, has maintained its position with heavy contributions from the Italian-based subsidiaries of American MNCs. In Holland, a small but very technologically advanced society with several hundred years of capitalist development behind it, the royal family is named as the recipient of a million dollar Lockheed corporation bribe. In powerful Japan, the former prime minister is similarly implicated. And these are nations with relatively powerful domestic bases of private enterprise. In the less developed and economically feeble Third World countries, the elites, possessing little or no domestic infrastructure of economic support, are, more often than not, the visible spokesmen and direct intermediaries of the resident MNCs.

Accompanying the corruption of political life is the political infiltration and utilization of the local media beyond the "normal" penetration effected through the commercial arrangements described earlier. In addition to the flooding of foreign economies with commercial TV programs, films, published materials, and tourists, foreign-based news organizations and publishing companies are infiltrated.

This accomplishment has the neat effect of controlling the flow of international information in *all* directions. One account (Horrock, 1976a) describes how the process operates:

> You place a story in Bangkok, for instance, in a small paper, maybe one with C.I.A. support, and it gets picked up by a larger paper and then, possibly by a foreign news service, or *Paris Match*. The next step will see it used by Reuters or an American news service and coming back to the United States.

In this manner the local (overseas) audience is first of all misinformed. The fact of publication then lends authenticity to relaying the misinformation to an American audience, which obviously has no means of checking its reliability.

The level at which these activities occurred (or occurs) indicates that this has been no erring single operation of misguided subordinates. Horrock (1976a) notes that: "Until July 1973, for example, the C.I.A. operated Forum World Features, a news syndicate in London, which bought articles from a wide range of journalists and placed them in English-language newspapers. The syndicate was registered as a corporation in Delaware and at different times such well-known American businessmen as John Hay Whitney, owner of *The International Herald Tribune*, in Paris, and Richard Mellon Scaife, the Pittsburgh banker, were listed as directors."

Other reports indicate widespread C.I.A. penetration of news organizations and several instances of agents working "as full-time correspondents with organizations that have 'major general news impact' " (Horrock, 1976b).

COMPUTER TECHNOLOGY, INFORMATION SYSTEMS, AND DEPENDENCY

A recent development, that can only be touched upon lightly but that already is affecting international information flows and threatens to deepen the condition of dependency of much of the world, is the onward march of computer technology, a new component of transnational media facilities.

Computers and computer systems now constitute a major category of U.S. commercial exports. In 1975, it was estimated that about $2.8 billion worth of computers and calculating equipment had been shipped out of the United States. Much more than profit from the sale of this equipment is involved. The installation of computer hardware is but the first step in a complex process of computerization. The programs of instruction to the computer and the assembling of data bases soon become larger and larger proportions of total costs (Harvard University, 1975, Vol. 1, pp. 8, 11).

Accompanying the sometimes unanticipated long-run costs subsequent to the installation of the hardware is the increasing dependency of less industrialized and less technically sophisticated countries on the programming of the computer and the control and organization of the newly established data bases. Informational dependence and vulnerability to external control of and access to the information stored in the system are already pressing issues. These may be expected to intensify. Consider the appraisal of a former director of the United States Information Agency (Marks, 1974):

> Long before a direct broadcast satellite becomes feasible, however, there will be electronic networks—some of them already in operation—which will pose realistic questions about information flow and cultural integrity . . . These networks will move massive amounts of information through high-speed circuits across national boundaries. Moreover, they will be effectively beyond the reach of the traditional forms of censorship and control. The only way to "censor" an electronic network moving . . . 648 million bits per second is literally to pull the plug. The international extension of electronic mail transmission, data-packet networks, and information-bank retrieval systems in future years will have considerably more effect on national cultures than any direct-broadcast systems. Our strategy will have to take this into consideration. (p. 66)

It requires little imagination to predict who will have control of and access to these electronic networks, especially in the initial period when basic institutional arrangements and structures are being established. The MNCs and powerful governmental bodies are the only entities with the resources and capabilities for developing and handling these systems. IBM now sits astride the global computer market. Poor nations and voiceless subgroups within countries, developed and nondeveloped, are and probably will be shut out from these powerful new capabilities of administration and governance. Unless there is social mobilization and awareness, not now apparent, further domination and dependency will be the likely accompaniments of the extension of the new information technology.

CONCLUSIONS

The transnational media are inseparable elements in a worldwide system of resource allocation generally regarded as capitalistic. They function as private profit-making enterprises seeking markets, which they term "audiences." They provide in their imagery and messagery the beliefs and perspectives that create and reinforce their audiences' attachment to the way things are in the system overall.

It is pointless, therefore, to attempt to measure the impact of any individual medium or message. Each is a contributor in its own way to a systemic process. All are mutually reinforcing and capable as well of absorbing occasional discordant messages and influences.

The consequences of the transnational media's heavy outputs are not measurable either. They are observable as typifying a way of life. For example, a minority report of a Brazilian governmental inquiry on the impact of the multinational corporation in Brazil, found that "the multinationals have concentrated on producing expensive goods, such as automobiles and color television sets, that demand a concentration of income . . . so more debts have been built up to finance the consumption of luxury goods instead of satisfying the minimum necessities of nutrition, health, housing, and employment'' (Greenwood, 1975).

This describes a developmental path. It is a familiar one. It is what has come to be recognized, with apologies to the Chinese, as the capitalist road to development. In this process, the media, now many times more powerful and penetrative than in an earlier time, are the means that entice and instruct their audiences along this path, while at the same time concealing the deeper reality and the long-term consequences that the course produces.

While the transnational media as constituents of international capital push and guide the developmental course favorable to capital, they are no stronger than the system itself. They cannot impose this pattern at will. In fact, with the general weakening of American capitalism, the future of the MNCs becomes problematical. One observer (Read, 1976) notes this carefully:

> After World War II, American transnationals flourished because the United States had the political power to keep the international system open (i.e., to assure freedom of operation) and transnational organizations had the necessary means of transportation and communication to pursue (their) strategies abroad. . . . But while technology has offered improved means (jet liners, computers, satellites), the ability of the United States to keep the system open—to enforce the general concept of freedom to operate and the specific principle of free flow of information by any medium—has been challenged.
> A crucial question is this: Will the concept of freedom to communicate endure the current phase of international affairs in which the United States is experiencing a relative decline of its international political power? (pp. 10–11).

This, indeed, is the crucial question. It is not surprising that in those places where resistance movements have developed, genuinely autonomous communications efforts have accompanied, and contributed significantly to, the larger liberation struggle.

REFERENCES

Bender, M. (1976). Marion Javits issue focuses unwelcome spotlight on publicizing of foreign clients. *New York Times*, February 27, p. 6.

Geneen, H. S. (1974). Foreword. *In* ''Advertising and Society'' (Y. Brozen, ed.), pp. 7–8. New York University Press, New York.

Greenwood, L. (1975). Multinationals drain Brazil, report says. *Los Angeles Times*, December 1, p. 11.

Harvard University. (1975). Program on Information Technologies and Public Policy. *Annual Report, 1974–75*.

Honomichl, J. J. (1976). For top 10 researchers, a good '75. *Advertising Age* (March 15), 1, 53–54.

Horrock, N. M. (1976a). C.I.A. infiltration of press overseas viewed as influencing news received by Americans. *New York Times*, February 9.

Horrock, N. M. (1976b). C.I.A. ties to journalists. *New York Times*, January 18.

Lyons, R. D. (1976). Marion Javits registered as agent on behalf of Iran. *New York Times*, January 5, p. 4.

Marks, L. H. (1974). International conflict and the free flow of information. *In* "Control of the Direct Broadcast Satellite: Values in Conflict," pp. 65–71. Aspen Institute Program on Communications and Society, Palo Alto, California.

Masson, P., and Thorburn, A. (1975). Advertising: The American influence in Europe. *In* "Superculture" (C. W. E. Bigsby, ed.), pp. 96–106. Paul Elek, London.

Morris, R., Mueller, S., and Jelin, W. (1974). Through the looking glass in Chile: Coverage of Allende's regime. *Columbia Journalism Review 13* (Nov.–Dec.), 15–26.

Mowlana, H. (1975). The multinational corporation and the diffusion of technology. *In* "The New Sovereigns: Multinational Corporations as World Powers" (A. A. Said and L. R. Simmons, eds.), pp. 77–90. Prentice-Hall, Englewood Cliffs, New Jersey.

Musgrave, P. B. (1975). "Direct Investment Abroad and the Multinationals: Effect on the United States Economy." Government Printing Office, Washington, D.C. (Report prepared for Subcommittee on Multinational Corporations, Committee on Foreign Relations, United States Senate.)

O'Gara, J. V. (1976). It's a record: U.S. agencies bill $14.6 billion. *Advertising Age* (Feb. 23), 1.

Read, W. H. (1976). "Foreign Policy: The High and Low Politics of Telecommunications." Program on Information Technologies and Public Policy, Harvard University, Cambridge, Massachusetts. (Publication P-76-3.)

Sauvant, K. P. (1977). The potential of multinational enterprises as vehicles for the transmission of business culture. *In* "Controlling Multinational Enterprises: Problems, Strategies, Counterstrategies" (K. P. Sauvant and E. Lavipour, eds.), pp. 39-78. Westview Press, Boulder, Colorado.

Schiller, H. I. (1973). "The Mind Managers." Beacon Press, Boston, Massachusetts.

Schiller, H. I. (1976). "Communication and Cultural Domination." International Arts and Sciences Press, White Plains, New York.

Shabecoff, P. (1976a). Closing in on pay-offs abroad. *New York Times*, February 15.

Shabecoff, P. (1976b). Ford sets review of bribes abroad by U.S. companies. *New York Times*, February 11.

Smythe, D. (1977). Communications: "Blind Spot" of Western Marxism. *Journal of Political and Social Theory* (In press.) (Paper presented at West Coast Critical Communications Conference, Stanford University, Dec. 1975.)

Wallerstein, I. (1974). "The Modern World System, Capitalist Agriculture and the Origins of the European World-Economy in the Sixteenth Century." Academic Press, New York.

3

Latin America and the United States: Flaws in the Free Flow of Information

Luis Ramiro Beltrán S.

Elizabeth Fox de Cardona

International Development Research Centre, Bogotá

Luis Ramiro Beltrán S. is Representative for Latin America of the Division of Information Sciences, International Development Research Centre, Bogotá. Dr. Beltrán was awarded a PhD degree in Communications by Michigan State University in 1965. He has been a newspaper editor, a member of the Information Office of the Cooperative Agricultural Extension Service in Bolivia, advisor to the Scientific Communication Service of the Inter-American Institute of Agricultural Sciences, and Director of its Inter-American Center for Rural Development and Land Reform. In addition, he has written extensively on communication for national development, Latin America's structural communication problems, national communication policies, and communication research in Latin America.

Elizabeth Fox de Cardona is Assistant to the Representative for Latin America of the Division of Information Sciences, International Development Research Centre, Bogotá, and holds degrees from Vassar College, Javeriana University, and the Annenberg School of Communications at the University of Pennsylvania. She has headed research projects for the Ford Foundation, UNESCO, the Development Center of OECD, and Instituto Colombiano de Desarrollo Social, and has also published papers on television, radio, and the structure of the mass media in Latin America.

This article is extracted from a paper presented at the Conference on the Fair Communication Policy for the International Exchange of Information, the East–West Center, Honolulu, Hawaii, March 28–April 3, 1976, and originally published in the Report on the Conference, *New Perspectives in International Communication*, edited by Jim Richstad, East–West Communication Institute, East–West Center, Honolulu, Hawaii, 1977.

The opinions expressed in this chapter are solely the responsibility of the authors and not those of the institution for which they work.

INTRODUCTION

In order to analyze the nature, influence, and role in national communication development of the international communication institutions operating in Latin America, it is first necessary to identify and classify the elements that constitute these phenomena. In this chapter we define institutions as those formal organizations with direct or indirect international communications activities in Latin America. We have selected only those institutions related to the mass media with special emphasis on "software" aspects; we are conscious of the fact that this election means narrowing our definition of communications.

Our interest is the structure and function of these nonnational institutions with regard to the national mass media of the region. In other words, we are concerned with how the organization and activities of these institutions influence the organization and activities of national media. We then study the influence of these institutions with regard to the achievement of the development of the countries.

The term nonnational is defined as those institutions not original to a specific society, be these international organizations or multinational corporations. Nonnational organizations can be classified into the categories of economic, political, and communications institutions. *Economic institutions* are those principally concerned with the production and distribution of wealth. For the purpose of this paper, *communication institutions* are those concerned principally with the production and distribution of messages at the mass level, whereas *political institutions* are those involved in the exercise of power by one state on some entity. We wish to emphasize that this classification has been developed to facilitate analysis and that the categories do not pretend to be mutually exclusive. Overlaps do occur, especially in free market economies. By employing them as basic categories, we hope to analyze the complex political, economic, and communication phenomena that constitute the international exchange of information.

We have narrowed the scope of this paper by limiting our analysis to the many manifestations of the United States in nonnational communication institutions of Latin America. This decision is due to the fact that, although evidence exists of operations of other countries in this field, North American activities are historically the most predominant.

IDENTIFICATION AND CLASSIFICATION OF NONNATIONAL MEDIA INSTITUTIONS IN LATIN AMERICA

Economic Institutions

Direct Investment in National Media by Nonnational Institutions

The main institutions of direct capital investment in the media in Latin

America have been the three U.S. national television networks. These began with radio in the 1930s and continued during the 1960s in television. The last five years have witnessed a reduction in direct investment, our first category of international information flow.

Colombian radio networks established in the 1940s and 1950s were set up and financed by CBS-owned Cadena de las Americas and the NBC-owned Cadena Panamericana, both of which operated throughout Latin America (Fox de Cardona, 1975). Chilean radio station, Radio Cooperativa Vitalicia, is an affiliate of the NBC Panamericana Network (Schenkel, 1973, p. 55).

In 1960, after the creation of the Central American Common Market, the ABC Worldvision group invested in five Central American stations, creating in this way CATVN, which simultaneously purchased programming, served as sales representative, and set up the network among these stations. In 1968, a similar strategy was applied to South America with the LATINO network. ABC led the other U.S. networks in this type of activity, and by 1969, their two networks included (Mattelart, 1973a, p. 136):

Channel 9 in Buenos Aires	Channel 5 in Tegucigalpa
Channels 13 and 4 in Chile	Channel 2 in the Dutch Antilles
Channel 9 in Bogota, Colombia	Channel 2 in Panama
Channel 7 of Costa Rica	Channel 12 in Uruguay
Channel 7 of Santo Domingo	Channel 4 in Venezuela
Channels 7, 6, and 3 of Ecuador	Channel 3 in Guatemala
Channels 2 and 4 of San Salvador	

CBS followed ABC's activities with direct investments in Latin American record companies, in addition to direct investments in three television production companies, including Proartel in Argentina, Proventel in Venezuela (both recently sold), and Pantel in Peru. CBS also owns stations in Trinidad and Antigua (Mattelart, 1973a, p. 137).

Time Inc. has interests with CBS in Venezuela and Argentina, where it has since pulled out, and yet continues with investment in Brazil through technical and financial assistance to TV Globo in Rio and TV Paulista in Sao Paulo (Mattelart, 1973a, p. 137).

NBC was less aggressive in its direct investment policy, perhaps due to the relation with mother company RCA which was involved with other activities in equipment sales and technical assistance to the emerging Latin American television companies. NBC has investments in Channel 2 of Caracas (20%), a television station in Monterrey, Mexico, and in Jamaica. NBC had previous investments in Channel 9 in Buenos Aires (Schenkel, 1973, p. 23).

The U.S. networks were not the only direct investors in the Latin American media. The U.S. Sidney Ross Drug Company set up and owned one of the first Colombian radio chains (Fox de Cardona, 1975, pp. 23–24), while in Chile, until 1971, controlling stock of Radio Network Minera, was in the hands of the three main U.S. mining companies, Anaconda, Kennecott, and Anglo Lautaro (Schenkel, 1973).

The 1970s have witnessed a decrease of North American direct investment in Latin America media, especially in television, due to a growing apprehension of possible political intervention. Other forms of investment that have developed are discussed below: for example, advertising and sales of programming, technology, and educational materials (Mattelart, 1973b, p. 175).

The U.S. television and radio networks have been the main nonnational institutions of direct capital investment in the Latin American media. During the 1960s they had significant investments in most major television stations of the region.

Direct Investments by Nonnational Institutions in the Financing of the Operations of National Mass Media

Our second areas of analysis is the financing of national media through nonnational advertising agencies and the multinational corporation as an advertising client. The strength of advertising, as practically the sole financer of the Latin American media, is illustrated by the following statistics.

Latin American dailies devoted 46% of their space to advertising (Kaplun, 1973, p. 29), while 86% of the radio stations in Latin America are commercial—93% if the Cuban stations are excluded (Kaplun, 1973, p. 58). Between 30 and 40% of the broadcast time on these stations is advertising (Kaplun, 1973, p. 64). Television channels in Latin America are commercial in 83% of the cases—92% if the Cuban channels are excluded (Kaplun, 1973, p. 54). Broadcasting time on these channels is 20% commercial (Kaplun, 1973, p. 76).

The following illustrates what part of this advertising is managed by nonnational firms in various countries of the region:

> In Central American countries such as Guatemala, Nicaragua, and El Salvador, advertising is practically in the hands of one firm, McCann Erickson.
>
> In Argentina, among the ten most important advertising agencies, six are affiliates or associates of North American agencies, representing 70% of the billings of these ten agencies (Mattelart, 1975, p. 87).
>
> In 1960, the top five U.S. advertising agencies controlled 35% of television commercials, while foreign advertisers (Ford, Standard Oil, Shell, Coca Cola, etc.) represented between 30 and 45% of all Argentine television advertising (Schenkel, 1973, p. 21).
>
> Sales of the two largest agencies in Brazil, McCann Erickson and J. Walter Thompson, represent approximately twice those of leading national companies (also associated with U.S. capital and agencies) (Mattelart, 1975, p. 87).
>
> Of the twenty leading Chilean advertising agencies in 1970, five were direct affiliates of North American firms, including the two top firms.

Forty-five percent of Channel 13 advertising was from nonnational firms, and the large majority of radio advertising was also foreign (Mattelart, 1970, pp. 56–57).

Three U.S. agencies in Colombia are among the seven top agencies, in addition to heavy U.S. investments in national agencies. The first five advertising clients in Colombia television are Colgate-Palmolive, Lever Brothers, American Home Products, Lotteries and Raffles, and Miles Laboratories (Fox de Cardona, 1975, p. 37). Over 50% of television advertising is dedicated to cosmetics, nonessential food stuffs, detergents, and supermarkets, the great majority produced by m· ˙nationals (Fox de Cardona, 1975, p. 41).

Of the 170 advertising agencies in Mexico, only four are solely in Mexican hands. ''The rest, dominated by United States companies, control 70% of the advertising business which finances the country's newspapers and the radio and television networks. Money spent on publicity in Mexico amounts to nearly $500 million a year, of which $400 million is handled by eleven large United States agencies'' (By the Way, 1976).

Malpica (1968) reported that 80% of Peruvian commercial advertising was controlled by seven North American agencies. In 1969 in that country, Sears Roebuck and ''Supermarkets'' occupied the first place in newspaper advertising while Procter and Gamble, Sears Roebuck, Sidney Ross, Colgate-Palmolive, Sherwin Williams, and Bayer were the top television and radio announcers.

The top ten agencies in Venezuela are either directly U.S. owned or controlled (Mattelart, 1975, p. 87). The national Association of Advertisers in Venezuela is made up of the leading advertising clients for radio and television and for the press. Of seventy-eight members, forty-two are multinational corporations (Venezuela, Comisión, 1975, p. 130). Over 210 million dollars is spent every year in the country in advertising. Among the top twenty-three agencies are the following U.S. agencies with their respective clients:

JWT: Ford, Kodak, Adams, Lever Brothers, Pan American, Cheesebrough Ponds, Kraft, Kellogg, Gillette, and Abbott Laboratories.
McCann Erickson: Westinghouse, American Express, EXXON, General Motors, Coca-Cola, Goodyear, Cyanamid, Max Factor.
Young and Rubicam: Chrysler, Procter and Gamble, General Electric, Mennen (Eliaschev, 1975, p. 16).

Public Opinion and Public Relations   The goal of commercial advertising is to sell companies' products. This, however, is not the only way the media are financed, for there are other less direct commercial uses of national institutions. The purpose of public relations is to sell the public image and good will of the company itself, an important function for nonnational corporations operating abroad. International public relations departments of multinational corporations prepare press releases for the national media. As Schiller (1973) observes: "National and local mass media systems are infiltrated by business messages not necessarily identified by their sources or origin" (p. 137).

The two other media services related to advertising in which nonnational institutions predominate, are international public opinion polls and marketing research institutions. Their functions are quite similar; the former is more concerned with political attitudes, whereas the latter serves to direct commercial activities. Both are extensively employed by the media to plan programming and to attract advertising investment. The firms themselves tend to be one and the same. The largest market research company, A. C. Nielsen, operates in twenty different countries in four continents, supplying research services to eighty-six organizations. Other firms within Latin American surveying operations are International Research Associates and Gallup International, which conducts periodic surveys of any sort in Argentina, Chile, and Uruguay (Schiller, 1973, pp. 133–134).

Matellart reports in a recent article that in 1968 Crompton Advertising (U.S.) managed the presidential campaigns of the Christian Democrats' candidate in Venezuela, Rafael Caldera. He continues to report that the 1970 campaign of right wing candidate Alessandri in Chile was managed by J. Walter Thompson, which also managed the 1972 campaign of General Alsogaray in Argentina (Matellart, 1975, p. 78).

Latin American media are principally financed by commercial advertising. U.S. advertising companies lead the field in most of the countries of the region. Among their main clients are the U.S. multinationals. Advertising-related service industries such as public opinion and public relations are also U.S. owned and managed.

Communication Institutions

The next category we will discuss is the production of messages by nonnational private institutions. This production has been divided in two types: those messages produced and distributed to national media institutions as intermediaries, and those directly distributed to the population. Messages distributed to the national media include news flow and programming. Direct distribution are the cases of film and magazines.

Indirect Distribution of Messages to National Media

News.   U.S. news services operating in Latin America and the rest of the world are the United Press International (UPI) and the Associated Press (AP).

A 1975 UNESCO–CIESPAL survey of Latin American Communication Institutions (UNESCO, 1975) showed that UPI serves sixteen out of twenty countries, and AP fourteen out of the same twenty. These two agencies dominate the international content of the Latin American news media. As Markham (1961) reported, foreign news in seven Latin American dailies was supplied almost entirely by the two U.S. agencies, plus France Press. UPI alone provided nearly half, 47%, of all story items to those dailies.

Corroboration for this data is available in three other studies. Diaz Rangel (1967) analyzed one day's content of fourteen Latin American dailies and found that AP and UPI contributed 72% of their foreign content. The Centro Internacional de Estudios Superiores de Periodismo para America Latina (CIESPAL) Study (1967) revealed that 84% of the foreign news in the twenty-nine dailies for the study was contributed by news agencies; less than 1% was contributed by ORBE, one of the few Latin American agencies; the rest was distributed among foreign news agencies, half by UPI, 30% by AP, and 13% by France Press. There was a total of 80% from U.S. agencies. Those three agencies were also found to be the primary source of news about the United States for twenty Latin American dailies (Wolfe, 1964). The role of the nonnational news agencies is described below in the different countries of the region.

In Argentina, AP and UPI manage the international news. UPI has exclusivity in *La Presa*, of Buenos Aires, and *Los Andes* of Mendoza, while AP serves *La Nacion* and at least four provincial dailies (Schenkel, 1973, p. 21).

In Colombia, international wire services filter news to and from the country, in addition to some of the internal national news. UPI and AP together account for 70% of international news in that country (Schenkel, 1973, p. 37).

The Chilean press, radio and television are also serviced by the nonnational news services, in particular by UPI, that maintain a monopoly on news leaving the country (Schenkel, 1973, p. 53).

In spite of the fact that Mexico has two national news agencies, one State owned, 90% of international news is provided by AP and UPI and AFP (Schenkel, 1973, p. 70). In addition, Telesistema receives photographic material from NBC and CBS.

Sixty percent of international news in Peru before the revolutionary government was provided by UPI and AP, although there are three small national agencies (Schenkel, 1973, p. 87).

The U.S. news agencies manage 80% of the international news in Latin America, and in many countries a significant percentage of national and regional news as well is controlled by these agencies.

Programming.   A survey conducted in 1970 examined one week of television programming in eighteen cities of Latin America. The study reveals an average of 31.4% of U.S. programming in Latin American television (Kaplun, 1973, p. 79), ranging from a high of 92.7% in Panana to a low of 21.4% in Argentina.

A worldwide study of the flow of international television programming (Varis, 1973; Nordenstreng and Varis, 1974) complements this data, analyzing the flow of U.S. programming in Latin America.

According to *Vision*, Latin America spends annually $80 million in U.S. television programming and film (Kaplun, 1973). With the exception of the Education Television Network, all the American companies seem to distribute about one-third of their total foreign sales to Latin America (Varis, 1973, p. 196). The main purchaser is Brazil, with almost a quarter of the total followed in 1970 by Peru, Mexico, and Venezuela (Varis, 1973, p. 196).

This phenomenon of commercial television programming sales has extended to the sale of noncommercial educational television programs in Latin America. For example, "Sesame Street" is financed by Xerox for the Spanish version, "Plaza Sesamo," which is administered by the company Producciones Barbachano Ponce S.A., owner of television chains, and distributed in the region by the Mexican private television monopoly, Televisa. The same occurred in Brazil, with "Vila Sesamo," financed mainly by Xerox, and coproduced by the television and newspaper monopoly, O Globo, of Rio de Janeiro, and the Company TV Cultura de Sao Paulo (Mattelart, 1973b, p. 172).

Television is not the only recipient of U.S. programming. In Argentina, according to Schenkel, (1973, p. 22) up to 85% of the music heard on the radio consists of imported records and tapes, principally rock and soul from the United States. Argentine newspapers contain U.S. comic strips, editorials, and articles from *The New York Times*, the *Los Angeles Times*, and the *Washington Post*.

In the Colombian press, 80% of the comic strips and 25% of the sports news are from the United States (Schenkel, 1973).

The Mexican press devotes 30% of its space to U.S. sports news, while 50% of radio time is music and soap operas from the United States (Schenkel, 1973, p. 71).

A list compiled on Sunday August 3, 1975, of the comic strips published in the two major Caracas dailies, *El Nacional* and *El Universo*, include thirty-one different strips, all U.S.-originated, distributed mainly by King, Walt Disney, and Field (Eliaschev, 1975, p. 15).

U.S. programming dominates an average of 31.4% of television programming in the region, including both U.S. commercial and educational programming. In addition, U.S. recorded music is heavily used in radio and U.S. comic strips almost completely monopolize the newspapers.

Direct Distribution of Messages by Nonnational Media Institutions

Magazines. The majority of the nonnational magazines distributed in Latin America are generated by the Hearst Corporation.

In Mexico, these magazines (*Cosmopolitan, Good Housekeeping*, and *Popular Mechanics*) are published in Spanish by Publications Continentales, and have a monthly circulation of 2 million copies.

In Chile, the edition and distribution rights are in the hands of Editorial Lord Cochrane of the Edwards Group.

Latin American publications elaborated in Venezuela of the Hearst Magazines are managed by Editorial America of the De Armas group. The De Armas chain, formed in 1967 from the Distribuidora Continental, is now the largest editorial house in Latin America. The De Armas chain has exclusive rights for the reproduction and distribution of the U.S. magazines *Buenhogar, Mecanica Popular, Cosmopolitan, Readers Digest*, and the *Almanaque Mundial*. Every month the De Armas releases 17 million copies among all their publications (Eliaschev, 1975, p. 17).

The Hearst Corporation is also co-owner of UPI and of MGM (Matellart, 1973a, pp. 127–128).

Readers Digest. This magazine has nine editions in Latin America, eight in Spanish and one in Portuguese. Ninety-five percent of the material of all nine magazines, which is rarely from Latin America, is the same for all editions. Total circulation of the magazine in the region reaches 900,000 monthly (Kaplun, 1973, p. 43).

Time circulates in all countries of Latin America. According to Matellart, Time-Life Inc. has investments in various magazines and editorials of the region (Matellart, 1973a, p. 131).

Comic Books. The largest editor and distributor of comic books for Latin America is Western Publishing Company, headquartered in Mexico. It circulates millions of copies of "Archie," "Batman," "Superman," "Walt Disney," "Dagwood and Blondie," "Tom and Jerry," and "Porky the Pig" among many others. In addition, Walt Disney directly licenses Latin American editorials to publish its production in Spanish, such as Editorial Andes in Bogota, and Editorial Tucuman S.A. in Argentina (Matellart, 1973a, p. 130).

Films. Of films shown in Latin America, an average of 55% are U.S. originated, ranging from 46% in film-producer Mexico to 70 and 73%, respectively, in Bolivia and Guatemala (Kaplun, 1973, p. 52).

Film distribution is dominated by MGM, Twentieth Century Fox, United Artists, Columbian Paramount, and Warner Brothers, all operating under the cartel of Motion Picture Export Association of America. the MPEAA is permitted under the Webb Pomerene Export Trade Act of 1918, which permitted domestic competitors to cooperate in trade by forming export associations which might otherwise have been held illegal under the Sherman and Clayton Antitrusts Acts. In effect, this exemption allowed American companies to combine and fix prices and allocate customers in foreign markets (Guback, 1974, p. 92).

In many countries international film companies also directly own the theaters to which their films are distributed (Matellart, 1973a, p. 139).

U.S. originated magazines and comic books are widely distributed to the Latin American public. U.S. films represent an average of 55% of films shown in the region.

Political Institutions

The production and distribution of messages by a nonnational government, in this case the U.S. government, is accomplished in two ways: (1) the distribution of messages to national media institutions, and (2) the direct distribution to the public of a country. We will discuss both types in relation to U.S. activities in Latin America.

The Office of Coordination of Inter-American Affairs.   During the second world war, Nelson Rockefeller was named Director of the Office of Coordination of Inter-American Affairs. When the United States entered the war, this office was concerned with open propaganda in favor of the Allies. According to Epstein (1976) Rockefeller convinced the Treasury Department to accept as tax free deductions funds spent by North American companies in advertising in those media sympathetic with the Allied cause. This tax free advertising accounted at one time for 40% of the earnings of the press and radio in Latin America. Newsprint was also selectively administered by this office to the "cooperative" newspapers. The Rockefeller office, with a staff of 1200 in the United States, included journalists, advertisers, public relations analysts, and pollsters, and had a budget of $140 million over a five-year period. They prepared editorials, photographs, and feature articles for the Latin American press, in addition to the direct distribution of magazines, pamphlets, books and films. A weekly commentary letter was sent to 13,000 preidentified "opinion leaders" in the continent. Rockefeller also organized trips to the States for influential Latin American editors and later provided scholarships for their children.

During the war more than 1200 newspapers and 200 radio stations received a dosage of 3,000 words a day of news in Spanish and Portuguese, administered by U.S. news agencies and radio chains through the Rockefeller office.

By the end of the war, the Inter-American Affairs Office calculated that over 75% of the world news that reached Latin America originated in Washington under their control and that of the State Department (Epstein, 1976, pp. 4–5).

Current U.S. activities of the type referred to above are under the auspices of the United States Information Office, established in 1953 as an executive office of the government. Total USIS staff is 9,800, 4,400 of whom are American and 5,400 nationals. USIS has twenty-two offices in Latin America, and employs 169 Americans and 660 nationals. The 1973 budget for Latin America was approximately 20 million dollars (Ficha de identificación, 1974, p. 6).

In a recent interview with *U.S. News and World Report*, Frank Shakespeare, former director of USIS, explained the principal facets of this organization as: (1) to assist the foreign policy of the United States by clarifying, seeking support for and diminishing opposition to this policy, and (2) to evaluate international attitudes to the degree that these are relevant to U.S. foreign policy and its formulation. The former function, he explained, is achieved through worldwide radio transmission (The Voice of America) in 35 different languages, production and distribution of films for television and theater, libraries, and art shows, and press and cultural offices all over the world. He gave no explanation for the latter (Shakespeare, 1974, p. 105).

USIS Latin American operations also include the direct distribution of films for television and theaters, and recordings for radio, art and music exhibitions, and free international cable service for national newspapers, in addition to the direct service of La Voz de las Americas.

According to Fresenius, USIS also directly distributes comic books in Latin America, among recent examples of which are: "La Palmada en la Frente," distributed in Chile on the eve of the last presidential elections, portrayed the situation in the country if the socialist Unidad Popular were to win the elections as a nation controlled by a huge arbitrary Soviet Bureaucracy, and "El Desengaño," 147,000 copies of which were distributed simultaneously in 1969 in eleven countries of the region. It depicted the urban guerrilla as a trap and a false solution to social problems. One year after this was anonymously distributed, USIS publicly acknowledged authorship (Fresenius and Vergara, 1974, p. 12).

The following are examples of the radio soap operas distributed free of charge in Latin America as they are described in the USIS Catalogue. *La Trampa* (The Trap) (52 episodes, 30 minutes)—each episode presents the story of an individual who fell into the trap of communism (recorded in

Mexico and Bogota). *El Lobo del Mar* (78 episodes, 30 minutes)—the protagonists, Captain Silver and Tex, combat subversion and extremism throughout the Latin American hemisphere.

The USIS is also involved in the edition and distribution of books in Latin America through agreements, among others, with Editorials Sudamerica, Paidos, and Troquel in Buenos Aires (Matellart, 1973a, pp. 151–159).

Alan Wells (1972), in his book on U.S. television in Latin America, reports the case of Radio Swan, which operated a 50,000 watt station from Swan Island in 1970.

> Like the other stations, Radio Swan (later renamed Radio Americas) had its own civilian "front" office in New York, in this case headed—none too tactfully for Latin sensibilities—by a former president of the United Fruit Company. Under allegedly "absolute CIA control," the station played an intimate part in the unsuccessful Bay of Pigs invasion of Cuba. (p. 101)

A recent official U.S. document provides extensive detailed information on certain activities of the CIA (Central Intelligence Agency) in relation to the mass media of one Latin American country. This document is the Staff Report of a special group of the U.S. Senate, the Select Committee to Study Governmental Operations with Respect to Intelligence Activities (U.S. Senate, 1975).

The information of the Select Committee of the U.S. Senate illustrates the operations related to the Chilean mass media that the CIA conducted between 1963 and 1973, and particularly during the last three years of this period when the first democratically elected socialist government in Latin America was in office. The report was presented by the Senate Committee during the special hearings in 1975, in which this legislative body reviewed the CIA activities in general.

The report commences affirming that in 1965, as indirect support for the Christian Democratic Candidate Eduardo Frei, "the CIA mounted a massive anti-communist propaganda campaign" and "a scare campaign which relied heavily on images of Soviet tanks and Cuban firing squads and was directed especially to women" (U.S. Senate, 1975, p. 15). The report considers this campaign to have been "enormous," provides details regarding its magnitude, and demonstrates that, "the CIA regards the anticommunist scare campaign as the most effective activity undertaken by the U.S. on behalf of the Christian Democratic candidate" (U.S. Senate, 1975, p. 16). The report continues to explain that the CIA supported various similar projects: one involving news agencies, another wall posters, leaflet campaigns and public heckling, a third supporting a right-wing weekly newspaper. "Other assets funded under this project placed CIA-inspired editorials almost daily in *El Mercurio*, Chile's major newspaper, and after 1968, exerted substantial control over the content of that paper's international news section (U.S. Senate, 1975, pp. 18–19).

The Senate report also includes considerable information on the media-oriented activities of the CIA during the elections of 1970, directed toward thwarting the victory of the socialist candidate, Salvador Allende. The strategy was the same as that employed before, "an Allende victory was equated with violence and repression" (U.S. Senate, 1975, p. 20). The report points out that the CIA undertook half a dozen projects, "an intensive propaganda campaign which made use of virtually all media within Chile and which placed and replayed items in the international press as well" (p. 21).

The report confirms that these campaigns had considerable influence on the public to which they were directed, and provides the following details of the size of these efforts:

> A few statistics convey the magnitude of the CIA's propaganda campaign mounted during the six-week interim period in the Latin American and European media. According to the CIA, partial returns showed that 726 articles, broadcasts, editorials, and similar items directly resulted from Agency activity. The Agency had no way to measure the scope of the multiplier effect—i.e., how much its "induced" news focused media interest on the Chilean issues and stimulated additional coverage—but concluded that its contribution was both substantial and significant. (p. 25)

After the electorial victory of Allende, the CIA directed its efforts toward opposition propaganda. The Senate Report states in regard to the cost of this campaign:

> Besides funding political parties, the 40 Committee approved large amounts to sustain opposition media and thus to maintain a hard-hitting propaganda campaign. The CIA spent $1.5 million in support of *El Mercurio*, the country's largest newspaper and the most important channel for anti-Allende propaganda.
> According to CIA documents, these efforts played a significant role in setting the stage for the military coup of September 11, 1973.
> The 40 Committee approvals in 1971 and early 1972 for subsidizing *El Mercurio* were based on reports that the Chilean government was trying to close the *El Mercurio* chain. In fact, the press remained free throughout the Allende period, despite attempts to harass and financially damage opposition media. The alarming field reports on which the 40 Committee decisions to support *El Mercurio* were based are at some variance with intelligence community analyses. For example, an August 1971 National Intelligence Estimate—nine months after Allende took power—maintained that the government was attempting to dominate the press but commented that *El Mercurio* had managed to retain its independence. Yet one month later the 40 Committee voted $700,000 to keep *El Mercurio* afloat. And CIA documents in 1973 acknowledge that *El Mercurio* and, to a lesser extent, the papers belonging to opposition political parties, were the only publications under pressure from the government. (p. 29)

Finally, in regard to the international aspects of the campaign, the report affirms that:

> The freedom of the press issue was the single most important theme in the international propaganda campaign against Allende. Among the books and pamphlets produced by the major opposition research organization was one which appeared in October 1972 at the time of the Inter-American Press Association (IAPA) meeting in Santiago. As in the 1970 period, the IAPA listed Chile as a country in which freedom of the press was threatened (p. 29).

U.S. political institution USIS extensively distributes information either directly or through the Latin American media in this region in the forms of radio soap operas, comic books, and radio broadcasts. In addition the CIA has carried out operations related to the Latin American mass media, directed toward financing messages against popular political movements of a reformist social democratic orientation.

Mixed Institutions

Satellite. One nonnational media institution that in effect constitutes a mixed institution—economic, political and communication—is the case of the regional satellite for Latin America. Ballochi (1974), in a review of the steps leading up to the educational satellite for Latin America, reports that:

1. In June 1967, Stanford University published a study on educational satellite use for Latin America.

2. In April 1969, a meeting was held in Santiago de Chile to consider a proposal by several U.S. institutions to use an educational satellite in the region. This meeting was attended by Latin American and U.S. institutions and various U.S. foundations and companies, among these COMSAT and General Electric. The product of this meeting was CAVISAT, an organization that was to perform studies and promote the design of the educational use of satellites in Latin America. Ten U.S. and ten Latin American universities were chosen by the meeting for the elaboration of the educational programs. This was the first and last direct nongovernmental effort in the area of educational satellites for the region (Ballochi, 1974, pp. 117–121).

3. In 1970 UNESCO published a preparatory study of educational satellite use for development purposes in Latin America which had been requested by the governments of Argentina, Chile, Colombia, Peru, Uruguay, and Venezuela.

4. Also in 1970, the Educational Ministers of the Andean Pact signed the Andres Bello Agreement for Scientific, Cultural, and Educational Integration of the region. The Andres Bello Agreement assigned to Venezuela the task of studying the feasibility of carrying out educational, scientific and cultural programming for the region via satellite. This study was undertaken under the sponsorship of UNESCO and the Inter-American Telecommunications Union, and financed by the United National Development Fund. The Venezuelan study included satellites and other systems of educational television production, transmission, and distribution and the legal, financial, and economic aspects of a regional educational television system. This study was published in 1973 and presented and discussed in Caracas by a group of experts in 1974 (UNESCO, 1973).

Brazil is the only country in the region where a satellite is actively functioning. The different stages of the establishment and development were designed in a 1967 study by Stanford University. A feasibility study was carried out by the Brazilian National Commission for Space Activities in 1968, and a UNESCO experts mission. Since then the project has been administered by the Institute of Space Research of Brazil. The first stage of the experiment used the NASA ATS-3 satellite and studied the reception of telephone and documents in the region; the second stage planned the utilization of the ATS-6 for an experimental program for educational television that reached 500 teaching centers and 1,500 students in North East Brazil (Sommerlad, 1975).

Other Institutions.   There are other areas that form part of the structure of the international exchange of information between the United States and the countries of Latin America, into which at this point it is impossible to enter in greater detail. One of these is technology, and another research and development activities in telecommunications in which the United States performs the active role of leader and exporter.

As the National Academy of Engineering, Committee on Telecommunications noted in a recent review of telecommunications research in the United States and selected foreign countries (National Academy of Engineering, 1973), prepared by the National Science Foundation:

> Certainly the recent levels of telecommunications research and development for the requirements of the Department of Defense (250 million/year), the National Aeronautic And Space Administration (100 million/year), the Bell Telephone System (400 million/year), and other major users of telecommunications has been adequate to maintain a technological lead for the United States in these mission areas. (pp. 7–8)

U.S. private enterprise and government institutions have also played important roles in financial and technical assistance and training for the design and implementation of national media systems, such as the role of USAID and the Peace Corps in the Colombian Educational Television System (see Bennett, 1964), and AID's role in the Educational Television System for San Salvador (see Hornik et al., 1973). Not to mention the role of hardware sales by U.S. tele-communication manufacturing companies, and supplier credits to national media institutions. Similarly U.S. Government institutions have also historically been instrumental in training and technical assistance in general audio-visual education and extension work in the region.

Summary: Identification and Classification

The nonnational economic institutions concerned with the media commenced their activities in Latin America with the direct investments of the U.S. networks and other companies in the radio and television for the region. This investment, which was quite important during the 1960s, has been gradually replaced by the nonnational investment in advertising agencies that support the media, and nonnational advertising clients as economic institutions that are influential in the Latin American media.

The management of international and regional news flow in the region has been assumed by U.S. agencies since the Second World War. During this time, programming sales and direct distribution also grew. The use of nonnational political institutions that involved the media also appears to have had its birth during the war and continues today. In summary, direct nonnational economic investment has been replaced by nonnational media "service" institutions, and more directly by nonnational communication institutions, as is the case of programming sales and news flow, in addition to nonnational political involvement with the media. Reference is also made to other areas that form part of information exchange, such as the transfer of technology and technical assistance on the part of the U.S. Government.

More specifically, U.S. advertising companies lead the field in the majority of the countries of the region, in addition to U.S. public opinion and public relations firms. U.S. news agencies manage 80% of the international news in Latin America and in many cases also the national and regional news. U.S. programming dominates an average of 31.4% of television programming in the region. U.S. records and comic strips also flood the market. The United States directly distributes magazines and films in the region, the latter constituting 55% of all films shown in Latin America. The political institutions of the United States, more exactly the USIS and the CIA, extensively distribute information, in addition to other activities in relation to the Latin American media.

INFLUENCE OF NONNATIONAL MEDIA INSTITUTIONS IN LATIN AMERICA

This section addresses how the organization and activities of the institutions described in the first section influence the national media in Latin America. This phenomenon is examined in three principal areas: (1) the influence of economic institutions (direct investment and advertising and services); (2) the influence of the communication institutions (news flow and programming flow); (3) the influence of the political institutions; and (4) the influence of the mixed institutions (satellite).

One type of influence that we do not attempt to gauge is how the international investment activities of the U.S. networks and the other organizations determined the predominantly commercial nature the media in Latin America assumed in the first place. In other words, would the Latin American media have been more like some European publicly-owned media systems if it had not been for the influence of the U.S. institutions on these? This point, in regard to television, is explored by Williams (1975) in a recent publication on television:

> . . . The "commercial" character of television has then to be seen at several levels: as the making of programmes for profit in a known market; as a channel for advertising; and as a cultural and political form indirectly shaped by and dependent on the norms of a capitalist society, selling both consumer goods, and a "way of life" based on them, in an ethos that is at once locally generated, by domestic capitalist interests and authorities, and internationally organized as a political project, by the dominant capitalist power. It is then not too much to say that the general transition, in the last twenty years, from what was normally a national and state controlled sound broadcasting to what now, in world terms, are predominantly commercial television institutions, is a consequence of this planned operation from the United States. (pp. 41–42)

The purpose of this section is to document with empirical evidence the influence of the U.S. media related institutions on existing Latin American media in three specific areas: economic, communication, and political, always referring back to the initial definition of these institutions stated in the introduction.

Economic Influence

We have examined two types of economic relationships between the United States and the Latin American media institutions: (1) direct investment, and (2) indirect investment through advertising and services.

Investment Influence

The fact that ownership is a determinant of bias of media content according to the vested interests of the owners was documented in a study by Luis Roca on economic interests and the orientation of news concerning the peasant movements in Peru (Roca, 1969), in which the hypothesis was proven that the interests of the owners, among these U.S. firms, conditioned the orientation of the information in the press.

Advertising Influence

Advertising influence has been examined in Venezuela by Diaz Rangel (1974), who documented various cases of intervention of advertising in the national press. One case was the advertising boycott of *El Nacional* between 1961 and 1962 because of its independent and at times sympathetic line with the Cuban revolutionary process. Leading multinational and national advertising clients carried out an effective boycott of the paper until the board of directors was forced to change the editor and the editorial line of the paper.

Specific news suppression cases were, according to Diaz Rangel (1975), the following: the case of the investigation by the Labor Ministry of corporal punishment practices by the Venezuelan General Electric subsidiary, which was not carried by any paper in spite of official news releases on the subject, and a banner headline on the illegal entry of television sets into the country by Sears of Venezuela, which was squashed because of advertising pressures against the paper.

Other cases were documented in Peru prior to the present government's arrival to power in 1968, and reported by Benavides Correa (1970) as examples of overwhelming advertising pressures against a radio station, a television channel, and a political weekly, which took a line favorable to the revindication of national interests from the domain of the International Petroleum Company.

Theotonio Dos Santos, in his book *La Nueva Dependencia*, documents "the expulsion of journalists from two Brazilian publications, *Correio de Manha* and *Manchete*, because their independent and nationalist position were not tolerated by foreign interests in the press" (Benavides Correa, 1970, p. 118). Benavides concluded, "Advertising has an eminently political character and it is only channeled to the media which defend the political positions that the group of large (particularly foreign) firms desires."

Muraro (1975) describes a recent advertising lock-out organized in Argentina by the multinational corporations for the purpose of creating a negative environment for the imminent nationalization of the television channels there. Through the massive decrease in advertising investment, they hoped to stimulate an economic recession during those precise months when employment was highest.

A U.S. marketing specialist, Leo Bogart (1959), reproduced a statement of advertising philosophy for Latin America, which Bogart found in a "brochure sent out by a large international publication":

> It is dangerous to spend advertising appropriations to appeal to the millions, most of whom have no buying potential. It is enough of a task for any advertising budget merely to concentrate on those who *do* have the buying power, and to aim *to turn these prospects into buyers of your particular product*. The goal of the advertiser in Latin America, therefore, should be to reach *not* the largest number of people, but the largest number of *prospects*. The advertiser in Latin America should concentrate not on turning *people* into *prospects* but in turning prospects into customers. (p. 161)

Communication Influence

Communication influences include the influence of news flow into and out of the region and the influence of direct and indirect programming flow.

The Influence of News Flow

The influence of news flow has been documented by various researchers within the region and in the United States. This influence has two directions:

one concerns the nature of news reaching Latin America from the rest of the world, and the other, the nature of the news about Latin America disseminated outside the region. As has been observed in the previous section, both these flows are almost exclusively regulated by nonnational news agencies, in particular United Press International and by Associated Press.

News Flow into the Region.   One of the few studies that examined the nature of news flow into the Latin American region is a 1967 book by Venezuelan Senator and journalist, Eleazar Diaz Rangel. In an analysis of the international and national news in the 14 major dailies of the region, he found on one specific day that the most important international items for the 14 papers were the U.S. offensive in Vietnam and the royal visit of a pair of newlyweds to the Dutch Parliament. A conference of African leaders held the same day was completely ignored. The news disseminated about the Third World consisted of a story of a confrontation between an African tribe and some gorillas, and "the discovery of Noah's Ark in Turkey." A military uprising in Ecuador and the Dominican crisis were passed over by the 14 papers. Other Latin American stories were the capture of a witch in Bogota, and the birth of a pig with two legs in Caracas (Diaz Rangel, 1967).

The Vietnam coverage in the Latin American press is a singular case of the role of the news agencies. The Latin American public received almost exclusively the U.S. version of the war, to the extent that even the more critical U.S. reporting of the war never reached the continent. The cables from the news agency of North Vietnam never appeared, and little news reached Latin America of the U.S. war protest within the country.

Information from the United States.   With regard to Latin American print media coverage of the United States, Markham (1961) found that Latin American dailies generally publish about twice as much foreign news as the United States. Latin American dailies devoted about 38% of their foreign news space (fifty column inches) to the United States, in contrast with the two to three inches per day U.S. dailies devoted to Latin American news.

A study of twenty-nine of the major Latin American dailies showed that of the proportion of space they allocated to information from North America, the largest portion was assigned to the United States, and only minimal attention went to Canada and to Caribbean territories (Centro Internacional de Estudios Superiores de Periodismo para América Latina, 1967).

Merrill (1962) concentrated on the image of the United States in ten Mexican dailies. He found that (1) very little, if any, was reported which gave the reader a real idea of how Americans live; (2) the heavy emphasis on official news of the United States makes the general picture of the country off balance; and (3) almost all the U.S. news is from Washington and New York City. Merrill noted, for instance, very little material dealt with the American man in the street, with religion and education, and with people in the small cities and in the rural areas of the United States.

There have been few studies of the image of the United States in exported television. From an analysis of some of these surveys, Browne (1968, p. 315) concluded that American television programs more often than not have given foreign viewers a rather favorable impression of life in the United States. This has been chiefly, he specifies, through the portrayal of harmonious family life, a high standard of living, and a general sense of freedom and equality for and among Americans.

Judging the inadequacies in both directions of the inter-American flow of news, Graham (1969) of the *Washington Post* observed: "It is this kind of mutual lack of knowledge that could cause the people of the United States to be astounded in 1958 when Vice President Richard Nixon was stoned and mobbed in Caracas, and again more recently when Governor Rockefeller met his stormy reception in Latin America" (p. 3).

Bias of U.S. Wire Services.   Two documented cases of the operations of the U.S. wire services against Latin American interests are those of Reyes Matta (1974), of Stanford Institute of Communication Research, and Bonilla de Ramos (1972).

The object of the Ramos study was the treatment given by the U.S. wire services to the 1972 United Nations Conference on Trade and Development (UNCTAD) meeting in Santiago de Chile. She found an overwhelming bias on the part of the AP and UPI toward covering the positions of the ten industrialized countries attending, although the participation of the Latin American countries was quite active. The Colombian press had sent no reporters to the meeting, and used only wire services in their reporting of the conference. They used mainly UPI and AP cables, in spite of the fact that agencies such as AFP gave slightly more coverage to the countries of the region in the conference.

Reyes Matta examined the conduct of the UPI in the February 1974 meeting of the Latin American Ministers of Foreign Relations with Secretary of State Henry Kissinger. The majority of the information that UPI dispatched from the meeting was used by Latin American papers. He examined such incidents as: (1) the publication by wire by UPI of a U.S. draft that contained concepts that had not been accepted by the Latin American delegates as the final text of the meeting, reporting that a proposition had been presented by the Latin Americans and accepted by Kissinger, when in fact it was just the opposite; (2) the complete silence of the UPI on issues planted by the Latin American delegations such as economic coercion, the balance of payments, and the role of the multinational enterprise; and (3) the selection by the wire services of key issues out of the context of the meeting. Reyes Matta (1974) concluded that: "The UPI selects information on Latin America according to a criteria of interest which coincides with the structure of U.S. domination, and informs Latin Americans of a reality which is not that which they live but which they end up believing given the communicative force of the agency" (p. 56).

An example of national news reporting by institutions that do not necessarily concur with national development goals is the case of oil exporting Venezuela, where all the information concerning Organization of Petroleum Exporting Countries (OPEC) in the National papers is originated in agencies located in petroleum *importing* countries (Pasquali, 1975, p. 20).

The control of news flow into the Latin American region is dominated by the U.S. wire services that systematically distort, through selection and manipulation, the image of the world outside presented to the Latin Americans through their papers. This distortion by the wire services also extends to the coverage of specific Latin American items.

Inter-American Press Association.   One last aspect of nonnational influence on the Latin American press is the case of the Inter-American Press Association (Sociedad Interamericana de Prensa), an association of newspaper owners and editors founded in 1926. Originally, the IAPA was organized on a country basis, in which each country had one vote. However, according to Mary Gardner (1965), "The communists attempted to manipulate the early meetings to their own advantage. . . . they wished to gain control of an international group whose membership would supply both the prestige and the organs for spreading communist propaganda" (p. 2).

After the 1950 meeting in New York, in which the IAPA statutes were revamped to allow one vote per newspaper, the United States gained control, with 424 of the 768 members (314 were Latin Americans and 22 Canadians and Europeans).

One of the principal activities of the IAPA is a yearly review of press freedom in Latin America, which began in 1946. One of the "principal targets of this analysis has been the Cuban regime" (Gardner, 1965). As reported by Fortunata de Barrios, and cited in Benavides, under Peron in Argentina the IAPA attacked the closure of *La Presnsa,* organ of the Argentine elite, but it did not attack the closure of other publications of different leanings by Peron (Benavides Correa, 1970, p. 149). Nor did IAPA censure the closure in Venezuela of La Republica, under Dictator Perez Jimenez, for which act IAPA official Jules Dubois was not permitted to return to that country when the democratic system was reinstated (Benavides Correa, 1970, p. 144).

A similar denial was issued by Peruvian ex-President Velasco Alvarado, who replied to George Beebe, president of the Executive Committee of the Inter American Press Association, regarding his request for an audience as follows (Benavides Correa, 1970):

> . . . The enactment of the Statute of Press Liberty is a sovereign act for which no Government has to give an explanation to a foreign organism, and even less to the Inter American Press Association, given that this is an entity that defends the interests of companies, and not the genuine liberty of expression as this is considered by the popular classes of America . . . in consequence, the President of the Republic does not grant you the audience requested in your letter of January 8. . . . (p. 148)

A recent review of IAPA activites between 1952 and 1973 in Bolivia by

Knudson challenges the assertion that "the IAPA has proved to be an effective instrument in maintaining and perpetuating freedom of the press in the Western hemisphere" (Gardner, 1965). Knudson (1973) argues that during the revolutionary government in that country between 1952 and 1964, IAPA denied that freedom of the press existed, whereas, after 1964, during the right wing military regimes, freedom was reported to exist by the IAPA. He concluded that:

> Every government—as every person—has the right to self-defense. . . . But to the IAPA that right seems limited only to conservative or reactionary governments pledged to the protection of private property. . . . The IAPA judgements on freedom of the press in the hemisphere should not, therefore, be accepted without question. (pp. 14–45)

Influence of Programming Flow

The discussion of available information on the influence of nonnational programming flow into the Latin American region includes two basic dimensions. The first is the analysis of the latent (not manifest) content of the programming itself, which potentially acts on the public, while the second is the measurement of this action on the public. In Latin America, the former, the analysis of the latent content of the programming, has in recent years been applied to various media, using variations of the tools of analysis of the science of signs, semiology.

Content Analysis. Ariel Dorfman (1973) and Dorfman and Mattelart (1973), carried out two analyses of this type with studies of the *Reader's Digest* and Donald Duck comic books. In the analysis of *Reader's Digest*, Dorfman identifies several key concepts that dominate the bulk of the articles.

> A false leveling and democratization of knowledge for the general public, coupled with the impression that, in the real world, knowledge and technology are also equally distributed among all members of the population in a society where science is neutral and good for everyone.

> A perception of achievement and fame linked with this idea of knowledge, in which everyone has the same opportunities for success.

> The lesson that in spite of the conditions explained in the first two concepts, knowledge and science only favor those who are good and ethical. In other words, they only help him who is deserving.

> Given this interpretation of science, progress and goodness, *Reader's Digest* depicts the state of the underdeveloped world as due to strange customs, fatality, bad climate, and lack of a tradition of great thinkers.

> The solution, therefore, for this part of the world, is the transfer of knowledge, the lack of which produces underdevelopment, for with knowledge, food will come along by itself.

Dorfman and Mattelart (1973) analyze the latent content in Walt Disney's creation of Donald Duck and others. They show the portrayal of a society without a family structure in which the main activities are leisure time activities; a society in which the economy has been reduced to primary and tertiary sectors; an underdeveloped world in which the only characters that are human in the stories are backward and silly, and for the most part dangerous; and a world in which material aspirations are the moving forces of society.

The book was first published in 1971 in Chile. After the coup (September 11, 1973), it was banned in that country. It has since had 15 editions, one of them was published in May 1975 in Great Britain in English. According to International General, upon attempting to import the book into the United States on June 1975, the United States Government seized the books and have been holding them ever since, pending legal action by the lawyers of Walt Disney Productions (International General, 1975).

A similar analysis was conducted by Delgado (1973, p. 65) of the "Flintstones" television series. The Flintstones live in a primitive society with all the characteristics of a modern consumerism. There are no class conflicts and all problems are presented on an individual level. Hence, development is shown as moving in one direction—toward modern capitalism. Success, competition and status are constant themes, all measured in buying power and coupled with escapist solutions to problems. The series is riddled with the general theme of conformism.

Analyses have been conducted on Film (Colina and Diaz Torres, 1972) in which the use of status, submission, and impotence against change, clothed in melodrama and sentimentalism, are identified in the films shown in the region (Colina and Diaz Torres, 1972, Table 3). In 1970, a study was carried out in Chile on movie fan magazines along similar lines (Piccini, 1970).

Effects on Audiences. Conclusive results on the actual behavioral effects of this latent programming content are difficult to achieve, given methodological problems such as the isolation of key variables and measurement over time. In spite of these limitations, there *is* empirical evidence that relates the content of media in Latin America and social phenomena such as conformity and the formation of stereotypes. One of the few effects studies was done in Venezuela by Eduardo Santoro, a psychologist from the Universidad Central de Venezuela, who researched the formation of stereotypes induced in children by imported programs. Among his findings were:

the fixation of 63% of foreign language terms;
the belief that the hero was a North American in 86.3% of the cases, or at least English speaking in 82% of cases;
the belief that the Chinese is seventeen times more bad than good, while the white man is eleven times better than the black;
the belief that the rich man is good in 72% of the cases, and poor is bad in 41% of the cases (Santoro, 1969, p. 12).

Another survey in Venezuela indicated that 68% of the programs in a typical week of television encouraged physical, emotional, and moral violence. This figure reached 83% on Saturdays and 73% on Sundays (Venezuela, Comisión, 1975, p. 171).

Political Influence

With the possible exception of nonhouse studies conducted by the United States Information Service, there are no studies available that have attempted to gauge the direct and indirect influence of the nonnational political institutions on the Latin American media and audiences. In short, the possible effects of U.S. propaganda on the audience are not publicly documented.

Influence of Mixed Institutions

The regional educational satellite for Latin America has not yet gone into operation in the region. However, various organizations and individuals have predicted a negative influence on the part of the satellite for Latin America.

The 1969 CAVISAT proposal met with opposition from the official educational and cultural sectors of the different countries (Ballochi, 1974, pp. 117–121).

Numerous national and regional meetings were held while the Venezuela study was being conducted, in which serious doubts were raised by the representatives of the countries and of the region as to the educational use of satellites for the region.

The study of a Regional System of Educational Television for South America was published in May 1973 and analyzed in Caracas in 1974 by representatives of the participating countries. Revisions were made according to these comments and the final document is now in limited circulation (Sommerlad, 1975, p. 10).

The use of satellites for educational purposes has been strongly attacked and defended in the region of Latin America. Jose Galat, an advisor to the Colombian president, in 1969 made the following statement (Santos, 1974) in regard to the pending regional satellite program.

> The North American project to educate Latin America by Television via Satellite appears to be a vast plan for the ideological occupation of the continent. (p. 135)

The Colombian National Planning Department concluded in 1972 in respect to the regional education satellite system that:

> The producers and salesmen of communication systems by satellite constitute a quasi-monopolistic offer, which implies for the buyer the acceptance of harmful conditions in prices and technological dependence. . . . The cost of the educational television via satellite project exceeds any financial possibility for Colombia. (p. 135)

Similar objections have been raised by representatives of other countries of the region. They ask who will do the programming and who will bear the cost, and conclude by questioning the use of the satellite itself before the other alternative educational systems are explored by the countries (Secretaria Ejecutiva Permanente del Convenio "Andres Bello," 1975).

The potentially harmful effect of the latent and manifest content of nonnational programming in the region has been shown. In some cases these effects have been actually documented as is the case of Venezuela with the formation of stereotypes and the induction of violence. In the case of the regional satellite, the call for a closer examination of the nature and origin of the programming illustrates the strength of this "programming" preoccupation in Latin America.

Summary: Influence of Nonnational Media Institutions in Latin America

This section reviews the influence nonnational media related *economic institutions* exercise through: (1) direct investment, and (2) advertising pressures. Specific cases of bias, censorship, and pressuring are documented in Venezuela, Peru, Brazil, and Argentina. The influence of nonnational *communication institutions* is reviewed in that which refers to news flow, in which the bias and manipulation of news flow into the region, the image of the life in the United States, and the distortion of the U.S. wire services are shown. The analysis of news flow out of the region reveals a similar distortion of life in Latin America portrayed in the U.S. media, especially in several cases of directed social changes in the region. The activities of the Inter-American Press Association are also briefly described.

Two dimensions of programming flow are explored, the latent, conformist, *pro status quo* nature of programming and their effects on audience in introducing negative stereotypical interpretations of reality. Data on the influence of *political institutions* is not available.

The last part of this section deals with the potentially harmful influence of the Regional Educational Satellite for Latin America.

In summarizing the data in the first two sections, we have explored the nature and influence of nonnational and particularly U.S. institutions operating in relation to the media in Latin America. *On the basis of this data*, we fully endorse the following statements made by Naesselund (1975):

Analysis and research on the international communication processes have established a picture of an *international flow* of information with the following characteristics (or defects): (a) The distribution of communication resources in the world is strongly disproportional to the distribution of population and the information needs of the people. Thus an imbalance of the potential. (b) Quantitatively it is estimated that the total flow of communication from the industrialized part of the world (with one third of the total world population) to the developing countries is 100 times the flow in the opposite direction. Thus an imbalance in the flow of information. (c) The fact that the media in many developing countries fail to diversify their content sufficiently to give it some significance to all audiences (in particular in rural areas) leads to an irrelevance of content to the social and cultural problems encountered in those countries. (p. 3)

GENERAL SUMMARY AND CONCLUSIONS

This has been an exploration of the multiple dimensions that appear to make up the international exchange of information in Latin America. We have found these dimensions to fall into the general categories of *economic, communication*, and *political* institutions. And, in light of the available empirical evidences, it reviewed the influence of these institutions on Latin America's mass communication system and its relationship to this region's development.

The review yielded the following:

Economic Influence

1. Direct U.S. investment has been significantly present in several of the major privately owned mass media of Latin America.

2. Most of the major mass media of Latin America derive much of their financing from U.S. advertising agencies.

3. The majority of U.S. investment in Latin America through advertising comes from U.S. based multinational corporations, whose operations have been shown to be negative to many aspects of host country interests (United Nations, 1972, 1974).

4. The role of advertising in Latin America, a business in which U.S. interests play a predominant role, has been perceived as undesirable for social change and national development in this region, especially in terms of fostering consumerism.

5. The information contained in advertisements and that contained in the messages financed by advertising is oriented toward that small percentage of the population economically able to consume the goods presented in the media. For this reason, the information, culture, ethnic, and social needs of the majorities are ignored by the media.

6. In addition, as by definition, advertising clients tend to support messages that reach a mass audience of consumers. Therefore, even within that limited audience to which the messages are directed, specific ethnic, cultural, and economic differences are ignored, and a mass uniform content and homogeneous audience are fostered. In this manner the cultural and ethnical complexity of a country, an important element for autonomous national development and survival, is reduced.

7. Nonnational clients utilize advertising investment as a tool to limit and manipulate the information that reaches the media audiences in line with their own commercial and political interests. In this way, an important principle of democracy, an informed citizenry, is thwarted.

Communication Influence

1. Direct U.S. influence on the Latin American audiences takes place mostly through films and Spanish versions of U.S. magazines and comic books.

2. On the one hand international news flow in the region is controlled, heavily and in all directions, by U.S. agencies. These firms, although they operate under commercial criteria, appear to perform a distortion more from a political than a commercial point of view. News is often manipulated according to a situation of political domination. The reality presented to the region and from the region tends to be distorted according to political positions of the United States. This is especially clear in the case of the presentations of efforts of directed and substantive change in the region.

3. On the other hand, the U.S. programming distributed either through the Latin American media (such as the case of television shows) or that which is directly distributed to the audience (such as films and magazines) operates under an unrestrained mercantile maximization and tends to play a more commercial than political role in their type of distortion of society. This type of programming is encouraged by the commercial structure of the media, and in particular by U.S. advertising companies and clients in that it fosters consumerism. This, however, does not deny the essentially conformist and pro status quo political orientation of this programming.

4. In both cases these communications portray the world in a way which thwarts the understanding of the national reality, in addition to distorting this reality in a direction that favors the economic and political dependency of Latin America on the United States.

Political Influence

Political institutions are much less subtle in their aims than are the communication and economic institutions. The empirical assessment of their influence is rarely viable. Their business is propaganda—the organization of the sale of a political doctrine, a value system, a way of life—a common enough practice of many nations of the world. The point when this practice becomes noxious for the development of the nations subject to it is difficult to ascertain; however, some information was found to indicate that, in some of the Latin American countries these activities of U.S. political institutions have at times reached a level where they are damaging democratic practices, as is the case of alleged CIA bribing of some newscasters and telecasters in Chile and the USIS distribution of photonovelas before elections in that country, as reported in Congressional hearings in the United States.

Communication Policies

Although efforts have been made to formulate national and regional policies in Latin America, those pertinent to the international communication situation that affect this region have been inappropriate up to now. This is true at country, subregion, and regional levels. With few exceptions, their provisions are clearly insufficient and inadequate to aptly defend the region from foreign domination. One of the reasons for their failure is that, for the most part, a fair and acceptable international exchange of information is perceived as an entity separate from any particular economic or political process. In reality, however, the international exchange of information, as has been shown in the preceding sections, is an end product of a complex economic and political system with multiple components and processes, inserted in concrete economic and political realities.

Therefore, special policies, going beyond a simply declarative function, must address all levels of the system in an integrated, explicit, and durable master policy guiding the overall communication process in a country in line with needs of national development based on social change and national independence.

Likewise, in addition to being internally systematic, national policies on international communication should aim in Latin America to be coordinated in a region-wide sense through inter-American cooperative mechanisms in which the United States does not have a dominating voice, for example, the newly-born SELA (Latin American Economic System) and the Andean Pact, including the Andrés Bello Agreement for cultural, scientific, and educational activities. This should greatly aid their implementation vis-à-vis the strength of the foreign and national interests at stake.

The inquiry paper for the April 1976 meeting on Fair Communication Policy for the International Exchange of Information at the East–West Communication Institute (East–West Center, 1976), wondered if there was any clear evidence of foreign penetration of a country's communication system. It appeared to doubt that a communication imbalance necessarily existed between developed and underdeveloped nations; specifically, it wondered whether alien materials from any source effectively outweighed those native to a given country or group of countries. Furthermore, the paper asked whether international communication had indeed any necessary effects on a receiving society. And finally, apparently wondering whether such imbalance and influence truly existed, it implicitly doubted that they were noxious.

We believe that the information from a number of studies on international communication in Latin America, which we have summarized and appraised here, does begin to answer such questions. And it does so affirmatively in every respect:

1. The mass communication system of Latin America is so strongly permeated by economic, political, and communication institutions of the United States of America that it is not unwarranted to talk of a case of foreign domination.

2. Most of the main mass media in this region, and especially the electronic ones, are directly and indirectly penetrated by major U.S. interests.

3. With regard to news sources in Latin America, U.S.-originated material greatly exceeds that of the region itself. In film, foreign originated material constitutes a little over half of the total films exhibited in the region. United States television programs make up approximately one-third of the total programming, with important variations among the countries. Although there are no global figures for comic strips, it is estimated that U.S. originated material constitutes over two-thirds of the total. This lack of proportion indicates that the superior position of the United States is sufficiently large to constitute a threat to the communication autonomy of Latin America, especially if qualitative factors of impact are taken into consideration.

4. Proportion aside, and even in those cases where the imbalance is not sufficient to cause concern, the North American materials can directly influence the public, or indirectly influence the system, by establishing models for production that are imitated by the Latin American producers. This potentially augments the impact of the foreign products above that indicated by the simple import figures. The qualitative aspect, or multiplier effect, of the undesirable material is more important than the purely quantitative considerations.

5. U.S. economic and communication institutions do appear to have some noticeable effects on the behavior of many of the major Latin American mass communication institutions. The audience selection and content policies of many of these latter are inseparable from those of the respective U.S. sources. They are criticized for promoting consumerism, alienation, banality, violence, racism, elitism, and conservatism. This is deemed to be in line with the ideologies and interests of the investors, and in discrepancy with the region's efforts to attain national development through social change, cultural autonomy, and political sovereignty.

6. Political influence is extremely hard to assess, but it is evident that U.S. propaganda and security agencies, not allowed by law to operate within the United States, actively function in Latin America, recoursing at times to truly unethical and undemocratic procedures.

7. The U.S. economic, political, and communication institutions, and their Latin American associates, subscribe publicly and militantly to classical notions of "information rights," "press freedom," and "free flow of news." Certain forms of their behavior, however, hardly appear consistent with such a creed. Some of them, for instance, fall at times into monopolistic, coercive,

and even extortive practices to secure the perpetuation of their power position. Those opposing them are labeled "totalitarian."

8. Moreover, some data suggest that such rights and freedoms exist mostly, if not exclusively, for the dominant native minorities and their foreign, mostly U.S. associates whose communication media activities are linked to the sizable interests in the means of production in Latin American society.

Thus, in summary, the free flow of information, hailed by the United States and the United Nations as the fundamental tenet of democracy, is not obtained in Latin America. Sadly, in this region it has no real enforcement.

REFERENCES

Ballochi, P. R. (1974). Algunos antecedentes sobre el satélite educativo para America del Sur. *Comunicación y Cultura* (Argentina) No. 3, 117–121.

Benavides Correa, A. (1970). "La Verdadera Libertad de Prensa." Oficina Nacional de Información, Lima, Peru.

Bennet, M. (1964). "Overseas Evaluation: Colombia E-TV Program." 1964.

Bogart, L. (1959). Changing markets and media in Latin America. *Public Opinion Quarterly 23*, 159–167.

Bonilla de Ramos, E. (1972). "Las Agencias Internacionales de Noticias y sus Procesos Informativos; El Estudio de Un Caso." (Documento presentado al Seminario Internacional "El Papel Socio-politico de los Medios de Comunicación Colectiva para la Sociedad de Cambio en América Latina," San José, Costa Rica, 19–25 de Noviembre 1972.) San José, Costa Rica.

Browne, D. R. (1968). The American image as presented abroad by U.S. television. *Journalism Quarterly 45*, 307–316.

By the way: Mexico. (1976). *Latin America* (England) *10* (No. 8), 59.

Centro Internacional de Estudios Superiores de Periodismo para América Latina. (1967). "Dos Semanas en la Prensa de América Latina." CIESPAL, Quito, Ecuador.

Colina, E., and Diaz Torres, D. (1972). Ideologïa del melodrama en el viejo cine lationamericano. *Cuadernos de la Realidad Nacional* (Chile) No. 14, 113–125.

Diaz Rangel, E. (1967). "Pueblos Subinformados; Las Agencias de Noticias y América Latina." Universidad Central de Venezuela, Caracas, Venezuela. (Cuadernos de Nuestro Tiempo, No. 3.)

Diaz Rangel, E. (1974). "Noticias Censuradas." Sïntesis Dosmil, Caracas, Venezuela. (El Hombre y la Comunicación.)

Diaz Rangel, E. (1975). La dependencia foránea y el sensacionalismo en los medios masivos de comunicación. *El Periodista* (Venezuela), pp. 8–11.

Dorman, A. (1973). Salvación y sabidurïa del hombre común: La teologïa del *Reader's Digest*. *Textual* (Peru) No. 8, 44–55.

Dorfman, A., and Mattelart, A. (1973). "Para Leer el Pato Donald; Communicación de Masa y Colonialismo." 5th ed. Siglo Veintiuno, Buenos Aires, Argentina.

East–West Center. Communication Institute. (1976). "New Perspectives in International Communication." East–West Center, Honolulu, Hawaii.

Eliaschev, J. R. (1975). Los Medios de comunicación; Un pais multimillonario en una nacion extraniera, *Crisis* (Argentina) No. 32, 12–18.

Epstein, E. J. (1976). Los Rockefeller: La familia y el imperio. *El Tiempo (Lecturas Dominicales) Bogotá* No. 18, 1–7.

Ficha de identificación de la Agencia de Información de los EE.UU. (1974). *Comunicación y*

Cultura (Argentina) No. 3, 5–10.

Fox de Cardona, E. (1975). "Broadcasting in Colombia: Communication Structures and Regulatory Frames." Bogota, Colombia. (Mimeograph copy.)

Fresenius, G., and Vergara, J. (1974). La Agencia Informativa Norteamericana (USIS) y sus boinas verdes de papel. *Comunicación y Cultura* (Argentina) No. 3, 11–82.

Gardner, M. A. (1965). The Inter American Press Association: A brief history. *Journalism Quarterly 42*, 547–556.

Graham, K. (1969). (Remarks at the Twenty-fifty General Assembly, Inaugural Reception and Dinner of the Inter-American Press Association, Washington, D.C., 28 October 1969.)

Guback, T.H. (1974). Film as international business. *Journal of Communication 24* (No.1), 90–101.

Hornik, R.C., Ingle, H.T., Mayo, J.K., McAnany, E.G., and Schramm, W. (1973). "Television and Educational Reform in El Salvador: Final Report." Academy for Educational Development, Information Center on Instructional Technology, Washington, D.C. (AID Studies in Educational Technology.)

International General, New York. (1975). "On Donald Duck's 40th Anniversary; United States-Style Free Flow of Information and Chile." International General, New York.

Kaplun, M. (1973). "La Communicación de Masas en América Latina." Asociación de Publicaciones Educativas, Bogotá, Columbia. (Educación Hoy No. 5.)

Knudson, J.W. (1973). "The Inter-American Press Association as Champion of Press Freedom: Reality or Rhetoric?; the Bolivian Experience, 1952-1973." Temple University, Department of Journalism, Philadelphia, Pennsylvania.

Malpica, C. (1968). "Los Dueños del Perú." 3rd ed. Ediciones Ensayo Social, Lima, Peru.

Markham, J.W. (1961). Foreign news in the United States and South American Press. *Public Opinion Quarterly 25*, 249–262.

Mattelart, A. (1970). Los medios de comunicación de masas; la ideologïa de la prensa liberal en Chile. II. Estructura del poder informativo y dependencia. II. La dependencia del medio de communicación de masas. *Cuadernos de la Realidad Nacional* (Chile) No.3, 52–73.

Mattelart, A. (1973a). "Agresión Desde el Espacio; Cultura y Napalm en la Era de los Satelites." Siglo Veintiuno, Buenos Aires, Argentina.

Mattelart, A. (1973b). El imperialismo en busca de la contrarrevolución cultural: "Plaza Sésamo:" Prólogo a la telerepresión del año 2.000. *Comunicación y Cultura*, (Argentina) No. 1, 146–223.

Mattelart, A. (1975). Hacia la formación de los aparatos ideológicos del "Estado Multinacional." *Comunicación y Cultura* (Argentina) No. 4, 73–115.

Merrill, J.C. (1962). The image of the United States in ten Mexican dailies. *Journalism Quarterly 39*, 203–209.

Muraro, H. (1975). La minija (III) el negocio de la publicidad en la television argentina. *Crisis* (Argentina), No. 22, 64–69.

Naesselund, G.R. (1975). Declaración inaugural. *In* "Seminario sobre Medios de Comunicación Social para Periodistas y Productores de Radio y Televisión, México, D.F., México, 3-4 de Julio de 1975. Anexo III." UNESCO, Paris. (COM-75/WS/29)

National Academy of Engineering. Committee on Telecommunications. (1973). "Telecommunications Research in the United States and Selected Foreign Countries; A Preliminary Survey. I. Summary." National Academy of Engineering, Washington, D.C.

Nordenstreng, K., and Varis, T. (1974). "Television Traffic—A One-Way Street?" UNESCO, Paris. (Reports and Papers on Mass Communication, No. 70.)

Pasquali, A. (1975). "On the Instrumental Use of Mass Media in America for Purposes of Dependence." (Paper presented at the New World Conference, San Antonio, Texas, 4-8 November 1975. Panel: Arts and Culture in the Americas.) Universidad Central de Venezuela, Instituto de Investigaciones de la Communicación, Caracas, Venezuela.

Piccini, M. (1970). El cerco de las revistas de ïdolos. *Cuadernos de la Realidad Nacional* (Chile) No. 3, 179–217.

Reyes Matta, F. (1974). América Latina, Kissinger y la UPI: Errores y omisiones desde México. *Comunicación y Cultura* (Argentina) No. 4, 55–72.

Roca, L. (1969). Los intereses económicos y la orientación de noticias sobre el movimiento campesino. *Campesino* (Peru) *1* (No.1), 37–52.

Santoro, E. (1969). "La Televisión Venezolana y la Formación de Estereotipos en el niño." Universidad Central de Venezuela, Facultad de Humanidades y Educación, Escuela de Periodismo, Caracas, Venezuela.

Santos, E. (1974). Tecnología, imperialismo y educación. *Comunicación y Cultura* (Argentina) No. 3, 135–146.

Schenkel, P. (1973). "La Estructura del Poder de los Medios de Comunicación en Cinco Países Latinoamericanos." Instituto Latinoamericano de Investigaciones Sociales, Santiago, Chile. (ILDIS. Estudios y Documentos No. 21.)

Schiller, H.I. (1973). "The Mind Managers." Beacon Press, Boston, Massachusetts.

Secretaria Ejecutiva Permanente del Convenio "Andrés Bello." (1975). "Convenio Andrés Bello y Resoluciones de su Órgano Máximo 1970-1974." SECAB, Bogotá, Columbia.

Shakespeare, F. (1974). Quién está ganando la guerra de la propaganda? Entrevista con Frank Shakespeare, Director de la Agencia de Informaciones de los EE.UU. (USIA). *Comunicación y Cultura* (Argentina) No. 3, 105–116.

Sommerlad, E.L. (1975). "Los satélites de Comunicación; Examen de los Sistemas Actuales y de las Futuras Aplicaciones para la Radiodifusión." (Documento presentado al Seminario Regional Naciones Unidas-UNESCO para América Latina sobre los Sistemas de Radiodifusión por Satélite al Servicio de la Educación y el Desarrollo, Mexico, 2-11 de Septiembre de 1975.) UNESCO, Paris. (UNESCO-COM-75/CONF.703/2.)

Tapio Delgado, G. (1973). "Los Picapiedra," aliados del imperialismo. *Textual* (Peru) No. 8, 63–66.

UNESCO. (1973). "Estudio de Viabilidad de un Sistema Regional de Teleducación para los Países de America del Sur; Borrador Informe Final." (PROYECTO RLA 223.) UNESCO, Paris. (UNESCO/PNUD/UIT.)

UNESCO. (1975). "Perfiles Socioeconómicos y de Medios de Comunicación en los Países Latinoamericanos." UNESCO and Centro Internacional de Estudios Superiores de Comunicación para América Latina, Quito, Argentina.

United Nations. (1972). "Restrictive Business Practices. The Operation of Multinational United States Enterprises in Developing Countries; Their Role in Trade and Development." United Nations, New York.

United Nations. (1974). "Restrictive Business Practices in Relation to the Trade and Development of Developing Countries; Report by the Ad Hoc Group of Experts." United Nations, New York. (E.74.II.D.11.)

U.S. Senate. Select Committee to Study Governmental Operations with Respect to Intelligence Activities. (1975). "Covert Action in Chile 1963–1973; Staff Report of the Select Committee to Study Governmental Operations with Respect to Intelligence Activities." U.S. Government Printing Office, Washington, D.C.

Varis, T. (1973). "International Inventory of Television Programme Structure and the Flow of TV Programmes between Nations." University of Tampere, Research Institute of Journalism and Mass Communication, Tampere, Finland.

Venezuela. Comisión Preparatoria del Consejo Nacional de Cultura Comite de Radio y Televisión. (1975). "Diseño para una Nueva Política de Radio-Difusión del Estado Venezolano (Proyecto Ratelve)." Caracas, Venezuela.

Wells, A. (1972). "Picture-tube Imperialism? The Impact of U.S. Television on Latin America." Orbis Books, New York.

Williams, R. (1975). "Television: Technology and Cultural Form." Schocken Books, New York.

Wolfe, W. (1964). Images of the United States in the Latin American press. *Journalism Quarterly 41*, 79–86.

4

Cultural Continuity and Change: Role of the Media

Elihu Katz

Hebrew University of Jerusalem

Elihu Katz is Director of the Communications Institute and Professor of Sociology at Hebrew University of Jerusalem. He received his undergraduate degree and PhD at Columbia University and was a member of the Bureau of Applied and Social Research at Columbia University from 1951 to 1954. In 1954 he became Professor of Sociology at the University of Chicago, and he held a Senior Research Fellowship at the University of Manchester in 1972–1973. Dr. Katz is the author and coauthor of many articles and books, including *Personal Influence; Medical Innovation; The Politics of Community Conflict; Bureaucracy and the Public; The Secularization of Leisure; The Uses of Mass Communication;* and *Broadcasting in the Third World: Promise and Performance*, of which this chapter forms a part.

Originally written for publication in a volume resulting from a Symposium organized by the Prospective Planning Project of National Iranian Radio and Television, Mashad, 1975. Reprinted by permission of the publishers from *Broadcasting in the Third World* by Elihu Katz and George Wedell. Cambridge, Mass.: Harvard University Press. Copyright (c) 1977 by the President and Fellows of Harvard College.

The thoughts and observations in this paper are from a research project on Broadcasting and National Development under the joint direction of the writer and Professor E. G. Wedell. The project, financed by a grant from the Ford Foundation to the International Institute, is based on an extensive survey of developing countries as well as intensive field work in a sample of eleven countries: Algeria, Brazil, Cyprus, Indonesia, Iran, Nigeria, Peru, Senegal, Singapore, Tanzania, Thailand. The full report of the study will be published in 1976, along with the series of case-study monographs by Katz, Wedell, Dov Shinar, and Michael Pilsworth. Field work was carried out during 1973–75, and no effort is made here to update the observations made at the time of the case study. I should like to add that the discussion in this paper profited greatly from the debate in the working group on "Cultural Continuity and Change" at the Mashad Symposium.

Theorists and policymakers on the subject of modernization have held high two hopes for broadcasting. One is that broadcasting should contribute to the process of integration, helping to forge a nation from regional, tribal, and ethnic loyalties. The other is that broadcasting should contribute to socioeconomic development, helping to motivate and to instruct in the problems that beset the peasant population of developing countries. To the extent that the mass media have been given a chance—that is, in those nations where radio and television networks have been extended to cover the countryside—there is a record of achievement, though it is very uneven, with respect to these two hopes. Apart from coverage, however, very few developing countries have harnessed the media seriously to their developmental goals.

Where the processes of national integration and economic development have taken hold, the side effects of modernization have become increasingly apparent to the planners and policy makers. Modernization brings in its wake a standardization and secularization of culture, such that the traditional values and arts, those that give a culture its character, are being overwhelmed by the influx of Western popular culture. Rock music and comic books and "Kojak" threaten not only local tribal cultures but the great traditions of societies such as Thailand, Israel, and Iran.

The traditionalists knew all along that this would happen: that is why they opposed modernization, and often, the idea of the nation state itself. The technocrats simply ignored the problem, and some of them remain untroubled by it even today. To them, emancipation from tradition is a price worth paying. For those who dream the dream of liberal democracy, there is too much restraint implicit in a commitment to the continuity of tradition. But for a lot of people in between—those concerned with modernization, on the one hand, but with authentic identity, on the other—the problem is serious. Geertz (1973) states it this way:

> Now that there is a local state rather than a mere dream of one, the task of nationalist ideologizing radically changes. It no longer consists of stimulating popular alienation from a foreign dominated political order, nor with orchestrating a mass celebration of that order's demise. It consists in defining, or trying to define, a collective subject to whom the actions of the state can be internally connected, in creating or trying to create, an experiential "we" from whose will the activities of government seem spontaneously to flow. (p. 240)*

The dilemma, according to Geertz, is in finding a proper balance between the

---

*Most developing countries have achieved full radio coverage, some only recently, but television tends to be limited to urban areas, even when the system is government operated and essentially not-for-profit. Direct measures of the effects of exposure to broadcasting are not usually available, nor does our own study include such measures. A strong case for the influence of broadcasting on modernizing attitudes is made in the recent book by Inkeles and Smith (1974), and in an earlier statement by Rogers and Svenning (1969, Chapter 5).

cosmopolitan, future-oriented "spirit of the age"—what he calls "epochalism"—and the common experiences that inhere in tradition—or "essentialism." The sources of the latter, says Geertz, are parents, traditional authority figures, custom, and legend, and of the former secular intellectuals, the oncoming generation, current events, and the mass media. For Geertz, the mass media seem inexorably opposed to "essentialism" (Geertz, 1973, p. 240).

We ask here whether this is necessarily so. Cannot broadcasting give voice to culturally authentic forms of expression? Looking at the screen, or listening to the radio, it certainly seems as if they cannot. But let us permit ourselves, at least, to ask the question.

MASS MEDIA AND THE CONTINUITY OF CULTURE: A NEW PROMISE

Asking the question is not simply an academic exercise. The nations' leaders are asking it too, and unlike the anthropologists, it has not occurred to them that the media may be unable to do it. Governments are demanding that broadcasters help solve the cultural problem. Language is the most obvious means; in Algeria, for example, since 1971 radio and television have substituted Arabic for French as the language of programming. Governments are insisting that broadcasters sharply decrease the proportion of programs which are purchased abroad: Peru, Nigeria, Algeria are ready examples.*

Increasingly, one hears explicit statements of policy on this subject. Thus, in establishing the expanded NIRT in 1972, the Council of Ministers gave as the first aim of Iranian broadcasting "to assist in safeguarding, developing and propagating Iranian culture" (20 March 1972, Law Establishing National Iranian Radio and Television Organization by Decree of Council of Ministers. "The raising of the cultural level," says the Algerian Quadrennial Plan, "which depends in the first instance on the educational effort, is equally dependent on the activities of the broadcasting system and on giving as many citizens as possible access to the national cultural heritage" (Secretariat au Plan, Algerian Democratic People's Republic, *Plan Quadrennial, 1970–73*, 1970, p. 77). More consistently than other countries, official Brazilian statements on broadcasting refer to the importance of cultural goals. But the first set of legal documents, following adoption of the Brazilian Code of Telecommunications in 1962, goes even further. The goals of broadcasting, it says explicitly, are educational and cultural "even in their aspects of information and entertainment" (Decree 52795 of 31 October 1963).

---

*These and the examples that follow—except where otherwise noted—are from the case studies detailed above.

What is happening, in effect, is that a third area of promise is being held out for the broadcast media. In addition to national integration and socioeconomic development, leaders are proclaiming that radio and television should promote the continuity of traditional culture.

The call for more indigenous self-expression in broadcasting is being sounded loudly in the developing world. It is, as we have said, the voice of those concerned with modernization, but not at any cost. Cultural nationalists have been saying this for a long time, sometimes in connection with broadcasting. The earliest broadcasting in Indonesia and in Brazil was organized by "cultural associations" interested in cultural creativity as the basis for national integration. The voices being heard today for mobilizing the mass media in support of cultural continuity are not concerned only *intrinsically* with authentic creativity for its own sake or for the sake of national respect. Some of them are concerned with the *instrumental* use of the themes of traditional culture as a more effective means of reaching people with the message of national integration and modernization. Peruvian rediscovery of their Inca ancestry, for example, relates to the fact that the Incas did have, in fact, a certain form of primitive socialism. Or again, there is a legend which tells how the participation of the people can "help" in the mending and resurrection of a great Inca king who was decapitated by the Spanish. Peruvian planners have created a festival around this revived legend to promote the idea of "participation."

Whether the motivation is intrinsic or instrumental, the call for more indigenous creativity on the part of those committed to modernization poses serious questions. First, there is the question already noted of whether the media are capable of answering the call. Second is the question, Which tradition? There are Zoroastrian and Islamic elements in Iranian culture; there are Indian and Spanish elements in Peruvian culture; there are French and Arab elements in Algerian culture. Which should be emphasized? The choice, of course, is related to the ideological and developmental goals of the choosers. But even within the tradition, there are problems of selectivity. Certain elements are more compatible with modernizing values than other; indeed, certain elements of the religious tradition are obviously antithetical to modernization. Related to this is a question also alluded to earlier: whether promoting the renaissance of traditional arts and values is not giving undue support to repressive elements in society which would deny freedom to others? Champions of pluralism and freedom of expression in their "epochalism" may be no less committed to the search for a national identity than the "essentialists." But each group is fearful, justifiably, of the other.

GLOBAL PEYTON PLACE: THE HOMOGENIZATION OF BROADCASTING IN THE WORLD

While those who favor freedom of expression cannot help but fear the call for an "essentialist" emphasis in broadcasting, study of the program schedules of radio and television in developing countries will at least serve to place the problem in an empirical—not just ideological—perspective. In Britain, the proportion of programs purchased abroad by either BBC or ITV is limited by convention to 14%. By contrast, in the eleven developing countries we studied, this proportion ranges from 30 to 75 and averaging about 55%. The proportion is even higher if one examines only prime-time hours. The United States, of course, is the major supplier. It is no news that television around the world is densely populated by American detectives, cowboys, and conniving housewife heroines. Two or more of our 11 countries were showing "Gunsmoke," "Ironside," "Family Affair," and "Streets of San Francisco" in July 1975. Summer Saturday nights on the national channel in Iran, for example, featured "Family Affair" at 19:30 and "Days of Our Lives" at 21:00, while the second channel was offering "The Bold Ones" at 20:05 and "Kojak" at 22:00. Cyprus, increasingly, is tending to balance U.S. imports with programs from Greece, even though Cyprus television considers its cultural level higher than that of Greece and was established several years earlier. Algeria, despite its arabizing policy, still imports heavily from France. Thailand is importing an increasing proportion of its programs from Japan. Nevertheless, the United States is predominant almost everywhere.

It is not simply the "imperialism" of the suppliers that explains the high rate of importing programs. Television stations, even small ones in poor countries, broadcast some six to ten hours per day; professional pride, if nothing else, requires it. That equals a minimum of 2000 hours per year. All things considered, it costs at least $1000 to produce even a rudimentary program of one hour. The cost of buying an hour of foreign programming is a function of the number of sets in the country, and of whether other countries in the same language or geographic region have adopted it. Thus Iran can buy Ironside for $300–$400, Thailand for $250–$350, and Peru can buy it for $250 (latest figures from *Variety*, 8 January 1975, p. 96). If these figures are doubled to make allowances for extra costs such as subtitling, the fact is that they are able to broadcast Ironside for far less than the cost of producing the most modest of their own programs and for a small fraction of the price it cost to make originally in Hollywood (about $200,000). Even if the money were available for so many hours of local production, the talent is not, nor is the infrastructure in the other arts—film, theater, graphics—well developed. For these same reasons it is not unusual for small countries in Europe to import as much as 50% of their programs.

So the problem is as much one of demand as of supply.* While radio is often more indigenous than television, the ravenous local demand for music to fill the hours is as good an explanation for the worldwide success of rock (or whatever else happens to be in fashion) as is the eagerness of the recording companies to sell their product. The complexities of television production—even where fewer hours are involved—makes the demand even keener.

In examining the situation of broadcasting in the developing countries, one must look beyond the importation of tape and films to the importation of program ideas and formats. What is not directly imported may be—at second glance—imported as a model or "stimulus" for local translation. Salesmen for the international television marketeers come equipped not only with packages of videotape but with catalogs of ideas which are also for sale. The quiz, the variety show, the soap opera are locally produced variants on the metropolitan models. In a certain sense these are "imported" too, although they may sometimes be adapted quite creatively, as we shall illustrate below.

The standardization of television around the world is further reflected both in the format of the program schedules and in the proportional distribution of programs by category. International travelers have very few surprises in store when turning on the TV in their hotel rooms. Wherever they go they will find that news occupies about 10% of television time, with an added 10% for current affairs and documentaries. Series and serials share about 20% of the time. Children's programs, light entertainment, and feature films are each assigned somewhat more than 10% of the schedule, while sports and adult education of all kinds are given somewhat less than 10%. Religion, music of all kinds, and plays each take about 2–5% of television time. And there is about a 30% chance of seeing Kojak some evening of the week at 9 p.m. The variations by country are only slight: the French tradition (Algeria, Senegal) includes more talk and current affairs; the South American tradition gives prime time to its home-made, and sometimes original soap opera, the *telenovela*. Countries like Cyprus and Algeria make more deliberate selections of foreign material in order to give explicit emphasis to their cultural ties.

The demand for local programming, and even more, for local programming rooted in tradition, is better understood in this perspective. It is not simply an expression of ideological commitment. It is a question of whether one wants one's culture to be overwhelmed and homogenized. The world is indeed becoming a "global village" in the sense of being exposed to the same television programs. The global village is Peyton Place, so to speak.

This problem is all the more urgent in view of the fact that television has

---

*It is in the importance of the demand side of the equation that we differ from Herbert Schiller (cf. Schiller, 1969). Nor is the demand merely a reflection of colonial dependence; it is at least as much related to the insatiable appetite of the media. Witness the high rate of importing of American programs in small European countries.

hardly been launched in many developing countries. Typically, it has been established in and around the capital city, but has spread no further yet. The huge cost of extending television coverage can be justified, if at all, only in terms of its potential contribution to development; political, economic, and cultural. Why then impose an alien formula? As the Brazilian Minister of Education says,

> "Commercial television is imposing on the youngsters and children of our country a culture that has nothing to do with Brazilian culture . . . Thus, instead of being a creative element in the diffusion of Brazilian culture, television appears as a privileged vehicle of cultural import, a basic factor in the 'de-characterization' of our creativity" (Oliveira, 1974, pp. 18–19).

Or, as Peruvian planners and educators are saying, if the Indians of the Sierra are to benefit from the introduction of television—now that the network is being expanded—the universal programming formula should not go with it. The Indians' expectations of development plans appear to be positive: health, education, agriculture, the Spanish language. These expectations can be helped in some measure by the broadcast media. Why not, they ask, provide a broadcasting service which will meet these expectations? Why ask these people to *change* their expectations so that when television finally arrives they will be looking at their watches expectantly on Saturday nights at 9 p.m. wondering why Kojak is late?

TAKING ENTERTAINMENT SERIOUSLY

It is interesting to note that this concern over the display of alien values on television and the demand for increasing attention to the promotion of indigenous creativity reflects a changed conception of the broadcast media on the part of policy makers. In proclaiming the goals of integration and modernization, attention usually focused on the informational and educational role of the media. News, current affairs, and programs for the farmer or the housewife were subject to close surveillance, while entertainment was usually considered trivial or neutral or, sometimes, more functionally, as a source of escape or relief from the strains of social change. Recognition of the promise of the media in connection with the problem of cultural identity leads to the realization that entertainment is *not* neutral but an active force in the communication of values.

Politicians and planners are not alone in this discovery. Like them, students of mass communication have also tended to give more attention to the role of the media as agents of information and persuasion than as agents of entertainment. It is ironic that there are very few television viewers who would make the same mistake. Perhaps not all viewers are aware or concerned that "Peyton Place" or "Sesame Street" contain alien values; but they surely know that the primary function of broadcasting, almost everywhere, is to entertain.*

The implication of all this—for planners, for broadcasters, for academics—is to take entertainment more "seriously." If broadcasting is to be harnessed to the goal of promoting indigenous values, it is important to understand how entertainment works. That means understanding what message is implicit in "Hawaii Five-O," what people perceive in it, what they enjoy, what it - "gives" them, and then, by contrast, analyzing the experience with home-made broadcast entertainment and with entertainment in traditional culture.† Doing so will immediately suggest that the performing arts in many traditional societies make no room for the distinction between information and entertainment. The Peruvian revolutionaries who want to harness the media to their ideas for creating a socialist society based on the rehabilitation of traditional Inca values insist that it is "alienating" to make the conventional Western distinction among information, education, and entertainment.

Incidentally, it is not true that American thrillers and Westerns are the most popular programs in any country. It is fascinating, admittedly, to see how easily such programs cross national borders. Visual action, not words, is part of the answer. It would be of great value—now that entertainment is being taken seriously—to study the meanings these programs carry in different cultures and the functions they serve. But their popularity notwithstanding, the fact is that certain home-made programs—especially the home-made soap opera—almost always outdraw them in popularity. This kind of indigenous competition does not often satisfy the "essentialists" or developmentalists either. Very often, as we have said, they are based on imported models. But they may contain some clues about how to make more authentic television. We turn now to consider some efforts in this direction.

INDIGENOUS PROGRAMMING: SOME CREATIVE EFFORTS AND THE ISSUES THEY RAISE

Everywhere, there have been attempts to create at least some programs which give expression to cultural authenticity and continuity. Programs for holidays are often of this kind, but before discussing special events of this kind we wish to marshall examples from several countries of relatively more continuous kinds of programming. Certain generalizations will suggest themselves as we proceed.

*We are not taking into account here the East European countries or China where the situation may be different: we simply do not know. But see Powell (1975) for evidence that the Russians face the same dilemma.

†For theoretical and methodological discussion of research in this tradition, see Blumler and Katz (1974).

South America is a good place to begin. From Mexico to Argentina, the thirty- or sixty-minute *telenovela*, five days a week and hundreds of episodes along, is the most popular form of television.* Its origin, apparently, is in the American soap opera translated and exported by pre-Castro Cuba and now made for television in Mexico, Venezuela, Argentina, Brazil, and elsewhere. Mexican television thrives on the export of its *telenovelas*. But the form is also being creatively used. In Mexico itself the *telenovela* has been adapted to the presentation of historical drama, to tell the story of Mexico's march to independence. It is interesting to note that during our visit in Algeria, broadcasters were debating this very question: how to translate Algeria's epic struggle for independence into television terms?

In Brazil, the largest of the networks, Globo, has commissioned some of the country's best writers to create stories in the *novela* form. The late-evening *novela* in particular (there are three novelas each evening) is now a "serious" affair, relating to real-life people (rather than escapist dreams) and contemporary social issues. It is an interesting example of a carefully considered and costly initiative to improve the quality of product on the part of an oligopolist. It is possible that the move is better interpreted as a response to the increasingly vocal concern of government with matters of television. But the achievement is real.

There are several lessons to be learned here. First of all, it reminds us that, in its various forms, the serialized soap opera seems to be the most popular genre of television the world over. It is much more widespread than the action-adventure story, for example, which is limited to the U.S., England, France, and Japan. Indeed, the first dramatic production attempted by many a new television service is a serial story set in a family or village, and incorporating heavy doses of folk wisdom and morality. Britain's "Coronation Street" is probably the closest Western analog. Thus, Iran's most popular program is colorful Morad Barghi's discourses to his family, while the story of a moralizing taxi driver, his clients, and comrades is one of Senegal's leading programs. Cyprus and Israel both began their dramatic presentations with a family soap opera. The characters are familiar, the setting is recognizable, the problems are real (if exaggerated and sentimentalized). Wherever there are measures of popularity, these home-made programs outdraw the most famous of American imports!

Second, it is worth noting—in connection with the Brazilian case—that the status and authenticity of broadcast art can be considerably enhanced when the best writers and directors are incorporated into the media. The glamor of broadcasting—even of television—is by no means uniformly high throughout the world. In certain traditional societies journalists and broadcasters are held

---

*Based on survey data. Recent analysis of the U.S. soap opera as a genre may be found in Katzman (1972) and in Newcomb (1974). The South American *telenovela* is studied in *Orbita*.

in rather low esteem because they are associated with an irreverence for authority, with a bohemian style in some places, and as mere civil servants in others.

Still another implication of the Brazilian experience is that the media cannot be genuinely creative unless they cultivate and exploit the other creative arts in society. It is extremely difficult to establish a western-style television system without good writers, a tradition of theater, a local film industry, and experienced craftsmen in the other graphic arts. As we shall note below in discussing Thai television, many of the Asian countries have highly productive film industries. In Senegal, too, we found that the active local theater and film studios were a great asset in the introduction of television, although the lack of formal agreement with the writers' and filmmakers' guilds has also impeded optimum cultivation of these alliances.

The introduction of television in Colombia, on the order of General Rojas, when he took office, made early use of a tradition of theater in the country, and the report of these early plans sounds interesting, if dictatorial.* Thai television immediately employed the dubbing troupes which, for years, have ad-libbed translations of imported foreign films in the movie theaters (and still do). Patronage by broadcasting of these allied arts is of central importance to creativity and authenticity on radio and television.

South American television has another original aspect: the ebullient celebrity presiding over a variety show of great duration, sometimes six or seven hours long. While this form seems to be on the decline, it is interesting to take note both of the folksy quality of these shows and of their open-ended character. It is curious that television came to the new nations complete with stopwatches, so that time could be divided into fifteen-, thirty-, and sixty-minute segments. In fact, it does not quite work out that way since the American series hour, minus advertising, takes only fifty minutes, while the addition of local advertising often stretches the hour considerably. It is worth asking whether creativity in broadcasting in the new nations would not benefit from more freedom from the rigidities of Western time frames.

Thailand, too, has an interesting story. As in Brazil and other countries, the earliest days of Thai television contained a much higher proportion of indigenous creativity and of televised material based on traditional art forms, such as the shadow play, the dance theater, puppeteering, and so on. The decline in the proportion of these original productions in Thailand, and elsewhere, followed the increase in the number of hours of broadcasting, the importation of foreign films and serials, the invention of the videotape, and perhaps just plain exhaustion. The fact is that Thailand has several classic dramatic forms which have not found their place in television; the national theater is the last

---

*From Elizabeth Fox de Cardona's report to the International Broadcast Institute meeting in Mexico City, August 1974.

preserve of the dance-drama for example. Instead Thailand is importing gory Japanese thrillers at a very high rate, vying with the importation of American series. One wonders why the native traditions of theater finds no real expression in the broadcast media. On the other hand, Thailand has a film industry which produces over one hundred films per year; television does show its share of these films, many of which are reminiscent, however, of the *telenovela*. Indeed, one wonders how much of these "easterns"—which are similar, we are told to the films produced in Iran, India, Turkey and the other Asian countries, each of which has a substantial film industry—are based on indigenous themes and how much influenced by western models.*

One of the traditional Thai forms has made it, both on radio and television. This is the Mau Lum folk opera or song-story of which Tambiah (1968) writes:

> A measure of the contemporary appreciation of it is that wherever the radio has spread into villages the programme most avidly listened to is *mau lum*. . . . The entertainment appeal of *mau lum* stems from the fact that much of its content is drawn from the pool of northeastern tales and myths . . . rather flexibly constructed rhyming songs . . . (with) room . . . to improvise and be adept at repartee. . . . The repertoire . . . includes courtship and love poetry, burlesque and earthy, bawdy jokes; it echoes and stimulates the romantic sentiments of the young men and women. . . . The *mau lum* singers not only preserve and propagate regional traditions; they are also the channels through whom certain stories and epics, popularly known and appreciated in central and northern Thailand, are passed on to the north-eastern villagers. They sing stories about the life of the Buddha which are nationally known and heard in a different form in the temple. (pp. 113–117)

Traditionally, these singers travel widely, particularly in the northeast of the country, appearing at all-night sessions of fairs held in the temple grounds. Efforts have been made to expand their repertoire to take account of campaigns of rural development, anticommunist propaganda, and other contemporary and development topics. "To the extent to which singers take to them" (the new texts), writes Dr. Tambiah, "a truly grass-roots propaganda machine will have been harnessed by the government to promote its political and socio-economic policies."*

Other broadcasting systems, too, have successfully incorporated traditional media. The *griot* of Senegal, for example, who sing of lineages and history as chroniclers of an oral tradition, are on the regular payroll of ORTS, Senegal.

Here, too, are several important principles for us to consider: (1) The dis-

---

*This is an important area for study. The story-within-a-story form together with the implausible coincidences which bring protagonists together does not seem Western, at least in modern terms, but the saga of the village girl who flees to the city in quest of the lover who deserted her, etc., seem familiar. But these are mere impressions, and the content analysis of popular Asian film and television stories well deserves attention.

*The harnessing of traditional performers to development and other instrumental goals is not, however, our primary interest here. For other examples of this phenomenon, see Rogers and Shoemaker (1971) and International Broadcast Institute (1975).

tinction between information, education, and entertainment is of no relevance to these artistic traditions. (2) An art form, the *mau lum*, which is associated with festivity and holiday, has been sufficiently secularized and routinized to fit the time slots and production formats of radio and television. (3) The incorporation of contemporary references apparently has a share in the goodness of the fit between the traditional and modern media. (4) Art forms which traditionally take place out of doors have been successfully moved into the studio.

Why is it so difficult, then, to marry the broadcast media to the classical arts?

One reason is that the classical arts are dying in the developing countries. As far as we are able to judge, this is not typically *because* of broadcasting.* The traditional storyteller of the Iranian teahouse or the Ruhozi theater-on-the-pool began to disappear before the rise of television, and even in places to which television has not yet penetrated. Perhaps radio is to blame. Local informants were uncertain. The classical dance-drama of Thailand, one of the great achievements of its high artistic traditions, survives only under the patronage of the national theater; and the theater is the only training school for artists. Similarly, the national theater in Japan is the only remaining school for Kabuki actors; the family tradition, which passed the art from father to sons, has been broken.

We do not know where to place the blame. Richard Hoggart blames the tourists for the westernization, if not the decline, of the dance-drama in Bali. It is not primarily a *performing* art, he claims. And the same may be true for other art forms related to religious traditions. They do not survive the process of secularization. Modernization in its various aspects, including literacy—but not just the broadcast media—is to blame.

A second reason for the difficulty in transposing these traditional forms has to do with their limited repertoire. Many of these traditions are built on a very small number of classical themes, and they are rapidly exhausted by radio or television. Those artistic traditions which do succeed over radio or television tend to have modes of refreshing themselves such as the contemporary allusions in the *mau lum* or the *griot* song histories.

Broadcasters and artists in several countries called our attention to the incompatibility between the traditional location on the village square of some of the best-liked of their performing arts and the constraints of the radio or television studio. This problem was emphasized in both Algeria and Nigeria. Part of the problem, of course, is in the lack of professional training and the dearth of equipment for outside broadcasting. Part of it is in a bias which leads professionals to think that the studio is where broadcasting belongs. But the

---

*A brilliant discussion of the confrontation of folk culture and popular culture is given in McCormack (1969). Unfortunately, it came to my attention too late for incorporation in the body of this paper.

problem goes deeper; there is a certain incompatibility between "inside" and "outside," because of the communal and participatory nature of the "outside" audience, on the one hand, and the freedom of movement of the artists, on the other. Perhaps there is more to it than that; we do not know enough of these traditional arts to be able to judge. The communal viewing of television may be of some use in this connection. The communal TV set is a necessity in any event in the developing countries, and perhaps it has certain advantages, not only disadvantages, over individual viewing. Coffeehouse discussions of the content of the newspaper were, and in some places still are, the breeding place of Western public opinion. (See Speier, 1950, and Tarde, 1901, Chapter 2.) Perhaps a certain kind of television deserves to be seen in the teahouse or the village square.

Still another difficulty in the transplantation of the traditional arts is the "festive" character of so many of them. They cannot easily be made into just another program on a Tuesday evening. Here, the broadcast media are caught in a basic paradox: the best—the most authentic—of their materials are appropriate to special occasions, yet the professional goal of broadcasting is enshrined in "continuous performance." Perhaps television would be better if it were less continuous; perhaps the aim should not be to be on the air every day for as many hours as possible. It is no coincidence that broadcasting is often at its best on holidays, when it has something "special" to say. The media often rise to these occasions with special bursts of creativity. They manage to catch the mood, and enhance the celebration, of both traditional and modern holidays. In the "engineering" of new national holidays, governments often show acute awareness of the potential role of the media.

ON THE "TRANSLATION" OF TRADITION

Our entire discussion of the problems of broadcasting and culture is anchored in the fundamental question of whether the media are capable of contributing to "essentialism" in Geertz' phrase—or whether they are its sworn enemy, agents of "epochalism," or worse. It is clear that the media are capable of "opening a window to the world," even if the view is distorted and, in the opinion of some, demeaning. It is clear that they are natural allies of the forces of modernization and development, however casually or unintentionally they pursue those goals. What is not clear is whether the values and artistic traditions of the society must also make way—along with the methods of subsistence farming—for the homogenized popular culture of the West.

In the last few pages, we have given some examples of successful coping by the broadcast media with the challenge of cultural continuity, and we have said something about the ingredients of these successful efforts: joining forces with the traditional performing arts through cultivation and patronage; drawing on those arts which can handle contemporaneity in the context of tradition; building on special occasions such as holidays; going "outside" the studio and the home for both production and reception. But the problem goes beyond specific programs, even special programs. There is a sameness in the style of television and radio presentations which has come packaged with the technology, almost as if the microphones and cameras came wrapped together with instructions for presenting a news program, or variety show. Indeed, we noted that these formulas are for sale as well, and tend further to standardize the broadcast media around the world.

One wonders whether this has to be: cannot Nigerian, or Peruvian, or Senegalese television be more indigenous, not just in programming, but in *style*? What are needed are more radical suggestions for making radio and television relevant for traditional people who have more important problems than those which can be solved by "Chief Ironside." Tanzania is an example of a country that has tried, and Peru is another which is talking about it. Their ideas are not based only on the content of specific programs but on a different conception of the role of the media. Radio and television need to be "reinvented," in a sense. But how? How can tradition be translated into the language of the broadcast media?

One idea is to make certain that producers have a deeper grounding in their *own* cultural traditions and not only in the traditions and technology of metropolitan broadcasting. Informants in several countries told us how ill-informed broadcasters are about the traditional arts of their own societies and about ceremonies and values of their own cultures. The techniques of producing and directing are mistakenly thought of as content. Sorting this out may lead to a more creative blending of the old and the new.

This idea, perhaps, can be further developed. A society concerned over the use of broadcasting for cultural continuity might try to experiment with the establishment of an "institute for the translation of tradition," whose members would give serious thought to traditional forms and content, on the one hand, and to the language of the media, on the other. Experts in the tradition, scholars and researchers, could sit together with producers and directors in an effort to find solutions to the problem of *domesticating* the broadcast media. What is needed are not programs *about* tradition, but a series of creative acts that will take the "mood" or style of a culture and translate it into broadcasting terms.*

For example, broadcasting systems everywhere have to solve the problem of how to mourn: there are holidays of mourning, such as punctuate the calendar of Islam, or commemorative mourning on the anniversary of wars, or

---

*The example of the Children's Television Workshop which created "Sesame Street" through interaction of a team of producers, child psychologists, and media researchers is relevant here. So are the working teams of Britain's Open University.

mourning as on the death of a leader or a great man. All cultures provide rules for such occasions. There are rituals to be followed and symbols to be displayed, pleasures to be denied, and a variety of enabling means through which people can commune with the living and the dead. These rules are not readily translated into the language of radio and television, yet the more modern a society becomes, the more broadcasting is expected to take the lead on such occasions. Spontaneously, or by imitating foreign models, broadcasting stations do their best. Often, they simply transmit the rituals and ceremonies as they are enacted outside the studio. The celebration of Shi'ite Islam of the deaths of Ali and Hussein, the death of John Kennedy in the United States, the mourning for the dead of the wars in Europe, the commemoration in Israel of the holocaust which brought death to six million Jews—are all improvised by the media. For example, replacing scheduled radio programs by the broadcast of classical music is the accepted form of broadcast mourning in Israel. But little or no systematic effort is given anywhere to finding "authentic" solutions to the problem of how broadcasting might capture the *mood* of the tradition.* Obviously, the answer is not to be found ready-made in the traditional sources, but rather in a creative melding of the old and the new.

Celebrations of the sabbath is another example. Christianity and Judaism have a day, each week, which is not simply a "day off" but one which is endowed with spirituality. Other cultures have similar days. Islam has an entire month of Ramadan. The challenge to broadcasting is to discover forms that capture the spirit of these occasions, more for the modernizing groups in the society than for the traditionals. The standard solution for the Sabbath is a music-and-variety show for the family, and sometimes, a program that is a little more highbrow than usual. But are there no more "authentic" solutions?

Creativity based on the interaction of research, tradition, and the media would be the primary charge of the institute. But within the context of an institute of this kind producers could also be trained in their own cultures. They could be sent out into the countryside to observe and record the traditional performing arts. They could be assigned to view television—indeed, to view their own programs—together with families and groups in traditional settings. They could be asked to analyze the meanings and the functions of different sorts of programs for these groups. They might study and observe the teahouse as a form of community center in which communication goes on. The issue of differentiating information, education, and entertainment in pro-

---

*Von Grunebaum (1955) poses the same problem with reference to the "Spirit of Islam as Shown in its Literature" (Chapter 5) and even gives an extended example from an epic poem on mourning (pp. 104–109). Analyzing what is "peculiarily Islamic" (not just Arabic) about this poem, he uses criteria of content (continual "need to live with one's death," "heedlessness"), outward form (the *maqama*), inner form ("abrupt transitions" of mood), attitude toward literature ("as a display of philological erudition and prosodical virtuosity . . . in invention of incident, repartee, or argument").

gram schedules could be thrashed out.

CONCLUSION

The performance of broadcasting in the realm of cultural continuity falls very far short of the promise held out for it. Indigenous self-expression in broadcasting is often little more than a copy of metropolitan models. There is a need to link the media with other arts, traditional and modern, from which ideas will flow. There is a need to create programs that will give authentic expression to the culture in the process of its confrontation with modernity. But more than this, there is the need to try—at least to try—to employ broadcasting in ways which will better fit the moods and styles of the national heritage and of its special occasions. Perhaps the luxury of immersing producers in their own cultures, and forming creative groups of broadcasters, scholars, and carriers-of-the-tradition to plan schedules and invent programs together, holds out a fragile hope that broadcasting might live up to its promise of contributing to cultural continuity.

It is all too easy, of course, to suppress free expression in the name of culturally authentic creativity. That is obvious. But even for men of goodwill, as was noted earlier, the commitment to authenticity in the media poses a dilemma. How does one reconcile this commitment with the equally compelling commitment to promote mass communications which permit the exchange of ideas among individuals and among nations? The dilemma is a genuine one, and therefore cannot be perfectly resolved. Rather rapidly developing societies must steer a practical course which refuses to sacrifice authenticity to modernity and refuses to sacrifice freedom to authenticity.

REFERENCES

Blumler, J. G., and Katz, E. (1974). "The Uses of Mass Communication: Current Perspectives on Gratifications Research." Sage, Beverly Hills, California.

Geertz, C. (1973). "The Interpretation of Cultures: Selected Essays." Basic Books, New York.

Inkeles, A., and Smith, D. H. (1974). "Becoming Modern: Individual Change in Six Developing Countries." Harvard University Press, Cambridge, Massachusetts.

International Broadcast Institute. (1975). "Seminar on Motivation, Information and Communication for Development in African and Asian Countries, Ibadan, Nigeria, 1–9 July, 1974." International Broadcast Institute.

Katzman, N. (1972). Television soap operas: What's been going on anyway? *Public Opinion Quarterly 36*, 200–212.

McCormack, T. (1969). Folk culture and the mass media. *Archives Européennes de Sociologie 10*, 220–237.

Newcomb, H. (1974). "TV: The Most Popular Art." Anchor, New York.

Oliveira, Q. de. (1974). "Television as a Medium of Mass Communication." (Lecture of the Minister of Communications at the Anhembi Faculty of Social Communication, Sao Paolo, 19 November 1974.)

Powell, D. E. (1975). Television in the USSR. *Public Opinion Quarterly 39*, 287–300.

Rogers, E. M., and Shoemaker, F. F. (1971). "Communication of Innovations; A Cross-Cultural Approach," 2nd ed. Free Press, New York.

Rogers, E. M., and Svenning, L. (1969). "Modernization among Peasants; the Impact of Communication." Holt, Rinehart and Winston, New York.

Schiller, H. I. (1969). "Mass Communications and American Empire." A. M. Kelley, New York.

Speier, H. (1950). Historical development of public opinion. *American Journal of Sociology 55*, 376–388.

Tambiah, S. J. (1968). Literacy in a Buddhist Village in North-East Thailand. *In* "Literacy in Traditional Societies." (J. Goody, ed.), pp. 85–131. Cambridge University Press, Cambridge, England.

Tarde, G. de. (1901). "L'Opinion et al Foule." F. Alcan, Paris.

Von Grunebaum, G. E. (1955). "Islam: Essays in the Nature and Growth of a Cultural Tradition." Routledge and Paul, London.

5

Culture in the Process of Dependent Development: Theoretical Perspectives

Raquel Salinas

Leena Paldán

University of Tampere

Raquel Salinas was born and educated in Chile and has lived in Finland since 1974. She received her Master's degree in Social Sciences from the University of Tampere. Her specialty is Latin American mass media, and she has published a monograph on this subject.

Leena Paldán received her Master's degree in Social Sciences from the University of Tampere. She is an instructor in the Department of Journalism and Mass Communication, University of Tampere. She has published several papers and reports on national cultural policy.

This chapter has been written specifically for this book.

"Development is multi-dimensional, and not confined merely to economic growth: economy, culture, education, science and technology are specific aspects, of course, but complementary and inseparable . . . (but) in order to develop, a society must remain true to itself, draw its strength from its own culture and ways of thought and action, and set itself objectives consonant with its values and felt needs . . ."

This concept was stated by the Director-General of UNESCO in his address at the closing meeting of the 19th session of the General Conference of UNESCO in November 1976 (M'Bow, 1977, p. 5). Moreover, the same conference adopted a resolution that called for UNESCO to assist "in liberating the developing countries from the state of dependence, resulting from specific historical circumstances, which still characterizes their communication and information system.''* Similar, though stronger and more analytical statements, have been expressed in forums in which the voice of the Third World has been more outspoken. One of the most important political programs against imperialism in the field of culture has been adopted by the movement of nonaligned countries in conferences in New Delhi and Colombo in 1976. Some of the basic problems to be overcome were formulated in these words:

> Just as political and economic dependence are legacies of the era of colonialism, so is the case of dependence in the field of information which in turn retards the achievement of political and economic growth.
> Nonaligned countries noted with concern the vast and ever growing gap between communication capacities in nonaligned countries and in the advanced countries, which is a legacy of their colonial past. This has created a *situation of dependence* and domination in which the majority of countries are reduced to being passive recipients of biased, inadequate and distorted information. *The fuller identification and affirmation of their national and cultural identity* thus required them to rectify this serious imbalance and to take urgent steps to provide greater momentum in this new area of mutual cooperation. (Emphasis added.)†

Obviously the present concern about the international information structure is an outgrowth of the expanding and intensifying dominance of the developed capitalist countries over the underdeveloped part of the world and its information systems. But, as the above statements indicate, the concern about information structures has been conceived within the framework of broader social processes, that is, within the whole process of development. Moreover, the questions pertaining to information are closely tied up with notions expressing different aspects of the role of culture in society and in its development process. This, in connection with the underdeveloped part of the world, is recognized as the process of dependent underdevelopment.

Within this context, expressions such as cultural dependence, cultural identity, preservation of national cultures, and people's authentic cultural needs have been given attention. Culture and dependence appear as the central words among those terms extensively used in present day political discussions about the cultural independence of the underdeveloped part of the world.

The present paper is an attempt to bring out some elements that might promote a fuller understanding of how the state of dependent development is created and expressed in the cultural sphere of societies subjected to an external domination system. Within this framework, the problem of the struggle against the state of cultural dependence will be given some attention. The

---

*Resolution contained in Document 19 C/123, Section 4.14, paragraph 8, for the 19th Session of the General Conference of UNESCO.

†Declaration of the Conference of Non-Aligned Countries on a Press Agencies Pool in New Delhi, July 8–13, 1976, which was adopted by the Summit Conference of Heads of State or Governments of Non-Aligned Countries in Colombo, August 16–19, 1976.

analysis will refer specifically to the present reality of the Latin American countries.

However, to provide a basis for a complete understanding of the ideas that have been introduced in the current discussion (e.g., national culture and cultural sovereignty) would require a comprehensive analysis, not only of the concept of culture itself, but also of the notion of national culture. This would necessitate separate treatment which, given the limited scope of the present paper, is not possible.* Our analysis rests on basic premises concerning culture and national culture.

Culture, as both a specific sphere of ideal reflections and a system of meanings attributed to the existing reality, cannot be separated from the basic socioeconomic structure of a given society. Culture is always an historically specific phenomenon, conditioned by the class structure of the society. Hence, culture exists as systems of representations and products that embody them, and as signifying practices and institutions which materialize them. In a capitalist society the conflictive class structure gives birth to a cultural sphere predominantly divided along class lines. It is a system comprised of dominated and dominant cultures, generated by the subordinated and dominant social groups and classes on the basis of their social experiences.

Within this general framework, national culture appears to possess an inherently contradictory nature. On the one hand, it is an expression of the basic relations of domination as they exist in the cultural sphere, the representative of the dominant culture itself, imposed upon and inculcated in the subordinated social groups. Basically, therefore, national culture cannot escape its class character. On the other hand, national culture provides the site for the subordinated social groups to struggle against the dominant culture; it is the realm that enables them to create a true unification and feeling of solidarity among themselves and to give birth to means and ways for the struggle against domination.

These basic premises however sketchy and limited, provide the general perspective from which to understand the concepts of culture and national culture in the following analysis.

CULTURAL DOMINATION IN THE CONTEXT OF IMPERIALISM

The analysis of the cultural sphere of the dependent societies is first and foremost to be conceived within the context provided by the international capitalist system, in its contemporary imperialist phase. It seems pertinent to

---

*Some elements relevant for an elaboration of the basic conceptualization pertaining to culture and national culture are given, for example, by Hall (1977) and Quijano (1971).

note that, although the Marxist tradition provided a sound analysis of the basic economic laws leading to the development of the imperialist phenomenon (e.g., the needs of industrial societies for cheap raw materials, for additional markets to consume rising levels of production, and for investment outlets to absorb accumulating capital), the cultural trends accompanying the capitalist accumulation in the dominant countries and the related processes in the dependent countries are yet to be thoroughly studied.

The term, "cultural imperialism," has been used to refer to this dimension of the relations existing within the international capitalist system. Golding (1977) refers to it as "the normative component to the structural relations of dependence between advanced and underdeveloped societies" (p. 291), which includes the impact of international media as well as of the educational and cultural systems. In Schiller's words (1976), it corresponds to "the sum of processes by which a society is brought into the modern world system and how its dominating stratum is attracted, pressured, forced into shaping social institutions to correspond to, or even to promote, the values and structures of the dominant center of the system" (p. 9). The notion of cultural imperialism, however, remains purely descriptive and is often loosely used with reference to a certain category of problems. A greater analytical effort and a more comprehensive theory of imperialism is called for if some explanatory power is to be given to it.

At the economic level, the existence of cultural imperialism is being increasingly connected to the role of the transnationals in the development of capitalism. Among those activities fostered by the development of transnational corporations, the growing role of the media has been a matter of increasing attention, because of its obvious relation to what has been called cultural imperialism. This concern is all the more justified, given the role that the media play in the reproduction of the capitalist mode of production, both at the economic and at the cultural–ideological level.* A significant body of data has been gathered concerning the activities of media conglomerates, although at the theoretical level the interpretative effort remains, to a great extent, to be done.

Recently, Boyd-Barrett (1977) has proposed the term, "media imperialism," as referring to "the process whereby the ownership, structure,

---

*In its modern form, the media accomplish two essential functions in the capitalist system. At the economic level, they are both an economic branch of their own and a link between production and consumption, by means of speeding up the commodity circulation and realization of surplus value (Pietilä, 1977, pp. 79–82). In the cultural sphere, they are crucial to the reproduction of the dominant culture and ideology that it conveys. This is done by providing the social knowledge through which the reality of others is perceived, so that an imaginary coherence is built, in which the contradictory elements are held within the frames of the dominant culture and ideologies. This transforms them into a formidable apparatus for the building of concensus and legitimacy (Hall, 1977, pp. 340–344).

distribution or content of the media in any one country are singly or together subject to substantial pressure from the media interests of any other country or countries without proportionate reciprocation of influence by the country so affected'' (p. 16). The notion is more restricted than the concepts of imperialism and cultural imperialism,* and the elements of cultural invasion, as well as the imbalance of power between the countries concerned, should justify the use of the term "imperialism." Thus, all major forms of media imperialism are considered to be an inevitable, or highly probable, outcome of the imbalance of power between the respective countries, and four modes of influence are suggested to guide further research. The country that originates an international media influence either exports this influence as a deliberate commercial or political strategy, or simply disseminates it unintentionally, or without deliberation, in a more general process of political, social, or economic influence. A country affected by media influence either adopts this influence as a deliberate commercial or political strategy, or simply absorbs this influence as the result of contact (Boyd-Barrett, 1977, p. 119).

Although this is an interesting effort to systematize an area of studies that remains scattered and predominantly empirical, the conception courts a certain formalism. Thus, for instance, the circuit of influence is located between the media system of one country and the media system of another, and the modes of influence, although referred to as an imbalance of power, are ranked along the dimensions of intentionality. At the empirical level, the analysis of media "interests" of the dominant countries has proved to be very difficult to separate from the interests of larger transnationals. But even more important, the two factors mentioned above tend to neglect important aspects of both the notions of totality and domination, which are central to an approach to any social formation. Indeed, although it is legitimate to outline a field of studies by separating it from related fields, the conception of the problem itself should contain reference to the existence of wider levels of determinacy. Additionally, there is a necessity for placing the analysis of systems of communication within the frames provided by the specific sociohistorical formations that embrace them. In this respect, generalizations offered by a study centered upon the core of the international system most assuredly call for the complementary analysis of the particular forms in which is contained the dependent situation of the peripheral countries. This complementary perspective will be presented in the following pages. It refers not only to the media but to society as a whole.

---

*Boyd-Barrett suggests that the range of phenomena covered by the term "media imperialism" is possibly the single most important component of cultural imperialism outside formal educational institutions, from the point of view of those who are actively engaged in extending or containing given cultural influences.

FROM IMPERIALISM TO DEPENDENCE: MAIN FEATURES OF DEPENDENT DEVELOPMENT

The relationships between the imperialist center and peripheral societies have been the concern of Latin American scholars, especially during this decade. This concern has been stimulated strongly by the theoretical and practical problems posed by the chronic underdevelopment of Latin American societies. A fairly substantial body of knowledge has been gathered around this perspective, which is generally referred to as "dependence theory" or the "dependence approach." Santos (1977a) presents an account "from within" the dependence approach, relating it to the existing theories of development. Fagen (1977) presents the view of an outsider and aims at summarizing the reasons for the emergence of such an approach in Latin America, as well as the main characteristics of it. The concept of dependence is central to these studies. It is thought of by de Moraes "as the dialectic unity of the general determinations of the capitalist mode of production and the specific determinations of each of the dependent societies and, thereby, as a synthesis of the 'external' and 'internal' factors" (cited in Cardoso, 1972, p. 17). More specifically, the concept aims at accounting for the relationship between the laws of development corresponding to an international structure of relationships, whose own level of determinacy is found in the dynamics of capitalist accumulation in the dominant countries, and their linkage to national economies. The accumulation processes of the national economies are conditioned by means of their insertion into the international economy and, simultaneously, determined by their own laws of development.*

Thus, the concept of dependence is inscribed within the more embracing theory of imperialism, and it represents the search for the multiple levels of determinacy that should explain the peculiar forms of development of the peripheral societies. This search for the concrete, which is a basic methodological premise of the dependency approach, is expressed in the analysis of the specific situations that derive from the existence of imperialist economic domination and the existence of nation states. At the same time, the nation states are thought of as expressing the relationships and interests of local classes who, although partly subordinated to the politicoeconomic international domination, determine in the last resort the behavior of the states.

---

*This presentation follows Don Santos, who explains the dialectic of the internal and external as follows. The internal contradictions—arising from the constitutive elements—of every phenomenon *determine* its laws of development and set the frame for its action. But the internal elements do not exhaust a given reality. They operate within given *external conditions* that modify its functioning, fostering the development of certain elements, closing off the path to others, increasing or diminishing the internal contradictions, or introducing new elements that call for the adaption of old ones, or may even provoke the break down of the existing structures (Santos, 1976, pp. 1–3).

This international approach, though it plays a central role, does not neglect the interaction in terms of regional and national socioeconomic structures, nor does it ignore the protagonistic role that the social classes and their contradictions have in the whole process.

Thus, there is a quest for the historical specificity of the social systems both at the national and international level, as well as for a consideration of the totality. The economic sphere and its respective trends must be studied in their relationship to the juridical–political and ideological superstructures.*

Thus, domination and dependence make up the history of the world economic system, whose unequal and combined development is continually renewing its exploitative and concentrating character.

In accordance with these premises, the characterization of the contemporary forms of relationship between the imperialist center and the dependent countries is a central concern of this approach. In what follows, we present some basic theses in relation to this problem. (For additional detail, see Cardoso, 1972, 1974.)

The present process of the international division of labor, impelled by monopoly capitalism and the reorganization of the multinational enterprises that start operating as conglomerates, opens possibilities for industrialization of some peripheral areas. There is a growing process of internationalization of internal markets and, because of this, industrialization of the periphery increases. Also enhanced is the role of local consumption in the absorption of the products manufactured by the dependent economies, as well as the capital generated by the internationalized sector. The metropolitan economies start importing rather than exporting capital. The contradictory character of the accumulation reappears in new fashions; it acquires new features in the growing external debt and simultaneously growing capitalization of the dependent economies. There is, therefore, a simultaneous process of dependence and capitalist development. Consequently, the composition of the productive forces, allocation of the factors of production, distribution of the labor force, and class relationships go through modifications in order to accommodate themselves more easily to capitalist structures of production. In this ongoing process, those who benefit from this type of "dependent development" are the state enterprises, multinational corporations, and local firms associated with both or either of them. In Cardoso's words, these social agents are the "tripod of the associated-dependent development."

This type of industrialization involves limited sectors of the periphery, and it coexists with older forms of dependence. But it is the "internationalization of the internal markets" that is the fundamental form adopted by the contem-

---

*This is a condensed and incomplete summary of some basic theoretical and methodological premises held by the primary authors working in the field. A complete analysis of these and other aspects can be found in Cardoso (1972) and Santos (1976).

porary situation of dependence.* It also reinforces the internal mechanisms of superexploitation, concentration, and monopolization, because it is incapable of absorbing the labor force liberated by the crisis in the traditional sectors of the economy. This is accompanied by growing inequality of income and consequent insurmountable limits to the internal market. In this manner, the dependent industrialization does not solve the basic socioeconomic problems, and the class contradictions become sharper.

Among the social forces involved in this process, the following are worth noting.† The state extends its activities and progressively adopts a vital role in the regulation of economic and political life. Its growing importance in the economic sphere gives rise to an important structure of power, which is formed by the whole set of state institutions and enterprises. In addition, a powerful coercive apparatus is developed, the decision-making capacity of which increases together with the acuteness of class conflicts. The common practices utilized by the state make the groups involved develop some forms of identification which, without being monolithic, are distinct from those assumed by other fractions and elements of the dominating classes. In ideological terms, this may give rise to nationalist ideologies of varying character, but always important in defining the course of society. As to the cultural institutions depending on the state, the educational system receives a new impulse, which issues from the necessity for a skilled labor force, local technicians, and managerial abilities required by the industrialization and its related activities.

The dependent development also benefits the local bourgeoisie and promotes their expansion. Despite the nonexistence of powerful industrial bourgeoisie, the local dominant class is supported by activities centered on industry and finance, commerce, transport, communications, and advertising. Some sectors are more closely related to the state and, therefore, are more supportive of state policies. Others depend more on the activities and interests of the transnationals, the result being a varied configuration in the political

---

*As to the apparent contradiction between dependence and development, Cardoso reminds us that sector I of the economy—especially that concerning the creation of new technology—is increasingly concentrated in the central economies, while the peripheral industrialization—mostly in sector II, production of consumption goods—is financially and technologically dependent on them. This process is accompanied by growing external debt, due to the necessity for loans in order to support the import of technology. Thus development and technological–financial dependence are processes both contradictory and mutually related, continuously reproducing, modifying, and expanding each other unless a political process stops them (Cardoso, 1972, p. 25).

†What follows is a condensed presentation of general trends accompanying the economic process described above. As such, it does not refer to any specific Latin American country, although it is based on specific analyses provided by the following authors: Bagú (1971); Cardoso (1972, 1974); Santos (1976, 1977a, b); and Sunkel (1971). These propositions cover the period starting from the fifties until today and are left in many cases undetermined deliberately, because specific sociohistorical systems are not referred to.

sphere. Thus, the local bourgeoisie does not constitute a monolithic entity, although the fact of sharing the benefits of the dependent development gives it some common features that are an essential linkage between the dominant groups is the society. The sector of the national bourgeoisie that owns the media is closely tied to the industrial bourgeoisie and constitutes a central link to metropolitan interests. This makes it an important pressure group on local governments, both because of its economic position and its capacity to influence consciousness, shape public opinion, and establish ideological control.

As for the dominated classes, some new sectors are incorporated in the sphere of industry and related activities, including those of the state. This contributes to the expansion of the market and, to some extent, unifies it at the national level. The industrial working class shows distinct features, which vary according to their inclusion in the modern or the less advanced sector of the economy. The process of marginalization, which is parallel with that of industrialization and urbanization, gives birth to specific social groups whose cultural features are determined by their level of socioeconomic and cultural deprivation. The dependent development also creates the conditions for the strengthening of important middle sectors, which, without having direct economic interests arising from ownership, may all the same appear closely identified with the dominating groups. These strata are also some of the main clients of the established cultural institutions.

CULTURAL EXPRESSIONS OF THE DEPENDENT DEVELOPMENT

The foregoing section has attempted to characterize briefly the structure of societies undergoing a process of readjustment to the new conditions of dependency relations. As such, it is necessarily schematic and a simplification of a complex process. Nevertheless, the discussion seems sufficient to suggest that the new stage in the development of the international order of domination—as it appears at the national level in the periphery—is producing distinct effects in the cultural sphere of the societies affected.

First, in terms of the classes and groups involved in the process of dependent industrialization, the import of productive facilities implies that larger sectors of the local population are susceptible to the influence of cultural models provided by the metropolis. On the one hand, the local ruling classes and groups who benefit from the dependent development come to constitute what Sunkel (1971, pp. 24–28) calls the "internationalized" social sectors, especially responsive to the demands of the metropolis. He refers to the national sector, which, due to the income distribution stimulated by this type of capitalist development, is able to share patterns of consumption and thereby life-styles and cultural affinities similar to those sustained by the dominant sectors of developed economies. On the other hand, the dominated classes and groups whose living depends on the activities fostered by the modern sector of the economy—specifically those of the affiliates of transnationals, but also of some state enterprises—also fall under the influence of normative elements that are transferred together with technology. Their own subcultures are shaken, both by the change of their objective situation in the sphere of material production, as well as by the cultural–ideological elements imported from the metropolis. Similarly, as in the case of the ruling classes and groups, the effects are different according to their inclusion in production as skilled workers, technicians, professionals, and so forth. What we are stressing here is the existence of common practices affecting them all.

Second, together with this increasing involvement of some sectors of the local population, there is a correlative movement of exclusion and marginalization of others. Thus, the domination affects both. Some are brought together under the influence of foreign cultural models. Others are submitted to levels of existence that prevent them from exercising minimal cultural rights, because of the imperatives that poverty poses to their survival. Quijano (1971, p. 52) mentions the existence not only of a "culture of poverty," as understood in the work of Oscar Lewis, but also of a "poverty of the culture," understood as the incapacity for the elaboration of a more complex vision of the relations between men and women and their circumstances, which is the result of the necessity of focusing all attention on physical survival.

Third, the domination by the metropolis has a differential effect on the varied cultural institutions, products, and practices. It may appear as (1) fostering and assimilating those that are functional to the model of development carried by the local and foreign elites, (2) relegating those that are unnecessary or nonsusceptible to assimilation by the dominant cultural–ideological patterns, (3) closing off the path to those that may play a role of resistance against the new style of domination, or (4) creating new forms of cultural expression that correspond to the realities created by the domination itself. Thus, for instance, the educational system and the media are shaped to adapt more closely to the requirements of the dependent industrialization; cultural manifestations of the working classes are either relegated or incorporated by the cultural industry to make them devoid of their original significations, etc.

Finally, the local cultural industry, because of its essentially profit-seeking nature, is especially responsive to the conditioning of the metropolis. However, this responsiveness varies according to the different levels of technological and financial control exercised by the metropolis on cultural production. As observed earlier, the electronic media are especially sensitive to external conditioning, given the sophisticated technology they need and their commercial character, which makes them depend on foreign advertisers and advertising agencies. Other branches of the cultural industry are not exempt from external conditioning, but their degree of autonomy may be greater according to the play of similar factors. Obviously, these conditioning factors affect not only the owners of the cultural industry, but all the sectors depending on it, so that the imprint of domination can be traced to the very moment of the creation of cultural products.

In comparison with former stages of dependency relationships, the contemporary stage seems to have a distinct character in the cultural sphere. In effect, dependent industrialization, accompanied by accelerated urbanization and the cultural features noted previously, can be seen as a drive toward cultural homogenization. This is associated with the strengthening of mechanisms that are designed to be nationwide distributors of social imagery and knowledge, e.g., the educational system and the modern media. Indeed, both the educational and media systems can penetrate throughout the culture and subcultures of society, and, without changing them completely, they provide a basic web of meanings common to all sectors of the population touched by them. In this sense, we can say that the social practices necessary for strengthening a nationwide culture are fostered by the associated–dependent development.

The dependent development is, however, a capitalist form of development. Hence, the trend toward homogenization is basically a process of modernization of the mechanisms for domination in the cultural–ideological sphere and, thereby, for the reproduction of the whole society as a system of domination. But none of the features pointed out can be interpreted as being the mere conveyor for the international order of domination. Basically, they appear so because there is an internal order of domination whose existence and reproduction depends on the existence and reproduction of the whole capitalist system.

CONTRADICTIONS AND CULTURE

The existence of domination is never without contradictions. Weakening of the levels of hegemony and correlative trends toward autonomy, or eventually liberation, appear. Thus, in connection with the trends singled out previously, we can mention at least some elements of contradiction that make the domination more like an unstable equilibrium than a total subjugation.

First, though the process of industrialization expedites the adoption of styles conveyed by technology, it also allows the possibility for the working class to acquire experience and to increase its organizational levels. Since this form of development is full of contradictions and periods of reversal, the experiences and cultural–ideological practices developed here may turn against the system itself.

Second, it has been mentioned that dependent development is, simultaneously, a process of incorporation and exclusion of different sectors of the population. Given the acute character of the polarization that the system produces in the periphery, the possibility for the appearance of cultural–

ideological practices expressing not only the polarization, but also the will to overcome it, is always present.

Third, for the same reasons, there is a possibility for those who create the cultural products to escape the limits and models imposed both by the metropolis and the local dominant culture by transforming their own practices into the expression of the lived reality of the dominated. This may happen, for instance, in the fields of art or literature, but also in the cultural industry itself. As such, it normally appears as a movement toward revitalization of indigenous cultures and as the search for alternative cultural forms to express the present reality of the working people. Thus, these trends introduce a contradiction within the dominant culture itself.

Fourth, although the development of the media has a decisive importance for the cultural homogenization and ideological control of the population, it cannot be assumed to have an all-powerful and homogenous effect. Indeed, the existence of mediating instances has to be considered in the generation of products as well as in their consumption. Above all, cultures and subcultures are the expression of men's and women's lived experience of their conditions of existence. Accordingly, the constant invasion of meanings that do not express this reality will often generate some limits to its assimilation. It is important, therefore, to study the conditions affecting the reception of the messages, as well as to examine the possible distance between the models of interpretation provided by the media and the real level of assimilation by the "audience" to them. The audience itself is a heterogeneous entity whose reality has to be inserted into the socioeconomic structure. Thus, the audience carries not only multiple realities, but also multiple histories of accumulated significations, whose importance to the interpretation of the media messages cannot be neglected. On account of these factors, the possibility for the appearance of alternative cultural products and models has to be taken into consideration. The possibility of overcoming the order of domination exists, and no cultural–ideological system has thus far succeeded in hiding this reality completely.

Earlier we said that the social practices necessary for the strengthening of a nationwide culture are fostered by the associated–dependent development. Now we have showed in which way this trend can be opposed by the reassertion of divergences in the cultural sphere. What matters, however, is to what extent the mechanisms of integration can absorb the germs of dissidence and resistance against the dominant culture.

In Latin America, the very frequent use of coercion is a manifestation both of the insurmountable contradictions of dependent development and of the weakness of the mechanisms for conditioning consciousness. Indeed, none of the institutions and practices of the cultural–ideological sphere so far have been able to conceal the tremendous exploitative nature of the dependent socioeconomic structure that operates as an obstacle against the economic growth that the private and public monopolies seek. Hence, the need for reinforcing the mechanisms for building legitimacy and consent.

There is a second aspect of this situation. Because the internal system of domination is also an expression of the international system of domination, the struggle against one often turns into being a struggle against both. When this occurs, nationalism may have a popular, antiestablishment character. Yet, while nationalism may have this popular character, it may also express mainly the effort of the dominating classes and groups to secure the legitimacy and consensus that their politicoeconomic projects require. In the latter case, it is the state and the groups related to it—the bureaucracy, the military, and the state entrepreneurs—who assume the basic role as supporters of the ideology. Here again, as was true for the economic level, the state appears as the fundamental entity for the reproduction of domination and dependence. Because of this dual dimension of nationalist ideology, as an ideology of domination and as an ideology of liberation—from internal as well as external domination—minimizing the importance of the struggle in this field would mean discarding an important element of the possible unification of dominated classes and groups. It would mean, also, ignoring a factor of real significance in the present day struggle over cultural–ideological questions, both at the national and international level.

THE STRUGGLE OVER COMMUNICATION POLICIES

To repeat, the media systems form a focal point in the cultural sphere of the dependent countries and their inadequacy in fostering development is a matter of increasing concern. In recent years, this issue has led to criticism as well as the formulation of proposals suggesting alternatives. So far, however, the situation remains unchanged and the issue continues as a focus of struggle. This section places this problem in the larger context provided by our previous analysis of dependent societies. This will allow us to define some of the contradictions at work in the sphere of Latin American communications.

For this reason, the main characteristics of the Latin American media are worth repeating. The industrialization itself requires an increasing role for local consumers and a consequent need for the creation and cultivation of consumer styles of behavior and, therefore, the necessity of advertising. This has given an enormous stimulus to the development of the media, especially broadcasting, which is the best channel to reach consumers who are not always literate. The institutional arrangements have followed the model provided by the metropolis—private and heavily commercialized broadcasting. Even the few media controlled by the state mostly follow the same commercial pattern. The commercial character of the media also has determined, to a great extent, the uneven geographical distribution of media. The media go where consumers are. This is especially true in the case of broadcasting, which is very much restricted to the urban centers. Given the dynamic role of the transnationals in the present economies, foreign advertisers and advertising agencies play a fundamental role in financing the media. Technological dependence, for its part, is all the more obvious in the electronic media, in which from hardware to software and technical assistance the foreign penetration is as evident as is its metropolitan origin. This appears not only as another manifestation of the global technological–financial pattern of dependence, but also as the necessity for matching as closely as possible, the sphere of production with that of consumption. Additionally, the media-related practices and objectives have been transferred to the dependent countries, and expressed ideologically as "media professionalism."

In recent years, strong objections have been voiced about many aspects of the media situation in Latin America; their uneven distribution—uneven from the point of view of geographical distribution and of the possibility of "consuming" them, the inadequacy of their contents for democratization of culture and as contributions to development, the massive penetration of foreign ideas and values, and so on. These complaints were in the background when the First Intergovernmental Conference on Communication Policies in Latin America and the Caribbean was held in July 1976 in San José, Costa Rica (UNESCO, 1976). This Conference, sponsored by UNESCO, was the most extensive regional effort carried out thus far by an underdeveloped region to foster self-reliance in communication matters. Among the proposals adopted by the meeting was an assertion of the right of states to install complementary communication systems and to tighten rules concerning the operations of the private sector. The creation of National Communication Councils and formulation of communication policies under the guidance of the state were also approved by the Conference. A related action was the reaffirmation of the principles of "cultural sovereignty" and the search for "cultural identity," as opposed to the obvious and ever-growing influence of foreign interests in the field of communications.*

The relative independent behavior of the states, together with their incapacity to accomplish the goals of their own resolutions, constitute an important problem, illustrative of the global situation of the region. To some extent, their relative independence weakened the power of the imperialist centers. Moreover, the chronic underdevelopment, the social unrest that accompanies

---

*Before, during, and after the Conference, both UNESCO and the most outspoken countries were subjected to strong and fairly aggressive attacks, launched by the major international media and the regional organizations of press and broadcasting owners. They were accused of aiming at "the totalitarian control" of the media on the continent. However, one year after the meeting, the situation remains unchanged, and not one of decisions made has been implemented. For a detailed account of the results of the Conference and the struggle surrounding it, see UNESCO (1977), Capriles (1977), and Salinas (1977).

it, and the power of the states—enlarged by the nationalization of some enterprises—give them, in some cases, the possibility of formulating neopopulist policies aimed at furthering development and building legitimacy around their regimes. Thus, the state becomes the site of an encounter of dominant class interests, and of some popular sectors that support the populist contents of some of their policies. In this sense, the need for communication policies arises not only as an imperative for the rationalization of the resources of society around specific development plans that the state advances, but also as a requirement for unification at the cultural–ideological level. To some extent, the popular, nationalist, and anti-imperialist feelings coincide with those of the state and reinforce its stand against communication and cultural invasion. Basically, however, the possibility for some states to adopt such a role and policies is contingent on the support of powerful groups, who are themselves sustained by state activities and are therefore able to advance their own specific political projects. In other cases, in which the dictatorial regimes give the popular forces no opportunity of expression, the state's position is much less consistent, though still concerned with communications. On the one hand, there is the generalized consensus about the role of communications in fostering economic growth. On the other, in some cases, states may have a special interest in having some means for controlling the media—tools other than those of repression.*

At the international level, the issue of communication policies reveals some contradictions between the metropolis and the dependent countries. Dependence in this field is but another aspect of the globally subordinated situation of all Latin American countries. So too the attempts to overcome it are a manifestation of the crisis of the global system, as well as of the interest of these countries in using the crisis to negotiate the conditions of their subordination. Naturally, these attempts may enlist some authentic anti-imperialism in the struggle, but this can not conceal the fact that the projects, as articulated by the respective governments, do not present a global strategy for the complete elimination of imperialist domination.

At the local level, the clash between the interests of the states and the media owners is evident. This can be explained in economic terms. The media form an important branch of the economy, and economic interests obviously play an important role in the confrontation. However, that issue hardly has been mentioned in the current discussion. What appears at the

---

*It is interesting to observe that only those governments that have the possibility of governing by means of consensus (or hope to) have positions on, and some understanding of, the role of communication policies. These are precisely those that have been accused of aiming at totalitarian control of the press. However, those governments that do exert dictatorship do not really show much interest in these matters. All the same, a basic element today, common to most of the dependent countries, is the existence of international crisis. It provides some room for independent maneuver.

ideological level is, instead, the confrontation between two different conceptions of the role of media in society. Thus, the media owners subscribe to, and aggressively advance, many positions that can be best understood in the context of liberal press ideology. These conceptions, until now, have been adequate enough for fulfilling the requirements of peripheral capitalist development on the continent. Indeed, Latin American governments have freely granted all kinds of concessions to media owners over the last few decades. The contradictions we observe now were not then apparent. But, as was noted earlier, there are now many factors compelling the states to take a stronger stand toward rationalizing the available resources in society. The earlier justification for the liberal role of the media no longer fits present requirements well. These new developments, however, should be understood as contradictions between sectors of the dominating groups in society, which, if left at this level, do not seem sufficient for producing real change in the communications situation on the continent.

The alternative position, however, especially in its ideological form, is much more than a mere expression of ruling class interests. In effect, an entire conception of a socially purposive use of the media is being developed and extended by the struggle. This, clearly, is in the interest of the dominated classes and groups of the society. The dominated classes and groups, all the same, have little or no direct participation in the struggle itself. Their interests are taken up and advanced mainly by progressive communication researchers and journalists.* But they, as well, remain out of the sphere of policy- and decision-making, so that the dominated groups can be said to be present in the struggle only at the ideological level, not as real participants.

The fact that the interests of the state cannot be viewed as purely democratic should not, however, diminish the importance of the ideological struggle. Once the necessary demands have been made, the fact remains that the position of the state does represent some democratic interests at work in the cultural–ideological sphere. Furthermore, the attainment of any of the proposals adopted, for example, by the Conference on Communication Policies (at San José), can only help to improve the present situation in the communication field. And, what is more important, these demands contribute to the steadily weakening hegemony of the dominating classes in the cultural–ideological field.

Within this framework then, present demands for fuller identification and affirmation of national and cultural identity, and the dependent countries' concern about their national cultures, offer real possibilities to dismantle the structures of internal and international domination.

---

*A manifestation of this is FELAP (Latin American Federation of Journalists), which was established in 1976 and immediately supported the objectives connected with the creation of communication policies.

REFERENCES

Bagú, S. (1971). Industrialización, sociedad y dependencia en América Latina. *Revista Latinoamericana de Ciencias Sociales* No. 1–2 (June–December), 172–197.

Boyd-Barrett, O. (1977). Media imperialism: Towards an international framework for the analysis of media systems. *In* "Mass Communication and Society" (J. Curran, M. Curevitch, and J. Woolacott, eds.), pp. 116–135. Arnold, London.

Capriles, O. (1977). "Actions and Reactions to the Policies of Communications within the Framework of UNESCO. Analysis of the Costa Rica Conference. (Paper presented at the seminar, International Communications and Third World Participation: A Conceptual and Practical Framework. Amsterdam, 5–8 September 1977.)

Cardoso, F. H. (1972). Notas sobre el estado actual de los estudios sobre dependencia. *Revista Latinoamericana de Ciencias Sociales* No. 4, (December), 3–31.

Cardoso, F. H. (1974). Las contradicciones del desarrollo asociado. *Revista Paraguaya de Sociologia* No. 29 (January–April), 227–252.

Fagen, R. R. (1977). Studying Latin-American politics: Some implications of a dependencia approach. *Latin American Research Review 12* (No. 3), 3–26.

Golding, P. (1977). Media professionalism in the third world: The transfer of an ideology. *In* "Mass Communication and Society" (J. Curran, M. Curevitch, and J. Woolacott, eds.), pp. 291–308. Arnold, London.

Hall, S. (1977). Culture, the media and the "ideological effect." *In* "Mass Communication and Society" (J. Curran, M. Curevitch, and J. Woolacott, eds.), pp. 315–348. Arnold, London.

M'Bow, A.-M. (1977). "Address . . . at the Closing Meeting of the Nineteenth Session of the General Conference, Nairobi, 30 November 1976." UNESCO, Paris. (UNESCO, 19 C/INF, 23, 18 January 1977.)

Pietilä, V. (1977). "On the Scientific Status of Communication Research." Institute of Journalism and Mass Communication, University of Tampere, Tampere, Finland. (Reports, No. 35.)

Quijano, A. (1971). Cultura y dominación. (Notas sobre el problema de la participación cultural). *Revista Latinoamericana de Ciencias Sociales* No. 1–2 (June–Dec.), 39–56.

Salinas, R. (1977). The Associated Press coverage of the Intergovernmental Conference on Communication Policies in Latin America and the Caribbean held in Costa Rica, July 1976. *In* "International News and the New Information Order" (T. Varis, R. Salinas, and R. Jokelin, eds.) Department of Journalism and Mass Communication, Tampere University, Tampere, Finland.

Santos, T. dos. (1976). "Relaciones de Dependencia y Desarollo Político en America Latina: Algunas Reflexiones." (Paper presented at the Seminar on Dependency Studies in Latin American Development, Helsinki, Finland, 8–10 September 1977.)

Santos, T. dos. (1977a). "Teoría del Desarrollo y Dependencia: Algunas Reflexiones Metodológicas e Históricas." (Paper presented at the Seminar on Dependency Studies in Latin American Development, Helsinki, Finland, 8–10 September 1977.)

Santos, T. dos. (1977b). "América Latina en la Coyuntura de la Gran Depresión." (Paper presented at the Seminar on Dependency Studies in Latin American Development, Helsinki, Finland, 8–10 September 1977.)

Schiller, H. I. (1976). "Communication and Cultural Domination." International Arts and Sciences, White Plains, New York.

Sunkel, O. (1971). Capitalismo transnacional y desintegración nacional. *Estudios Internacionales 4*, No. 16, 3–61.

UNESCO. (1976). "Intergovernmental Conference on Communications Policies in Latin America and the Caribbean. Final Report. San José (Costa Rica), 12–21 July 1976." UNESCO, Paris. (COM/MD/38.)

6

Realism in the Arts and Sciences: A Systemic Overview of Capitalism and Socialism

Dallas W. Smythe

Simon Fraser University

Since 1948, **Dallas W. Smythe** has been teaching and writing in the political economy of communications, a subject he pioneered in North American universities. A Canadian by birth and nurture, and with an AB and PhD from the University of California, Berkeley, he was an economist in the U.S. government from 1937 to 1948, the last six years as chief economist for the Federal Communications Commission. In the next fifteen years, Dr. Smythe was Research Professor, Institute of Communications Research, and Professor of Economics, University of Illinois, Urbana. Between 1963 and 1973 he was Chairman of the Division of the Social Sciences at the University of Saskatchewan, Regina, Canada. After a year at the University of California, San Diego, he was chairperson, Department of Communication Studies, Simon Fraser University, where he is now Professor of Communications. Dr. Smythe is the author of many monographs, articles, and reviews.

An earlier version of this chapter was presented at the International Symposium, "New Frontiers of Television," Lake Bled, Yugoslavia, June, 1971. It was published in *Lo Spettacolo*, Vol. 22 (Jan.–Mar. 1972), pp. 1–18.

The advent of socialist societies, embracing some 30% of the world's population in the twentieth century, has raised the question, what have been the essential features of the arts and sciences for the capitalist system? The controversy, which began in the Soviet Union in the first decade after the 1917 Revolution, was an overture to a policy debate that will continue for at least several centuries. This statement rests on the proposition that historically the capitalist system cultivated characteristic features of the arts and sciences. Just as those features were distinct from those of the culture of medieval Europe and of Imperial China, so they may be expected to differ from those of socialist societies. At issue here is the question of what aspects of the art of ancient Greece or of ancient China, of medieval Europe, of modern nationalism, are universal and timeless, and what aspects are specific to the class cultures that produced them? In what respects may socialist art be different?

It is too early to tell in detail yet. But we are a century or so late in understanding the necessary contribution that the institutional system of art and science, developed in the Western world since the Renaissance, has made to the development of the modern capitalist system. This chapter is a modest attempt to identify and analyze those unique features and that contribution. It assumes that the context of the arts and sciences in any social system is the "cultural realism" of that system. Cultural realism means the central values of the system as expressed in its artifacts, practices, and institutions. These central values may be thought of as the rationalization that informs and is implicit in the relations of the components of the system. By "cultural screens" I will be referring to the aspects of a culture or system that serve to protect its cultural realism against extraculture disruption, whether they be the protective features of a particular language, or restrictions on movement of people or things.

The urgency of addressing the problems of cultural realism for artists and scientists arises from two major "fronts" in the world today. The first and historically unprecedented front is the emergence of socialism in, chronologically, the Soviet Union, Eastern Europe, China, North Korea, Cuba, and parts of Indo-China. The second is the accelerated penetration by the cultures of developed capitalist nations of the so-called less developed parts of the world. In the former case, the core of the problem is how to decide which new elements of culture are required immediately to build socialist mankind, and which elements of the culture of capitalism should be rejected, which transformed, and which accepted into the cultural realism of socialism. In the latter case, the core of the problem is to determine the basis for admitting or rejecting alien and often destructive cultural artifacts, services, and values in favor of preserving and transforming traditional styles of life and the accompanying material artifacts. In fact, the two major fronts have overlapping problems. The socialist nations face the problem of screening (the second case), and in some less developed and presently nonsocialist nations there is the problem of making the cultural transition directly to socialism, while also concentrating on the screening problems.

A major barrier to directing appropriate talents of artists and scientists to solving these problems is the fact that there is inadequate understanding of how their systems have served to develop capitalist realism. Before artists and scientists can build socialist realism they should be aware of how capitalist realism trained them to serve it.

WHAT DO WE KNOW ABOUT THE SYSTEMIC ORIGINS OF CAPITALIST REALISM?

Science and art inevitably arise out of human life, social and individual. Both science and art have tactical and strategic levels of existence. At the tactical level, art and science have the ordinary human problem-solving procedure in common: Define the problem (or job), study it, try to do it, and review or evaluate the results. The respective methods at the tactical level differ, but there is a large degree of overlap between them. At the strategic or institutional level the systems of art and science have structural similarities. Both are cumulative and self-renewing. Both are embodied in associations that have their own institutional inertia, being themselves political organisms, and depend for their existence on the social power structure extant, and hence inevitably respond to such logistical support with mixtures of accommodation and resistance. Further, art and science at both the tactical and strategic levels are inescapably political in nature. In both it is necessary to choose the problems or concepts to be dealt with, and the methods to be employed in relation to them. Such choices arise out of, and are conditioned by, the ongoing social structure of power relationships, and hence have political significance by reason of the choices made. Following the completion of the artistic or scientific exercises, such choices have consequences for the social power structure. Apart from the political bias imparted by the choice of problem and method, there is the further political bias arising from the lure of effective opportunity for the scientist and artist to "do his or her thing." The availability of funds to support scientific research, of financial support whether from patrons or the market for artists, and the availability of recognition, honors, and so forth, combine to impart a bias in favor of the sources of such support and recognition.

A. What central values are fundamental to the growth of capitalist realism in art and science over the past seven hundred years? How does art and science relate to the ideology of modern capitalism? There are three central values:

1. *Man and the world are natural systems*. They are to be thought of as perpetual motion machines, susceptible to rational understanding. This is the fundamental view of man and the world held in modern times. The point of view and the practice of both art and science were common in this respect in the fifteenth century. Only in the sixteenth century and afterward was art held to be autonomous from science and learning (Hauser, 1957, Vol. 2, p. 75).

Being natural systems, man and the world might be manipulated if one learned how the system functioned. The Copernican mechanical model of the world, according to Hauser (1957, Vol. 2), manifested itself in the baroque art of the sixteenth century:

> The whole of the art of the baroque is full of this shudder, full of the echo of the infinite spaces and the interrelatedness of all being. The work of art in its totality becomes the symbol of the universe as a uniform organism alive in all its parts. Each of these parts points, like the heavenly bodies, to an infinite, unbroken continuity; each part contains the law governing the whole; in each the same power, the same spirit is at work. (p. 182)

If man and nature are essentially machines, technique is the key to understanding them. Beginning with the Renaissance it is obvious that technique becomes the central issue for art in capitalist realism. All the conventions of art (e.g., perspective) were rationalized. In contrast with the Middle Ages, when art was based on an objective "What," art in the Renaissance and after was based on a subjective "How" (Hauser, 1957, Vol. 2, pp. 16, 64, 70). The reciprocal of the technical preoccupation was the view of the individual as unlimitedly manipulable. Madison Avenue's cynical view of the individual as infinitely plastic when properly brainwashed was already held in the baroque artistic salons of France in the seventeenth century, when it could be said of the individual ". . . stripped of all extraordinary qualities, he attains an average, handy, easily manageable size" (Hauser, 1957, Vol. 2, p. 204).

For science, the mechanical view of man and the world seemed to be true—at least as the fruit of physical science had a spectacular payoff—and as applied to man as a social being it inevitably took the form of "scientism": a mechanical view of man with implicit denial of the reality of man's consciousness, and his apparently disorderly political behavior. Parallel to the trends in art, the science of man, likewise, took a manipulable view of man and looked for technique to control his behavior. Logical positivism has honored predecessors in capitalist realism. Hobbes's theory of knowledge anticipated it in its rejection of metaphysics and its insistence on semantic precision. His psychology anticipated the mechanistic shape of behaviorism, and his political philosophy rationalized a mechanically conceived society in which authoritarianism ensured the successful manipulation of the common man. Spinoza considered man's actions and desires "in exactly the same manner as though I were concerned with lines, planes and solids."

In the eighteenth century, Adam Smith, Joseph Townsend, and the physiocrats developed systems of economic thought in which atomic individualism was the basic assumption about human beings. The mechanics of hedonism and the ideological rationale for consumerism—the basis of Madison Avenue—were refined by the utilitarian system of Bentham and James Mill in the nineteenth century. The positivism of Saint Simon and August Comte envisioned society as a manipulative, mechanical, rationalized technocracy, with intellectuals like themselves running it. Herbert Spencer, William Graham Summer, and Ludwiz Gumplowicz happily incorporated Darwinism into similar scientific systems of methods and theory.

Psychology became positivistic with the associationism of Hume and Hartley long before the behaviorism of Watson, Hull, and Skinner developed the "S–R" school, which regards man essentially as a robot. Behavioral science is the cross-disciplinary unity of those (such as Lasswell) who would reduce the social sciences to the means by which man is treated as a conditioned and manipulated animal.

Communications theory and research—which might be expected to be applicable to art—falls mostly into the behavioristic category of science that takes a Newtonian mechanical view of life. Bernard Berelson (1956), in speaking approvingly of a quarter-century of work in public opinion research, said:

> . . . the field has become technical and quantitative, a-theoretical, segmentalized, and particularized, specialized and institutionalized, "modernized," and "group-ized"—in short, as a characteristic behavioral science, Americanized. Twenty-five years ago and earlier, prominent writers as part of their general concern with the nature and functioning of society, learnedly studied public opinion not "for itself" but in broad historical, theoretical, and philosophical terms and wrote treatises. Today teams of technicians do research projects on specific subjects and report findings. Twenty years ago the study of public opinion was part of scholarship. Today, it is part of science. (pp. 304–305)

Such has been the systemic view of man as part of nature in capitalist realism for the arts and sciences.

2. *Science and art are "pure"* —*that is, value-free and nonpolitical.* They are therefore ecumenical in the sense that they are universal, timeless and benign. This metaphysical concept is unique to the capitalist system.

In the sciences, this notion did not develop until the nineteenth century, when science became formally institutionalized in academies, societies, and universities, and when access to the ranks of scientists became effectively open to young people from social classes below the controlling bourgeois power structure. In the earlier centuries of the Renaissance and Enlightenment, the scientists were more closely knit to the ruling groups and did not deceive themselves as to the political nature of their scientific activities. Francis Bacon put it candidly (quoted in Bernal, 1939):

> The roads to human power and to human knowledge lie close together and are nearly the same; nevertheless, on account of the pernicious and inveterate habit of dwelling on abstractions, it is safer to begin and raise the sciences from those foundations which have relation to practice and let the active part be as the seal which prints and determines the contemplative counterpart. (p. 6)

Scientists prior to the nineteenth century understood that the Platonic idealist notion that science was concerned with pure thought was self-contradictory. As Bernal (1939) says:

> If the contemplation of the universe for its own sake were the function of science as we know it now it would never have existed, for the most elementary reading of the history of science shows that both the drive which led to scientific discoveries and the means by which those discoveries were made were material needs and material instruments. (pp. 5–6)

As far as the political consequences of science are concerned, it is unnecessary to do more than refer to the overseas period of imperial conquest from the fifteenth to twentieth centuries, which was made possible and efficient thanks to the scientific solution of transportation-and-weapons-related problems (including the astronomical contributions of Galileo, Copernicus, and Newton, which were essential to modern navigation), to the development of the textile industry in western Europe in the eighteenth and nineteenth centuries (made possible by the chemical scientists), and to the development of nuclear power within living memory.

Social science, however, was heir to the naive notion of science's apoliticalness developed in the nineteenth century. When he faces the area of political life, the capitalist behavioral scientist has, as Floyd Matson (1964) says, three choices, each of which is allegedly value-free and apolitical:

> First, he may choose to concentrate upon those mechanical and peripheral details of the political process which can be readily manipulated by the quantitative methods of sampling, scaling, testing and content-analyzing—such matters as electoral statistics and mass media research ("who says what to whom through which channel"). Second, the behaviourist may take up his measuring rods and push on into the central areas of politics, ignoring their ambiguity and trivializing their content; in the words of Hans Morgenthau, he 'can try to quantify phenomena which in their aspects relevant to political science are not susceptible to quantification, and by doing so obscure and distort what political science ought to know.' Finally, the behavioural scientist may abandon political realities altogether and retire to the heights of pure Method—with the vague intention of some day returning to the world when the master formulas have been computed and the tests for statistical significance are in. (p. 70)

I say "allegedly value-free and apolitical" because any commitment of resources, whether material or personal, in the context of the real world obviously has a dialectical political consequence—either in some fashion to support or to change the ongoing social system, or to clarify or obfuscate political issues, or both. As Mark Twain asked, "Who are you neutral against?" Behaviorism and logical positivism have provided a rationale for conservative, conformist, and escapist activity. By limiting knowledge to the perceptually verifiable, they have made it socially respectable for intellectuals to find busy-work, to make comfortable careers for themselves by the ready rewards for "counting" more and more about less and less. By treating the individual as an isolated atom, they provide a model for the academic world that coincides ideologically with the model of free-enterprise capitalism.

This is not to say that I am antiscience, that I oppose the use of mathematical and statistical tools, or that I would "throw out the baby with the bath." I welcome mathematical and statistical tools. But I want them to be used to attack questions stated correctly—that is, I want them to be used to pursue questions that are framed in a realistic policy context. Far from being value-free and nonpolitical in their application around the world, the great bulk of what passes for social science today is culture-bound and highly political in its consequences, both in its home country and in other nations.

The alienation of art and artists from the collective concerns of mankind was one of the necessary but most tragic consequences of capitalist realism. In the Renaissance, artists ". . . . lost the connection between artistic forms and extra artistic purposes, a simply and absolutely unproblematical reality taken for granted in the Middle Ages (Hauser, 1957, Vol. 2, p. 84). The subordination to the ruling classes during the Renaissance confronted artists and humanists with the twin dangers of Bohemianism or servility, and they succumbed to both dangers. If the artist does not adopt a servile role openly (Hauser, 1957, Vol. 2),

> He abstains from all political activity, in order not to tie himself down, but by his passivity he only confirms the holders of power. This is the real *"trahison des clercs,"* the betrayal of intellectual values by the intelligentsia, not the politicization of the spirit for which it has been blamed in recent times. The humanist loses touch with reality, he becomes a romantic who calls his estrangement from the world aloofness, his social indifference intellectual freedom, his bohemian way of thinking moral sovereignty. (p. 83)

The result in terms of allegedly nonpolitical art has been the "art for art's sake" rationalization of political escapism. And because technique is the politically safest and most attractive feature of modern capitalism, "art for art's sake" tends to center on technique. It thus provides the basis for the brainwashing by popular culture, especially advertising, which today is so blatant.

3. *Individualism, private property, and market organization are systemic necessities for the arts and sciences.* The notion of the dignity of the individual, when linked with its ideological counterpart, private property, became the foundation of the Renaissance, of modern capitalism, and of Protestantism. Acquisitiveness, competition, and dependence on the market mechanism became the operational mode for capitalist realism. The arts and sciences both embraced these institutional innovations, though with somewhat differing manifestations and consequences.

Possibly the most obvious feature of the capitalist system for the arts was the systematic cultivation of possessive individualism. The commoditization of art objects fitted them into the class structure appropriately along with all other commodities. Like all commodities, the production of art commodities became separated from their "consumption" by institutionalized markets, replete with critics able to appraise (and shill for) the art products, middlemen and brokers, and, in time, a myriad of specialized trade journals. Just as individualism became the ideological hallmark of production in business enterprise in trade and industry (note the centrality of the entrepreneur in business), so in the arts the doctrine of individualism took the quintessential form of genius. The system provided for the division of artists into the geniuses (or stars) and the much larger number consigned to "Grub Street." Capitalism made art a commodity identified with the bourgeois class ("High Art"). And aesthetics became the area of knowledge in which knowledgeable amateurs amongst the bourgeoisie and their philosophers provided the rationale for their behavior in the art markets, be they concert halls, opera houses, or art galleries.

The notion of artist as genius helped to depoliticalize art for the common person by making a myth about the exclusive capacity of alienated geniuses to produce "high art," and the analogous capacity of the "refined" bourgeois consumers to appreciate it. The Greeks never had this myth.

The artist-as-genius was also a useful concept to the capitalist system because it served to justify the "star" system. Based on that multifaceted notion of personality (or character), the star as genius could receive and seem to deserve unusually high income. We find that early in the Renaissance (fifteenth century) star artists (e.g., Michelangelo) received very high stipends or salaries for their work. In interesting analogy to physical capital goods, the mere capacity for reputed work of genius became the basis for income: the creation of new markets (as compared to the Middle Ages) in the *uncompleted* sketches or drawings of printings or sculptures. The precedent set in the fifteenth century was duly followed in music, literature, poetry, architecture, sculpture, and of course by the motion picture, radio, TV, and press.

When art became a commodity, as market dependence required, its main market was the elite upper class, for only they would have the amateur's expertise to discriminate properly in such a market (as well as the ability to pay the price). The result was that the typical art market product would be of the quality of "high" art, that is, the best. The pleasure in art of the upper class would thus be ensured, and the propaganda results of having a system that produced "high" art would be maximized. Never before the Renaissance was the pleasure principle made the basis of a massive system of culture such as modern capitalism. Its incorporation as the basis of modern aesthetics justified the application of the pleasure principle throughout the system (in popular culture, in personal attitudes, in family relations, etc.). For this reason the capitalist system focused on analysis of the arts its interest in developing theories of feeling, sensitivity, and beauty—the net effect of which was to glorify the cult of the personality and of pleasure. Out of this process came typical capitalist market phenomena for art, including the notion of intellectual private property in the commodities produced. Throughout, this side of the rationale for capitalist realism in the arts combined Machiavellian cynical amorality in acquisitiveness and the expression of individual creativity, within limits of what the market would take.

For science, the rationale for capitalist realism relied on individualism and private property much as did the arts. For science, the role of the market was less significant than for the arts. Leaving aside the commercial market for books and journals, the major dependence of scientists has been on employment by industry, governments, and universities. They have thus dealt with the tensions between influences toward servility and intellectual freedom without all the major confusions introduced into art by market phenomena.

B. What was the nature of the process of institution building for capitalist realism in the arts? It was part of the historical process by which modern capitalism and the modern nation state emerged from the medieval/feudal system in Western Europe. Capitalist realism in art matters, like policy on science, lay close to the seat of power. What concerns us in this analysis of its processual character is the fact that city states and later nation states used their power and resources quite openly to develop styles and structures for the arts, which would serve the capitalist system realistically.

Art academies, combining the function of teaching and debate, were created by the state for the development of standards, styles, and skills in the arts, first in Florence and Genoa in the sixteenth century, then in France, England, and the Low Countries a little later. The very *identity* of the fine arts was the subject of a debate lasting over three centuries—a debate ended in principle by the publication of the *Encyclopedia* and Immanuel Kant's *Critique of Judgement* in the late eighteenth century. Looking ahead to the process by which socialist realism will be developed, one could benefit from observing that for capitalist realism (1) the development was directly the result of state intervention in the interest of the dominant class, (2) new class-linked institutions were created to conduct the development, and (3) the process took a long time (Kristeller, 1970, p. 127).

C. What were the consequences of the system set up by capitalist realism? I do not speak in any detail here about the consequences for the arts themselves, but rather for the capitalist system which were as follows:

1. The very long period of time over which capitalist realism developed imparted to those living in it the impression of timelessness and universality. For these individuals, minor controversies within the system (naturalism vs. impressionism, new directions in cinematic art, etc.) might be analogized to the significance of a movement within living memory of a few feet in the extension of a glacier over the northern Great Plains in Canada in the last glacial age. But it must be remembered that the task faced by the builders of capitalist realism was no less grandiose than the time scale of the effort: how to revise the knowledge and ways of thinking of a thousand years since the breakup of the Roman Empire.

2. The fine arts provide cultural legitimation for the capitalist system and for their own lives for the middle class people able to enjoy the fruits of the system.

3. The fine arts are an adornment for capitalism and effective advertising for it in the world community. The consequence would be mitigated to the extent that socialist realism engaged the attention and respect of artists and other intellectuals throughout the world.

4. The arts in general (including not only the fine arts, but other arts lower in the pecking order) provide the spark of novelty incorporated in the plan-

ning, production, and marketing of all consumer goods and services under capitalism by means of design, packaging, and advertising, thus contributing to the planned obsolescence that makes the consumership system function.

WHAT IMPLICATIONS MIGHT BE DRAWN FOR SOCIALIST REALISM FROM THE ANALYSIS OF CAPITALIST REALISM?

If my analysis of capitalist realism is reasonably valid, perhaps the following implications for cultural realism flow from it:

1. The task of building socialist realism will be continued over a long period of time. People who expect quick results from this task will be disappointed. It may continue for centuries before it is even substantially completed. With the general acceleration that appears evident in human affairs in the past thousand years, however, one might expect the functional equivalent of the *Encyclopedia* within one or two centuries, barring a nuclear war.

2. The scope of the task is comprehensive. Nothing short of a total reassessment of human knowledge is required. Just as the medieval view of its own culture had to be revised and rewritten by capitalist realism, so will the socialist realism need to revise capitalist realism's view of itself.

3. The strategy for socialist realism might borrow from capitalist realism the idea of an appropriate institutional form for the conduct of the dialogue over the review of capitalist culture and the development of the necessary new modes of socialist culture.

4. An appropriate institutional form for the conduct of the dialogue over the development of socialist realism would be different from the elite-based academies used in the development of capitalist realism. For socialist realism to develop consonantly with its own ethic, it would probably require an institutional form for this purpose that involved the effective participation of everyone—a nice dialectical problem, to design a specialized institutional form for public decision-making. To date the most successful process for achieving this objective is that which the Chinese have developed since liberation, especially during the Great Proletarian Cultural Revolution. The process rests on the proletarian dictatorship, the mass line, and democratic centralism. It recognizes the interrelationships of all forms of culture, and the fact that the development of unselfish socialist people will involve a long struggle between the two lines: the revisionist (in which bourgeois and feudal tendencies persist), and the socialist. Their repeated emphasis that the process will take a long time and many dead ends is recognition that they are planning a systematic development spanning generations and perhaps centuries before it reaches its major objective, communism.

5. It is clearly impossible to forecast the outcome of such a public decision-making process now, but some guesses as to the nature of socialist realism are possible:

(a) Public welfare, rather than private gratification, will be the yardstick to be employed in making policy and standards for the arts.

(b) The present "fine arts" category will be revised to eliminate the pejorative and class-bound distinctions that flow from it. This does not mean degradation for the present arts classed as "fine arts"; it means that in socialist realism terms, the classification will be different.

(c) The notion of genius in the production of art will be abandoned and with it the star system. Collective creativity will be given greater emphasis than it has had in capitalist realism. For example, one might expect that under socialist realism, architecture would become a prime art form. Involving as it does the needs of people in groups as users, and the skills of many kinds of specialists as creators, architecture has languished sadly under capitalist realism. Its social character has ill-fitted architecture to fit into the system of capitalist realism, and one suspects it is only formally in the charmed group of the fine arts because of the authority of antiquity and the Middle Ages.

(d) Aesthetics will be revised to fit social criteria rather than those of the elite mediated through a market. The use of art will be reunited with its production.

(e) The role of the market in dictating taste will be eliminated and public decision-making will enter the process in some form.

(f) In the policy for producing art, a new blend of the "What" and the "How" will replace the capitalist realism's preoccupation with technique. Rather than the medieval "What" of a spiritual hereafter, perhaps for socialist realism the theoretical principle might be built on a triad: "Now/Then/How," in which the "Then" refers to both past and future. As of the present, one might expect the future "Then" to stand for an unhostile ecologically balanced world in which respect for human beings was evenly accorded. The "How" would be the release of the previously systematically-sabotaged human creativity and human decency perennially available and thus far repressed; the "Now" would be the present joy in building that kind of world. The neat trick will be to winnow out the basis for preserving and stimulating the elements of individual creativity that capitalist realism so ruthlessly exploited in the arts and which, in its reaction against capitalist realism, socialist realism may tend to deny in the interest of protecting the social ethic.

(g) Cultural diversity at all levels of human organization will be prized rather than destroyed by the present practices of capitalist cultural realism with its homogenized sensationalism (e.g., "Peyton Place," "I Love Lucy," "Mission Impossible"). This naturally leads to the consideration of the next section.

THE STRUCTURE AND POLICY OF CULTURAL SCREENS

At the outset cultural screens were defined as the policies and procedures that a social system such as a nation employs or might employ to protect and cultivate elements in the nation consonant with the common welfare of its people. Such screens are inevitable if the nation is to experience domestic growth or even to retain its existing cultural values, and if it is to contribute to the family of nations. Indeed one may say that when a "developing" nation permits a developed nation to impose its cultural imperial policy on the life of the weaker nation, the weaker nation is merely adopting as its own the particular cultural screen of the developed nation.

That this needs to be said is surprising only to those who have uncritically accepted the propaganda notion of a "free flow of information." Like its twin, "free trade," "free flow of information" had been the self-serving policy of the British Empire during the last half of the nineteenth century and of the United States empire since World War I. The history of protectionism for national trade in commodities and for cultural purposes is, of course, long-standing. In their own development, Western capitalist states, through practicing the policies called "mercantilism," erected national screens that protected their developing national and colonial systems from rivals, and the justificatory literature surrounding it laid the pre-Adam Smith basis of economics. Friedrich List, the German-American economist, writing in the first half of the nineteenth century, advocated systematic protectionism for developing nations (List, 1841).

The need for attention to cultural screens rests particularly on the vulnerability of nations with substantial remaining traditional cultures to assault by commercial mass media—particularly TV, radio, motion pictures, popular music, and comic books. As Herbert I. Schiller (1969) has shown, communications are the present equivalent of the nineteenth century gunboats in obtaining imperial control over the peoples and resources of developing nations.

Possibly, a theory for an optimal policy for cultural screens is one of the most difficult to devise, because it involves all kinds of international intercourse—from hardware of all sorts (military and nonmilitary) to software of all sorts, even to language, religion, tourism, migration, and geographic factors, all operating over space and with millenia of history behind them. It is possible for a socialist nation (e.g., China) to enunciate a general policy to govern its international intercourse. A recent statement of a long-standing Chinese policy stated (Chen, 1972):

> We stand for the normal growth of cultural, scientific and educational exchanges and cooperation among the peoples of all countries so as to increase their mutual understanding and friendship. We hold that progressive cultures of all nations, regardless of the length of their history, have their respective characteristics and merits, which should be

the cultural nourishment of other peoples and serve as examples in their cultural development. There can be mutual assimilation and overcoming of one's own shortcomings by learning from the strong points of others. Of course, this assimilation is by no means uncritical eclecticism. An analysis should be made of foreign cultures. Even their progressive elements should be appropriately adapted to the specific domestic conditions according to the needs of the people and conveyed through national forms before they can answer the purpose of serving the people at home. It is inadvisable to the development of national cultures to have blind faith in foreign things and transplant them in toto.

But any such policy is extremely difficult to apply in practice. How should the ecological consequences of importing industrial equipment be assessed before they can be observed in reality? For any country with its historical traditions still extant, what will be the ideological consequences of the introduction of almost any kind of machinery? Technology is never morally or politically neutral. When one speaks of introducing foreign technology and catching up with the developed European nations, how does one balance the contradictory advantages and disadvantages? And the development of cultural realism for a nation or for a socialist system requires an exquisitely delicate analysis of the dialectical process, both within the nation or socialist system and with regard to its external relations.

REFERENCES

Berelson, B. (1956). The study of public opinion. *In* "The State of the Social Sciences" (L. D. White, ed.), pp. 299–318. University of Chicago Press, Chicago, Illinois.

Bernal, J. D. (1939). "The Social Function of Science." Routledge and Sons, London.

Chen, H. (1972). From a speech, as Head of the Delegation of the People's Republic of China, at the 17th Session of the UNESCO General Conference, Oct. 25, 1972.

Hauser, A. (1957). "The Social History of Art." Vintage Books, New York.

Kristeller, P. O. (1970). The modern system of the arts. *In* "Problems in Aesthetics" (M. Weitz, ed.). Macmillan, London.

List, F. (1841). "Das Nationale System der Politischen Oikonomie." J. G. Cotta, Stuttgart, Germany.

Matson, F. W. (1964). "The Broken Image." Anchor Books, Doubleday, Garden City, New York.

Schiller, H. I. (1969). "Mass Communications and American Empire." A. M. Kelley, New York.

Part 2

Direct Satellite Broadcasting: Exemplar of the Challenge to National Sovereignty

Introduction

Kaarle Nordenstreng

Herbert I. Schiller

Whereas the preceding chapters have approached national and international communications from a general sociological perspective, the remainder of this book has been arranged to focus on specific issues closely related to international politics, law, and diplomacy. Ordinarily, it is in the latter context that the question of national sovereignty has been connected with practices and principles of international communication. But again it should be stressed that not enough scientific analysis is available on these problems; at this stage we can observe primarily the symptoms, notably through political debate.

An outstanding example of such political symptoms is provided by the broadcasting of television programs directly to home receivers in a foreign country by means of a telecommunication satellite. Although this technological innovation has not yet become an everyday practice, even as a potential technique it has triggered a heated debate covering not only the problems of conventional foreign broadcasting, but the very principle of the freedom of information across national borders. As was observed by two Finnish scholars (Grönberg and Nordenstreng, 1973) after the adoption in 1972 by UNESCO of a Declaration on direct satellite broadcasting, the crux of the matter

is not the urgent introduction of new communications technology but the principle of free flow of information: are we to set out from a principle of completely unrestricted communications alien to any notion of national or international legislation, or from a concept of freedom imbued with certain rules of the game designed at once to secure the desired mediation of information and control the spread of undesirable material. The former conception holds sway in the West, above all in the United States: the entire social and economic structure of the West is based on the effort to impose as little as possible official restriction on individuals, groups or countries. In the socialist communities and the developing countries, on the other hand, the approach is the converse: controls imposed on the individual are not regarded as restrictions—censorship in communications, for example—but as a guarantee that freedom will not become the monopoly of the rich and will not be exploited for undesirable ends for the society as a whole. (p. 6)

Furthermore, in the United Nations arena the question of direct satellite broadcasting has come to signal and symbolize the shift in relation of overall forces which has been taking place so prominently on a global scale during the past decade. To the United States, this is an issue demonstrating the decline of its hegemony in the world political and ideological arena—defensiveness has replaced initiative after a quarter of century of aggressive and successful "free flow" policies, in trade as well as in communications.

Ithiel de Sola Pool's chapter presents a history of the emergence of this issue on the international agenda over the past ten years, with some samples of the political arguments accompanying it (including Pool's own positions). Edward W. Ploman, for his part, approaches the issue from the perspective of telecommunication law, thus introducing the next part of this volume, which will focus on the legal aspects of international (mass) communication.

As will be made clear in these two presentations, the issue of national sovereignty has, in this context been crystallized into the concept of *prior consent*: the issue of whether or not the consent of the receiving country (through its government) should be understood as an internationally legitimate precondition for transmissions over direct broadcasting satellites. Benno Signitzer (1976) has recently summarized the positions of those thirty-one governments that have been actively involved in the drafting of an international convention within the U.N. Outer Space Committee (after the general debate reported in Pool's chapter). Noting that by 1975 "the question does not lend itself to compromise and successful bargaining", he classifies twenty-five countries "for prior consent" (from USSR to Brazil and Sweden) and six countries "against prior consent" (p. 80, Table 5) (from USA to Japan and Italy). His summary of the two main views is as follows:

> The advocates of the principle of prior consent argue that the principle of sovereignty gives to a state the right freely to select and develop its own political, social, economic, and cultural systems. The concept of exchange implies that the flow should be bilateral and not in one direction only. States have uneven opportunities in using the direct broadcasting technology and this factor strengthened the need to ensure that activities in this area are conducted on the basis of prior consent.
>
> The opponents of the prior consent principle base their objections to a system of prior consent on the argument that it would legitimize international censorship and stifle technological progress. Some of them also pointed out that the application of this principle would involve domestic constitutional problems. (p. 79)

Despite their antagonistic approaches, the opposing views have been converging considerably at the diplomatic level. In fact, a consensus agreement on the wording of the prior consent principle was almost reached in June 1977 at a meeting of the Outer Space Committee. The compromise wording of the principle, now called "Consultation and Agreements Between States," under debate in this Vienna meeting, reads in its essential paragraphs as follows (United Nations, 1977b):

1. A direct television broadcasting service by means of artificial earth satellites specifically directed at a foreign State, which shall be established only when it is not inconsistent with the provisions of the relevant instruments of the International Telecommunication Union, shall be based on appropriate agreements and/or arrangements between the broadcasting and receiving States or the broadcasting entities duly authorized by the respective States, in order to facilitate the freer and wider dissemination of information of all kinds and to encourage co-operation in the field of information and the exchange of information with other countries.

2. For that purpose a State which proposes to establish or authorize the establishment of a direct television broadcasting service by means of artificial earth satellites specifically directed at a foreign State shall without delay notify that State of such intention and shall enter into consultations with that State if the latter so requests.

Yet even this diluted formulation was too strong for the extremist free flow position, most forcefully advocated by the USA. But at this time there were also some new tactical reasons to oppose the introduction of international legislation on this crucial point. As reported in Ploman's chapter, the principle of prior consent in direct satellite broadcasting had been passed by the international community at a "technical" level—that is, by the World Administrative Radio Conference (WARC) of the International Telecommunication Union (ITU, a U.N. agency)—in early 1977. Therefore, in the Spring 1977 meeting of the relevant working group of the Outer Space Committee, the USA and United Kingdom supported the view (United Nations, 1977a)

that as a result of the Agreement and Plan concluded at this Conference as well as other ITU instruments there would be little intentional State-to-State direct television broadcasting and minimal spill-over problems and thus no need to draw up a principle on consent and participation. (Annex II, p. 1)

Not surprisingly, the same WARC decision was used by the defenders of prior consent to support their tactical aims, since it was viewed

that the ITU had done useful work in resolving technical problems, which would undoubtedly promote orderly utilization of satellites for direct television broadcasting, but that the results of the ITU Conference reflect broad international recognition that direct television broadcasting should be based solely on prior agreements between the interested States, and thus confirmed the necessity for a principle on consultation and agreements. Other delegations considered that there was no contradiction between the principle of free flow of information and the principle of respect for State sovereignty and non-interference in internal affairs of States. (Annex II, pp. 1–2)

It should be noted that the WARC decision itself has not been challenged in these most recent debates in the U.N. Thus, the most persistent defenders of the principle of the unqualified free flow of information across national borders have been confronted with a *fait accompli*. For example, in the USA, a group of policy makers observed in March 1977 that (see Dizard, 1977):

it seems clear that the recent actions of the ITU may well deny the use of satellites for international broadcasting, unless prior consent is given by the intended recipient and by all other countries that may be technically affected. Regretfully, this closes what could have been a wonderful window on the world for broadcasting, even before that window was ever opened. Even more seriously, this now leaves the existing shortwave bands as the only arena in which international broadcasting can take place. As a nation, now more than ever before, the United States must muster its technical, political, and policy resources at the highest levels to make certain that this last outlet for the free flow of broadcasts between nations is not blocked at WARC '79, where these wavelengths next come up for international reappraisal. (p. 7–8)

It should also be observed that most of this debate has been taking place at the politico-ideological level (although within the framework of drafting provisions of international law), and that little concern has been expressed about a "censorship mentality" from the legal experts. (See, for example, McWhinney, 1974). In fact, much of the international control which has been under discussion in this connection "can dwell in the tent of the first amendment," as pointed out by Price (1976):

> What is the appropriate American stance with respect to international ordering of direct broadcast satellite content? Clearly, it accords with domestic policy and with the spirit of the first amendment for the United States to urge passionately an international regime which fosters the flow of information. But it is also clear that, as interpreted and administered, the first amendment is consonant with an international scheme that classifies the spectrum available for direct broadcast by satellite so that only particular categories of programming could be used. The international community might determine, for example, that initially satellite frequencies could be used only for educational programming. The first amendment would not be hostile to provisions permitting each state to adopt regulations that legitimately protect its own domestic television system from foreign competition. Nor would the first amendment be inconsistent with international regulation of commercial messages. Certain content regulations would mirror specific or implicit constraints on American broadcast media. These include restraints on obscenity and pornography. The extent to which an international constraint on content would be consistent with first amendment norms would depend on the stage, mechanism and degree of sanction for the breach of an internationally set regulation. (p. 901)

REFERENCES

Dizard, W. (1977). "WARC '77: Implications for the Future." (Occasional Paper (CSIS NOTES) reporting a Conference at the Center for Strategic & International Studies, Georgetown University, March 1977.)

Grönberg, T., and Nordenstreng, K. (1973). Approaching international control of satellite communication. *Instant Research on Peace and Violence* (published by Tampere Peace Research Institute, Finland) *3* (No. 1), 3–8.

McWhinney, E. (1974). The antinomy of policy and function in the institutionalization of international communications broadcasting. *Columbia Journal of Transnational Law 13*, 3–27.

Price, M. E. (1976). The first amendment and television broadcasting by satellite. *UCLA Law Review 23*, 879–903.

Signitzer, B. (1976). "Regulation of Direct Broadcasting from Satellites: The UN Involvement." Praeger, New York.

United Nations. General Assembly. Committee on the Peaceful Uses of Outer Space. (1977a).

''Report of the Legal Sub-Committee on the Work of Its Sixteenth Session (14 March–8 April 1977).'' United Nations, New York. (Document A/AC. 105/196.)

United Nations. General Assembly. Committee on the Peaceful Uses of Outer Space. (1977b). ''Texts Formulated by the Working Party on 27 June 1977 (Twentieth Session, Vienna, Austria).'' United Nations, New York.

7

Direct Broadcast Satellites and the Integrity of National Cultures

Ithiel de Sola Pool

Massachusetts Institute of Technology

Ithiel de Sola Pool is Professor of Political Science and Director of the Center for International Studies, Massachusetts Institute of Technology. He received undergraduate, MA, and PhD degrees from the University of Chicago and was Chairman of the Division of Social Sciences at Hobart College from 1942 to 1949. Following four years as Associate Director of the RADIR Project at the Hoover Institute, Stanford University, Dr. Pool became Professor of Political Science at the Massachusetts Institute of Technology in 1953. He is the author of many articles and books, including *Satellite Generals; American Business and Public Policy; Candidates Issues and Strategies; Contemporary Political Science; The Prestige Press*; and *Talking Back*.

The major part of this chapter was presented at the "Airlie House Conference on International Communications: The Free Exchange of Information and Ideas and the Integrity of National Cultures," February 7–9, 1974, and published in *Control of the Direct Broadcast Satellite: Values in Conflict*, by the Aspen Institute Program on Communications and Society in 1974. To that paper (in somewhat abbreviated form) is added, in the section headed, "Conclusions," an extract from the author's "The Influence of International Communication on Development," a paper presented at the International Conference on Communication Policy and Planning for Development, April 5–10, 1976, East–West Communication Institute, East–West Center, Honolulu, Hawaii.

I. THE ISSUES

Should we take seriously the allegation that direct satellite TV broadcasting represents an active threat to the integrity of national cultures? It is hard to do so when we are aware that there is no imminent prospect of direct satellite TV broadcasts to countries that do not wish to receive them. It is also hard to do so when there are many much more significant threats to the integrity of national cultures, e.g., syndicated reruns of TV tapes. Nonetheless many people are alarmed by the prospect of direct satellite broadcasting and so it becomes a political if not a physical reality. Ghosts, when they are believed in, become real, at least as influences on human behavior.

To propose to protect the integrity of national cultures by restricting direct satellite broadcasts is comparable to proposing to solve the energy crisis by turning off traffic lights. In both cases the proposed solution addresses a trivial corner of a real problem. And in both cases the proposed solution does much harm in the process.

Yet, justifiably or not, the issue of satellites and cultural integrity has become an intense one, widely discussed, and exacerbating international discord. Minor as the reality behind the issue may be, diplomats must take the discussion seriously, for beliefs, whether well grounded or not, are the main realities in international relations; these beliefs are sincere and firmly held.

We have asserted two preliminary conclusions that we must document before we turn to our main topic: (1) Direct satellite TV broadcasting is not a threat. (2) There are, however, other legitimate sources of concern to those who would protect their cultures. We can, in the light of these facts, then discuss the normative issues of American policy toward the defense of cultural integrity.

A. Why Direct Satellite TV Broadcasting Is not the Threat

A sharp distinction should be made between direct TV broadcasting *with the cooperation of the receiving country* and direct broadcasting to a country that does not wish it. The former may be practicable in the visible future; the latter probably not. Any economically rational use of direct broadcasting requires that the receiving country allocate one of the few suitable wavebands to that purpose and distribute sets and antennas designed appropriately to receive such signals. The sender must choose to launch a rather large satellite capable of radiating much more power than is required for broadcasting to sophisticated earth stations.

For American domestic communications, for example, a national satellite TV distribution system could be created in one of two ways: One way would place something like 10,000, $3000 antennas around the country so that in every city and town broadcasters and cablecasters could pick up the national programs and redistribute them over the air or by cable. The other system would require only a $100 to $300 antenna and amplifier at every set, i.e., 50 to 100 million of them. Clearly the latter (or direct broadcast) system is ridiculously expensive, costing perhaps 100 times as much as the former.

There is, therefore, no reason to expect direct TV broadcasting in the continental U.S. Direct TV broadcasting does make sense, however, for other countries and situations. For remote sparsely populated areas like Alaska or

Siberia it may be economical to provide each of the relatively few scattered sets with antennas and other special equipment at a cost of several hundred or even a couple of thousand dollars apiece so as to eliminate the need for ground stations and retransmitters. In India, too, if the policy of one set per village can be enforced, then in the parts of the country where villages are widely scattered, direct broadcasting to enhanced community receivers makes sense. Such situations favorable to direct broadcasting are few, however. More satellite broadcasting will, it seems, be distribution to redistribution ground stations, and not just for the near term but for the indefinite future.

If that is true, then a country that wished to disseminate direct TV to others would have an extremely small audience, limited to those few individuals who own enhanced receivers of their own. To reach those few persons, the sender would need to launch a large expensive satellite capable of beaming high radiation, and if to more than one country, then with different standards of signals to different countries and in each case on a band (a) not otherwise in use in that area but (b) suitable for satellite transmission and (c) receivable by sets currently in use. These requirements would rarely be met on any significant scale. To invest in direct satellite TV broadcasting to countries that do not cooperate would therefore require great expenditure for trivial results. The situation is entirely different from short wave broadcasting, which takes little bandwidth, relatively cheap transmitters, and cheap receivers, which many people own anyhow for other purposes than to listen to the propagandist. Direct satellite TV broadcasting to countries that do not wish it is not an attractive option for either governments or commercial broadcasters. It is not something rational men should be worrying about.

B. It Is True that the Integrity of Established Cultures Is Challenged by International Communications

Media, such as radio, TV, and motion pictures, have an important effect in this regard, even if direct broadcast satellites do not.

The value judgment of when and whether cultural integrity *should* be protected against outside challenge is a complex one to which we shall return below. The answer, as with all important value issues, is not simple; different people would answer in different ways for different times and places. Should South Africa be protected from Tanzanian and other broadcasts against apartheid? Should Soviet Jews be able to listen to Kol Israel? Should scientific knowledge be made available to schools and universities in developing countries? Should Asians and Africans be subjected to Christian missionary efforts? Should UNESCO promote cultural exchanges and contact among intellectuals? Should advertisers be able to promote their products in foreign countries? Should X-rated movies be exported to countries holding to traditional sex mores? Should modern art be available in galleries in all countries? Few people would answer all those questions in the same way. But whatever one's value position, the fact in the modern world is that there is international cultural intrusion.

Foreign influence, it can be argued, is but a special case of the disruptive impact of intellectual and cultural media in general. All through history intellectuals have been called subversive and their products attacked as assaults upon the established culture. Socrates was seen as "an evil-doer, and a curious person, who searches into things under the earth and in heaven, and he makes the worse appear the better cause, and he teaches the aforesaid doctrines to others" (Apology 19). They attacked him as "a doer of evil, who corrupts the youth; and who does not believe in the gods of the state, but has other new divinities of his own" (Apology 24). And in answer he described himself as "a sort of gadfly, given to the state by God" (Apology 30). For this he was made to drink the hemlock.

Poetry, philosophy, literature, and the media are perennially labeled immoral, corrupters of youth, disrespectful of tradition. Those conservative charges have an element of truth. Intellectuals are gadflies. They claim a right to seek the truth and evaluate the good by some light of their own other than the writ of established authorities.

They are also, and always have been, conduits for foreign ideas. From the days of Greek slave tutors in Rome, through the wandering bards and scholars of the Middle Ages, to the refugee or brain drain scholars of today, communicators and men of intellect have been rootless cosmopolitans and introducers of alien ideas.

We are not arguing that nothing has changed. Phenomena that have been with us from time immemorial are magnified by the emergence of telecommunications and the mass media. That is a quantitative change so great as to also become a qualitative change.

The mass media and electronic communications obliterate many of the impediments that served in the past to slow down changes in ideas and mores. Barriers of time and space that once protected the status quo are easily penetrated or circumvented by modern media. These eliminate the cushion of time between when an event happens and when it is known worldwide. People have become ringside observers to dramatic news events, be they wars, moon-landings, hijackings, or riots; the public follow them hour by hour while they are taking place and while the outcome is still unknown. So, too, the barrier of distance is gone. We watch the oil crisis unfold on a worldwide stage, on which what happens in Singapore is as visible as what happens in Rotterdam or Caracas. Distance is not per se a significant factor, though there still is a vast difference in how we view something foreign or domestic.

Electronic communication and mass media also serve to widen the units in which political, economic, or social action takes place. A peasant who sells his crop in the local marketplace may ultimately be linked to the world market by a series of trading intermediaries, but that is quite different from the situation of the farmer who receives world price quotations on the morning newscast. He is operating directly in a regional or national, if not world, market. The village headman who established his legitimacy by his ties to local lineages and shrines operates in a very different way from the national politician who has to formulate issues as abstract platform planks that will be meaningful in national journals or national broadcasts.

For our present topic—the integrity of national cultures—the important point about the way in which electronic and mass media operate is the fact that as new sources of information or belief they create counterweights to the established authorities. Simultaneous radio coverage of a war, or moonwalk, or whatever absorbs and fascinates the mass audience is given directly, cutting out the traditional local purveyors of information and interpretation. It is not the imam or the chief of state who tells the people what happened and what it means. The people were there, along with the VISNEWS camera crew. So, too, the broadening of the arena of action transfers authority from the village bigwig returned from a visit to the district town, to nouveau powerful national leaders, and eventually beyond them to world figures.

In the 1950s Daniel Lerner, in a classic study of communication and development (Lerner, 1958), described the difference between three types of men and three orientations found in the Middle East. Illiterate villagers he described as traditional men. The world they could understand stopped at the limits of their first-hand experience. They could not conceive of what national politics was all about. Recent migrants from country to city he described as transitional men. They relied heavily on radio even in that pretransistor era, but they selected domestic broadcasts with familiar themes. They knew about national politics but only as it affected them. A good ruler was one who got them jobs or repaired their town. Educated urbanites Lerner described as modern men. For them foreign radio was a major medium. They understood the issues of the cold war and ideological movements and followed world affairs with interest. World media enabled them to raise the scope of their empathy well beyond their personal experiences.

Note that Lerner described all this in the 1950s without reference to direct broadcast satellites. The process was taking place without them. Every year the world communication system becomes more integrated.

A worldwide focus on common news is not, however, the kind of homogenization that exercises those who are alarmed about the violation of national cultures. The examples they typically cite are movies, TV, literature, songs, hairstyles, clothing styles, patterns of respect, etiquette, and religious observances.

Popular songs are a common issue between the upholders of tradition and its violators. Stylized traditional music tends to give way to more expressive modes such as jazz, rock, or movie themes conveyed on radio, records, or movies. In India, to preserve traditional musical forms, the All India Radio has put quotas on movie themes—the most popular program item—a genre that crosses familiar indigenous ragas and the soupy personal sentimentality of Western popular songs. India is not unique. In Japan and most non-Western countries, tin pan alley has proved to have a wide appeal, often in the same hybridized way.

Dance manifests similar tendencies toward cultural assimilation. The dance is generally a stylized, controlled indulgence in tabooed behavior, whether in boy–girl relations or in expression of other passions. So new style dances, imported from or influenced by the West, express feelings and break taboos in ways that are bound to shock many who see them.

So, too, with dress; it symbolizes one's identity. To refuse to wear one's proper tribal or caste dress, or to assume the dress of a foreign elite, or to bare one's legs by a miniskirt is to express a challenging assertion of changing identity.

Eating habits, manner of address, and place of residence all often become highly charged items in the conflict of generations. In most countries the principal battle between traditional culture and modernity is fought over the independence of the young from parental authority. The battle most often reaches its zenith on the issue of arranged marriages and the locus of habitat of the new household, but skirmishes are fought over every sign of self-assertion by the young: impoliteness, staying out late, wearing their hair oddly, drinking Coca-Cola, reading bad books, and so on. The central issue is the power of the old versus the autonomy of the young. Nor is the fight just an ego trip by either. In a traditional economy the social security of the whole family and the maintenance of its elder members may depend upon the carrying out of family obligations. At the same time, the chance for the young to get ahead depends upon their being able to free themselves from such family obligations. These issues cut deeply and are keenly felt. In Japan, under the occupation, virtually every novel, soap opera, or movie dealt with the clash between filial piety and the liberation of youth. That, not defeat in a war, was the central issue of people's concern. So, too, in many countries, the clash of generations is the most universal of conflicts.

Religion is another area in which the conflict between tradition and innovation gets expressed. Piety is the most common rationale offered in defending established relations of respect. At the same time reformations, scepticism, or militant atheism are common attacks upon the traditional culture.

New tastes created in the process of social change provide an economic opportunity to merchants. Commerce seizes upon the chance to stimulate tastes for what it can sell, and to produce for sale what people will buy. Thus, advertising and the monetized economy become major agents of the process of change, and serve to undermine family-centered traditional culture. The marketer is a willing panderer to the tastes of transitional men moving naively into a cash economy. Those merchants who sell what is popular among those new strata are in turn attacked by traditional authorities as unscrupulous corrupters who will do anything for a price.

These are examples of the areas in which the fight over cultural integrity most often takes place. The media in which novel, expressive, emotionally-laden matter that undermines the traditional culture most often appears are art, drama, literature, reform religions, and radical ideologies. All of these appear in movies, soap operas, songs, TV, advertisements, pamphlets, and evangelical tracts. It is such media, when they come from abroad containing controversial messages, that most upset the defenders of the integrity of national culture.

C. The Quality of Mass Media Material

The usual charge by the defenders of the integrity of national cultures is not only that the new mass media material is new, but also that it is "junk." That it will violate existing cultural taboos, whether on violence, sex, politeness, or sacrilege, is clear. But the additional charge is made that the shocking mass media material is also without artistic merit—it has no redeeming qualities of excellence.

Intellectuals in the West join in that chorus of complaint, and there is certainly something to the charge. The kitsch dispensed in recently modernized countries is often a horror when held up against the art of the traditional culture. But a fair judgment must be much more complex than that.

In most societies, excellent traditional art was made only in very small quantities. The environment in which the populace lived usually had few things of beauty in it. It is far from obvious that the average movie or manufactured object is aesthetically worse than the average traditional ritual or craft object if one makes a genuine comparison of the averages, not of a few great objects against mass produced ones. But even if that is conceded, there are numerous examples of clear artistic deterioration as a by-product of modernization. Colorful, beautiful clothes give way to mass-produced hand-me-downs. Well-done carvings give way to poor ones and then to plastic dolls.

A case to be made for the mass media is that they bring to the masses cultural products previously available only to the few. Stage plays are rare events; movies can be shown in every small town or village. Orchestras and performances by great musicians are luxuries of the capital; records and radios bring them to every home. But the obvious critical comment, which can hardly be rebutted, is that standard mass media bring but little of such quality in relation to the amount of "junk." And so it is that the defenders of cultural integrity may argue that they are defending the excellent against the mediocre.

D. The One-Sidedness of the Flow

Finally, and most important of all, the defenders of cultural integrity against free-flowing information point to the highly one-sided balance of exports and imports of mass communication. The developed countries, and particularly the U.S.A., export messages; the LDCs import them.

The best documentation of this fact is the University of Tampere's "International Inventory of Television Programme Structure and the Flow of TV Programmes between Nations" (Nordenstreng and Varis, 1974). In that study it was estimated that total foreign sales of U.S. program material was 100,000 to 200,000 hours, about one-third to Latin America, another one-third to the Far East and East Asia, and the rest mainly to Western Europe (p. 201). The dollar amounts look quite different because the rates charged Europe are much higher than the rates charged LDCs.

TV export sales by the U.S. fell from about $100 million in 1970 to $85 million in 1971. In general, the dominant role of American material is declining, as one would expect. The U.S. was the first into the massive TV production business; gradually other countries built up their capabilities. The Tampere report, the implicit viewpoint of which is somewhat to the left and somewhat negative toward the U.S.A., tries to reject this interpretation of the data, but the data speak clearly for themselves. They show a gradual decline in U.S. dominance, as one should expect. But they also show that there is a continuing imbalance in the direction of flows with large and more advanced countries being producers and small and less developed countries the importers.

There is enormous variation in the proportion of programs that are imported. A few countries show shockingly low figures: e.g., U.S.A., 1–2%; U.S.S.R., 5%; Japan (NHK), 2½%. On the other hand, about half of Latin American programs are of foreign origin; a similar figure holds in the Middle East, and in Asia, excluding Japan and China; in Western Europe the figure is 30%, and in Eastern Europe, 24% (pp. 33–34).

Similar, though less lopsided, data could be compiled on motion pictures, print syndication, and publishing. To cite some 1967 UNESCO figures: of 39,483 titles translated in that year, 15,279 were from English, 5368 from French, 3892 from German, and 3822 from Russian. All other languages ran far behind.

The facts as of the early 1970s are clear. Underdevelopment means underdevelopment in media production as in everything else. Development means leadership in the media field as in everything else.

More important than the facts, perhaps, which could be taken as simply an injunction to get on with the work of development, are the emotional reactions to these facts. One could fill a volume with heated quotations from unhappy nationalists, guilt-ridden Westerners, worried reactionaries, and angry radicals attacking the free flow of information as a Western plot to impose its culture on helpless people. Paranoid fantasies on the subject, particularly by some American writers, leave the realm of serious discussion. Extraordinary statements can be found by very sober men who in their own eyes are liberal and believe in freedom. As a sample, let us pick the quotations that appeared in a single issue (No. 3, 1973) of *Intermedia*, the bulletin of the International Broadcast Institute. President Kekkonen of Finland in a major speech said:

> These facts make one question the principles of freedom of communication in just the same way as one has cause to reevaluate the concept of freedom of speech. Could it be that the prophets who preach unhindered communication are not concerned with equality between nations, but are on the side of the stronger and wealthier? My observations would indicate that the United Nations, and its educational, scientific, and cultural organisation UNESCO have in the last few years reduced their declarations on behalf of an abstract freedom of speech. Instead, they have moved in the direction of planing down the lack of balance in international communications.

He went on to say that the developing countries are at the mercy of information exports by the industrialized Western countries: "I have read a calculation that two-thirds of the communication disseminated throughout the World originate in one way or another in the United States." He argued for "trying to achieve a 'balance of payments' in communication between the States to the largest degree possible."

The international symposium of scholars at which President Kekkonen talked adopted a resolution asserting:

> Each nation has the right and duty to determine its own cultural destiny within this more balanced flow of information within and among nations. It is the responsibility of the world community and the obligation of media institutions to ensure that this right is respected.

In the same issue the Prime Minister of Guyana is quoted: "A nation whose mass media are dominated from the outside is not a nation." Mr. Christopher Nascimento, his Minister of State, added:

> How many times greater must be the responsibilities of the media in developing countries than in affluent established societies. How much greater the danger and the threat to development and independence when huge mass media multinational empires own and control the media in, and strive through the use of their vast financial resources and immense international influence to exercise and maintain monopolies, in developing nations.
>
> It is the presence and the power of foreign owned multi-national mass media empires in developing nations that poses one of the greatest threats to independent development. . . .
>
> The alternative for many a poor developing nation is going to have to be, at least for a time, government ownership of the mass media.

Finally a report on an Asian regional meeting of IBI asserted:

> On the other hand, statements from industrialized or post-industrialized societies, with their specific life-styles, penetrate into the developing countries—creating additional difficulties for societies which already have problematic expectations and aspirations. . . .

A practical problem was the increasing commercialisation of distribution channels; even non-commercial broadcasting organisations have set up enterprises or departments for the selling and buying of programmes. This is to treat television as just another export; "exchange" can only work between organisations in roughly the same situation as each other. . . .

In so far as governments can claim to speak for the people, broadcasting in a developing country cannot fall outside government policy.

Indeed, it seems fair to say that, irrelevant as it may be, the real steam behind the attacks on direct satellite broadcasting is concern about cultural intrusion. The Soviet Union may have other political motives for introducing and pushing its draft convention, but it does not have the votes. The votes come from countries that have been frightened by the specter of cultural imperialism. There can be no doubt of their sincerity. They are scared. One may question the technical wisdom of their concerns about direct satellite TV. One may dissent from their value judgments. We, in our tradition, give a higher value to individual freedom than do most political activists around the world. But one cannot question their sincerity or the depth of their feelings. An examination of the history of the direct broadcast satellite issue in the U.S. and UNESCO makes clear the sources of the concern of most nations. Their reflexes are automatic once the issue is presented as one of cultural intrusion. We turn now to examination of that history.

II. THE DEBATE IN THE UN

Suggestions that satellites might be used to broadcast directly to home receivers in foreign countries first appeared along with Sputnik. Then the suggestions of the new things to come were expressed with some enthusiasm by writers in the U.S.S.R. (Parry, 1960): "With the help of a large Sputnik . . . Moscow television programs could easily be relayed not alone to any point in the Soviet Union, but also far beyond its borders" (pp. 208–9).

Attitudes more like those now heard in the UN began to be expressed from various sources in the 1960s. In 1962 and 1963 the dangers of foreign propaganda broadcasts were discussed in the UN. Brazil raised the issue in November 1963.

Active debate on the issue in the reported proceedings of the UN began two years later at the time of the discussion of the Outer Space Treaty.

The lineup of the subsequent debate forecast many debates to come. On July 26, Mr. Khallaf of the UAR submitted a new article for the Treaty to provide worldwide regulation of direct satellite broadcasting and that the nations should "undertake to refrain from using communication satellites for direct broadcasting until such regulations are set by the competent international organizations." He was backed by Mr. Morozov of the U.S.S.R., who raised the argument that would be heard repeatedly as an appeal to the Third World: "We would wish that other States, especially the developing countries . . . would not be placed in a position where they would have to adopt, without criticism or comment, whatever is handed to them" (quoted in Jones, 1967). Also supporting the Soviet and UAR position were Carvalho Silos of Brazil, Krishna Rao of India, and the Mexican representative.

The Outer Space Treaty was unanimously adopted on December 19, 1966 without the Egyptian clause or any reference to direct broadcasting. However, at the same time the UAR, Chile, and Mexico proposed a resolution asking that the Committee on the Peaceful Uses of Outer Space study space communication.

So by 1967 the issue had been defined and was being discussed, especially by Third World countries.

Any narrative of a single idea, such as the story of the fear of cultural intrusion by direct TV broadcasts is inevitably misleading. It selects out of a noisy background a few relevant occurrences, creating the impression of high attention and deep concern. The truth is quite different. Among the various comments on satellites that do occur, only a portion are expressions of fear of violation of sovereignty. The positive statements hailing the great new prospects are more frequent and often exaggerated in portraying the educational and cultural improvements that satellites can bring especially to the developing nations.

On November 15, 1972, the 17th General Conference of UNESCO adopted a "Declaration of Guiding Principles on the Use of Space Broadcasting for the Free Flow of Information, the Spread of Education and Greater Cultural Exchange." The philosophy of the Declaration is strongly restrictive, stressing sovereignty, the requirement that news broadcasts be accurate, the right of each country to decide the contents of educational programs broadcast to it, the need for broadcasters to respect cultural distinctiveness and varied laws, and the requirement for prior consent especially regarding advertising.* The Declaration was adopted by a vote of 55 to 7 with 22 absentions. The U.S. was in the minority.

The French position was particularly influential. Pompidou had picked up

---

*II. "1. Satellite broadcasting shall respect the sovereignty and equality of all states.

"2. Satellite broadcasts shall be essentially apolitical."

VI. "2. Every country has the right to decide on the content of the educational programmes broadcast by satellite to its people."

VII. "2. Cultural programmes . . . should respect the distinctive character . . . and the right of all countries' peoples to preserve their cultures."

IX. "1. It is necessary that States . . . reach or promote prior agreements concerning direct satellite broadcasting to the population of countries other than the country of origin . . .

"2. With respect to commercial advertising, its transmission shall be subject to specific agreement between the originating and receiving countries."

the satellite broadcast issue in a speech at UNESCO's 25th Anniversary, giving the issue some salience to the Quai d'Orsay. They became the most active lobbyists.

The French motivation was, in part, their concern to maintain a communications relationship with the Francophone states, especially in Africa, and not to permit the American lead in space activities to give the U.S. a wedge into that relationship. This stimulated what became a strong, solid, and emotional African support for adoption of the Declaration. Egyptian influence was also of some importance.

India also pressed for action. The Indian delegate, the Minister of Broadcasting, took a strong stand not well attuned to the fact that the Indo–Pakistan border is one of the few places where spillover problems may be genuinely important.

The role of the Soviet Union was somewhat enigmatic. Earlier at the Meeting of Experts the Soviet participant had tried to introduce into the draft language about the right to destroy offending satellites, to eliminate references to the Declaration of Human Rights, and to strengthen the language on prior consultation. However, in the U.N. September 1972 discussion of the UNESCO Declaration, they took a neutral stance. In the Paris preplenary discussions at UNESCO they supported the Declaration, only to abstain on the final plenary session vote.

Clearly the adoption by UNESCO of the Declaration, despite the Soviets' ambivalence, and American opposition, was clearly one expression of the intensity of views on the subject by African, Asian, and Latin American countries and of neutralist and antisuperpower sentiments there and in Europe too.

The consolidation of attitudes on the satellite broadcast issue in UNESCO can be better understood if we look at some background events.

The regional broadcasting unions have been an important factor in the picture. The unions are not united. The European union, which is by far the most important, has played a liberal role, providing, along with the U.S. representatives, some of the few opponents to restrictions and regulations. They have their own vested interest against regulation. That attitude is well represented in their negative comments on the draft Declaration.

However, the European Broadcasting Union, while the strongest, is not typical of the rest of the world. In Africa, the Arab states, and Asia there are fewer outside expert voices and so the broadcast unions may get even more exposure. And they are less liberal. For example, the Rome meeting of the unions adopted the following weak statement:

Article 11:

The reception within one state of a programme distributed by direct broadcast satellite from another may be regulated by an agreement between the appropriate bodies in the states concerned.

At the Arab States Broadcasting Union meeting, held shortly after, a resolution endorsing the UNESCO draft was adopted that also approved the Rome Conference declaration with the following qualification:

> The Arab States Broadcasting Union found that Article 11 would be unsatisfactory unless the word "may" is changed to "must."

In the meeting of the ABSU, the main enthusiasm about satellite communications was as an instrument for unifying "the Arab nation." A basic document for the First Arab Conference on Space Communication (Amman, September 23–26, 1972) says that, "In the '80s satellites will be capable of transmitting television programs directly to developed TV sets in homes or in remote areas." It asks:

> Are we threatened by the use of this technology for propaganda purposes and are we—the developing countries—threatened to become the scapegoat of such space propaganda machinery which is controlled by the major states?

In Africa, this nationalistic reaction was apparently triggered by the French through the Francophone countries. In the Arab world the most active agent was the ASBU. What about Latin America? In Latin America the key incident that shaped attitudes of the small community involved in satellite communications was the CAVISAT project.

The CAVISAT project was developed by Father Neill P. Hurley of Notre Dame University and of the Instituto de Communicaciones Sociales in Santiago, Chile. It was a proposal to use a dedicated communication satellite for educational broadcasts to the Andean nations. The project was to be joint between a group of U.S. and South American universities. The text of the proposal itself was not unreasonable, and the proposal won sympathetic backing from COMSAT, but what happened reflected not so much the text as the alleged personal behavior of the North Americans involved.

In September 1969 the plan fell apart. There was to be a meeting of the Ministers of Education of the countries of the Andean region in Bogota, January 26–31, 1970. Before the meeting Colombia prepared a paper for confidential circulation at that meeting attacking the CAVISAT plan, and circulated it at a prior Quito meeting of the Directors of Educational Planning. Annex 3 stated that the sponsors of CAVISAT, when asked about the balance of control of programming as between the North American and South American participants, said, "We have the technique to carry out the plan and we are going to carry it out, come what may, if needed at our own expense, whether the Latin Americans like it or not." By January 29, 1970, these allegations had broken into the press. *El Tiempo* (Bogota) of that date carried a story with the lead: "The plan of the ministers of education of the Andean Group for international education in Latin America by satellite may possibly be blocked by the veto of the United States on sharing its space technology." It cited the Colombian document to the effect that the U.S. would not sell its technology, that the six ministers had secret information about the financial plan for private commercial North American control of the satellite. CAVISAT, it said, was to be the agent for American corporations, universities, and commercial interests. It concluded that the Ministers had been warned of "a serious danger to our cultural identity and to sovereignty in educational materials."

Once the controversy exploded, and the charges were generally accepted, it is surprising that the Andean project continued at all. But it did, though without North American participation. The Andean educational satellite study has continued to this date, under UNDP and UNESCO encouragement, not North American. The mood of the ministers meeting is illustrated by a proposed resolution:

> Unilateral management of transmissions by satellite, either by state or by non-governmental entities, can easily be misused to disturb the habits, the standards of values and cultures of the receiving countries, with the sure danger of arriving at a condition where the ideas and judgments are against human dignity and rights. . . .
>
> Foreign enterprises, and organizations not employed by the Latin American governments develop activities intended to transmit television programs for education by satellite, destined for our countries, and which would be transmitted from the territory which is not Latin American, and without the participation or supervision of the competent authorities from our governments.
>
> Concerning the use of satellites for broadcasting educational and cultural programs directed to other nations, it is also necessary to apply the principle enumerated by President Nixon, according to which the relations between our countries have to be of equal partnership and not of the ruler and subordinate.
>
> The principle of non-intervention has to be respected, such as education being within the internal jurisdiction of each state so the freedom of the use of outer space in the field of satellite broadcasting is qualified freedom, i.e. limited by the rights of other countries.
>
> Broadcasting by satellites from one country to another even if emitted by non-governmental-entities, requires the previous, and explicit consent of the governments, obtained through bilateral or multilateral agreements.

The impact of the CAVISAT crisis on UNESCO had already been felt before the Colombian document leaked to the press. At a December 1969 meeting in Paris, numerous delegations—particularly Colombia, Brazil, Bolivia, Argentina, India, and France—were (to quote an observer) "up in arms concerning the 'protection' of countries and populations against unwanted programmes from direct broadcast satellites. Behind this is evidently the reaction against the CAVISAT proposal."

According to the same observer it was at that point that Latin Americans in UNESCO became solidly aligned behind the idea of "protection of audiences."

Since that time any proposal for international direct satellite broadcasting produces a strong Latin American vote for requiring prior consent. One clause of Article VI in the UNESCO Declaration is a reference to the CAVISAT issue.

> Each country has the right to decide on the content of the educational programmes broadcast by satellite to its people and, in cases where such programmes are produced in cooperation with other countries, to take part in their planning and production, on a free and equal footing.

In the UN itself the major discussions of satellite television began in 1969 with the formation of the Working Group on Direct Broadcast Satellites. Under the Committee on Peaceful Uses of Outer Space, the CPUOS family of committees have certain traditions unique in the UN system. They proceed by consensus, never taking a vote.

The United States and other states supporting the minority position in favor of free flow of information are thus protected from being overruled in either the CPUOS or in its Working Group, which has the same membership.

The balance of views in the Working Group is shown by Table 1. It shows clearly where the developing countries lie.

TABLE 1
Approximate Positions of 28 States in Working Group

Countries with a liberal position on international broadcasting	Countries for regional or organizational controls	Developing countries concerned about cultural imperialism	Developing countries with particularly legalistic approach	Strongly legalistic
Strongly: USA	Sweden	Morocco	Brazil	France
Less strongly: UK	Canada	Lebanon	Argentina	USSR
Australia[a]	Italy	India	Mexico	Albania
Belgium	Austria	Chad	UAR	Bulgaria
Japan		Sierra Leone		Czechoslovakia
		Iran		Hungary
				Mongolia
				Poland
				Romania

[a]Has shifted since Airlie House presentation of this paper.

The First Session of the Working Group was in February 1969. Working papers submitted to the session included a joint one by Canada and Sweden. In the first 50 pages it based its argument entirely on technical considerations such as broadcast interference. By page 54, however, it gingerly introduced the political considerations.

In that respect the document is typical of Canadian statements throughout the past few years. Fundamental to Canada's concern about unregulated direct broadcasting has been worry about the colossus of the South undermining the regulated Canadian system of broadcasting by advertently or inadvertently pouring U.S. broadcasts over the border. However, though concerned, the

Canadians, with a strong democratic tradition, have not been prepared to advocate a rigid censorship system. Also the strong tradition of civilized relationships between these English-speaking neighbors, plus a degree of dependence of Canada on the U.S. space program for its own space activities, have inhibited Canada from the kind of sharp rhetoric that some other countries have adopted. So the Canadian statements have systematically and as a matter of formal policy avoided using arguments about "propaganda" in their reasoning as to the importance of regulation and prior consent. Canadian spokesmen have tried to base their reasoning always on more specific and pragmatic considerations less offensive to the Anglo-Saxon tradition of media freedom.

Thus, the Canadian–Swedish paper moved from physical considerations of spectrum management to the issue of maintaining regulatory systems intact, which is Canada's own deeply felt concern. "It is a recognized principle that each country has the sovereign right to regulate its own telecommunication and broadcast services" (p. 54). From there it moved to the problem of stability in the developing countries. It quotes the U.N. Space Conference:

> No single development can perhaps alter the face of the developing countries as television via satellite can. (p. 9)
> The probable impact of direct broadcast systems in a national context could be particularly profound in developing areas with undeveloped communication systems where broadcasting from satellites could dramatically change the entire outlook of millions of people who at present have little contact outside their immediate surroundings. (p. 55)
> It is also probable that the introduction of television programming, based on practices, from one social context to another and greatly different one, might result in a cross-cultural shock whose consequences are not yet fully predictable. (p. 74)

And from there the argument moved to problems of libel and advertising in countries with diverse laws, and to considerations of social and cultural autonomy.

In its second session, held in Geneva, in the summer of 1969, the Working Group received working papers from Canada and Sweden, France, Argentina, Australia, Czechoslovakia, Mexico, the U.K., and UNESCO. All of them raised the specter of abuses by direct television broadcasts and proposed steps toward regulation.

In the French paper the rationale that is offered for taking such action is the inequality of capability between the space powers that will have the satellites, and other nations that will not.

> This inequality will further increase the possibility of interference in the internal affairs of foreign States: television broadcasting can be a peculiarly effective medium for political propaganda or for advertising. Similarly, false reports can easily be propagated on an immense scale so as to confuse public opinion throughout entire regions. Lastly, national cultures, civilizations, and social systems will be presented with a further means of imposing themselves on others, through the suggestive power of television.

Most themes that have come up in the direct broadcast controversy, and that are likely to come up again may be illustrated from the debate in the First Committee in October 1972.

> DIAZ-CASANUEVA (Chile): . . . None of us believed that men would be walking on the moon as soon as they did . . . a great Power . . . employing subterfuge and fallacy and appealing to a false conception of what is known as "freedom of information" seeks to consolidate its domination over the passive masses of the dependent or underdeveloped nations. (1867, pp. 47–51)

> DIAZ-CASANUEVA (Chile): . . . In the dependent countries our libraries are poorly stocked with books, our publishing houses are financially poor, and we have millions upon millions of illiterates and semi-illiterates. Into this world there enters television, which fascinates and hypnotizes both the literate and the illiterate masses; television, to a large extent commercialized, rarely subject to the influence of universities or the State; television which feeds on the worst, on the most vulgar, on the dregs of mass culture— violence, pornography, triviality, and mediocrity. Commercialized television, with the rivalry among the channels and the necessity of satisfying the tastes of a public that has had no opportunity to raise its cultural standards, constitutes a source of concern for our educators, sociologists and statisticians and for all of us who participate in a cultural policy that seeks to ennoble rather than to degrade our peoples. (1867, pp. 52, 53–55)

Such worries about the effects of TV broadcasts keep appearing in the debates.

The steam behind the feelings about sovereignty were, beyond doubt, the genuine imbalance of power between the countries with space satellite capabilities and those without.

> ALI (Pakistan): Unlike wireless broadcasting, satellite telecasting will be, and is likely to remain, the preserve of only a handful of technologically advanced and economically affluent countries. It may, therefore, accentuate the cultural and intellectual gulf which is already beginning to widen between the developed and the less developed parts of our globe. We would suggest, therefore, that ways should be examined of enabling the developing countries to share in the use of television satellites. (1868, p. 72)

> BAROODY (Saudi Arabia): There is an Arabic proverb, which I will quote: "If you cannot get what you want, settle for what you can get." We, the small countries, are trying to settle for what we can get for our own protection, neither less nor more, and we appeal to the highly technologized Powers, if I may use that term, to see our point of view and not to subject us in the future to any controversy that might be translated into a sort of television war between them. (1868, p. 92)

> GRIGOROV (Bulgaria): Television broadcasting could become a means of political and ideological blackmail, violation of sovereignty of States, and interference in their internal affairs. (1862, p. 42)

> KOROTKEVICH (Byelorussian SSR): It is well known that developing countries which in the past were under colonial subjugation by the imperialist Powers—Powers which consciously delayed their economic development—do not as yet have their own technical means for engaging in direct television broadcasting from space or to prevent broadcasts containing material directed against their national interest. It is easy to see that in such conditions and in the absence of the legal regulation of space television programmes developing countries could fall prey to intensive foreign propaganda from technically stronger States which, having obtained a monopoly of such an important mass-information

medium, could use it for their own selfish ends—for influencing the public opinion of other States, for protecting their commercial interests, for pressuring economically weaker countries and for imposing their will upon them. (1863, pp. 23, 24–25).

The fear that was overly and frequently expressed was of "cultural imperialism" as a force tending to destroy indigenous traditions and values.

DE GUIRINGAUD (France): . . . every state should have the means to preserve the cultural originality of the community for which it is responsible; likewise, national economic activities related to culture, such as the film and record industry, for example, are entitled to protection. (1862, p. 7)

DIAZ-CASANUEVA (Chile): Television is a double-edged sword. It can be a violation of the masses, as it might also lead them to liberation and dignity. Thus, we are justified in wondering what it might mean to the people of Latin America to be bombarded by imperialist monopolies through direct television broadcasting, by means of artificial earth satellites, freed of all and any control and without any thought given to international law. (1867, p. 56)

POHL (El Salvador): Under the impact of these new technical resources the underdeveloped nations might suffer a crisis of historical and cultural identity . . . they would be left with nothing of their own and would be following blindly in the footsteps of the developed countries, even though the latter countries believed in political ideologies other than those of the countries receiving the broadcasts. . . . The underdeveloped countries could even increase their dependency if these technical means remain entirely in the hands of national States. . . . Their survival as historic and cultural identities would be at stake. Surely the appropriate time to do all this is now. If we wait, it may be too late. (1862, p. 7)

AZZOUT (Algeria): We could hardly overemphasize the need to protect the sovereignty of our youthful States from all foreign interference. In fact, television broadcasting by satellites raises the question of the preservation of the cultural heritage of peoples and the originality of our national cultures. . . . We must make sure here and now that the circulation of ideas and information will not be in a single direction and that it will not become an instrument of cultural imperialism, particularly when we know that this new technique will for a long time to come still be held solely in the hands of a few, more advanced nations. (1867, p. 56)

TAYLOR-KAMARA (Sierra Leone): Coming from a developing nation which has recently emerged from colonial status, my delegation fully appreciates the concerns of the Soviet Union. We know what devastating effect cultural imperialism can have on the customs and traditions of the peoples of Asia and Africa. (1869, p. 46)

From such fears stemmed the demand to be protected from broadcasts entering from abroad unless they receive government consent. There was also a more positive form of reaction besides the impulse to ban unwanted broadcasts. Some delegations raised the demand that all countries should have access to satellites for broadcasting.

The Soviet draft contained an allusion to the desire of nonspace powers to access. Article I says:

All States shall have an equal right to carry out direct television broadcasting by means of artificial earth satellites. . . . All States shall have an equal right to enjoy the benefits arising from direct television broadcasting by means of artificial earth satellites, without discrimination of any kind.

It is not clear what this right implies. It is far less specific than the clause about prior consent. Some countries have tried to make the right of access more specific. A number of countries raised that issue and a few have suggested that the U.N. or regional international organizations operate in such a fashion as to provide broadcasting facilities to less developed countries.

> DIAZ-CASANUEVA (Chile): The system of satellite communications should, for example, provide technical assistance, increase worldwide objective information, and serve to encourage international cooperation. These new instruments of progress must be placed at the service of all mankind, without regard to selfish interests. (1867, p. 61)

> POHL (El Salvador): It might be thought that broadcasting stations . . . might provide access to the underdeveloped countries, in the same way as launching pads for rockets are already being used for scientific satellites from countries other than those in which the launching pads are located. (1868, pp. 13–15)

While protection of sovereignty was the main impetus to support of the Soviet draft declaration, there was also one other significant impetus, namely, dislike of the kind of material emanating from radio and TV.

This was illustrated in attacks on political propaganda, pornography, violence, and commercialism.

A. Propaganda

> AKE (Ivory Coast): . . . the system can just as easily be used for the . . . purposes . . . of subversion and propaganda, which might harm both the sovereignty of States and internal public order.
>
> LARQUI (Tunisia): . . . We . . . share the fears expressed by some here that free and systematic dissemination of information might be used for other purposes.
>
> In saying that, I am thinking of what has been said here about subversive, immoral broadcasts . . . (1869, p. 6)

> GRIGOROV (Bulgaria): . . . There is . . . justification for the desire of other countries not to condone the appearance of such stuff on its territory and their demand to regulate this kind of activity, which is another kind of aggression, without bombs or bullets but with consequences at least as serious for the security and welfare of the peoples. . . . It is possible that television programmes aimed at other States could openly praise war and aggression, justify colonialism, present in a favourable light abhorrent systems such as *apartheid*, advocate racial hatred and so on. Confirmation of the reality of that danger can be found in the rather recent past. We remember the radio broadcasts of Hitler's Germany, or another and even more blatant example in this field: the propaganda carried on by television in favour of *apartheid* and racialism in South Africa. (1862, pp. 43–45)

B. Pornography and Violence

> MALIK (USSR): Further, the representative of Belgium spoke of the free flow of information. But a question arises, whose flow? A clean flow, a creative flow in the interests of

peace and mankind? Or is it to be polluted by sex, violence, propaganda, misinformation, slander, interference in international affairs, against the culture and civilization of every single nation? This is what we are talking about. (1870, p. 46)

POHL (El Salvador): . . . It is not by any means a question of trying to set up yardsticks—which would not work anyway—for the evolution of ideas, including the evolution of ideas about good standards; rather it is a question of taking care that there are no extreme cases; of avoiding bad taste, vulgarity, the commercial exploitation of sex and other excesses which characterize not liberty but licence. (1868, p. 16)

DIAZ-CASANUEVA (Chile): The people of Latin America are rebelling against imperialism that tries to stifle their cultural personality through the export of certain inferior elements for mass information. An effort is being made to impose upon us standards of life, of style, of ideology, that are contrary to our very way of being: the glorification of the cowboy, the slaughter of the Indian and the buffalo, sex, violence, representing the Chinese as dark and evil beings, the customs of the consumer society, the models of a bourgeois society, conformity, hatred towards those who rebel against capitalist societies, cheap sentimentalism, and mediocrity. (1867, p. 57)

BAROODY (Saudi Arabia): . . . in the free enterprise countries the motivation of newspaper men or broadcasting companies, privately owned, is gain and profit; so they pander to the cheap—or perhaps "sensual" is the word rather than "cheap." They pander to the sensual and give people the things they like to read about, peddling sex, sex motion pictures, or sex programmes.

I was told recently that there was a programme—and I am not going to mention where because it is obvious, and you can reach your own conclusion—which, owing to the fact that in a certain country the teenagers have become promiscuous, in school and out of school, and are contracting venereal diseases, was about using the condom. (1864, p. 37)

Commercialism was often described in the debates not only as a source of such depraved programming, but also as a vehicle by which corporate invasion of weak countries could take place.

III. WHO ARE THE CULTURAL NATIONALISTS?

Nationalism is the doctrine of the right wing that most easily coopts the left. Historically, liberals and radicals have been internationalists. Marx's statement, "the workers have no fatherland," epitomizes that view. Liberal intellectuals have fought for freedom of movement, freedom from censorship, world cultural exchange, and condemned ethnocentrism and prejudice. Right-wing nationalists, on the other hand, have glorified the unique heritage of their own ethnic group. The right has fought foreign influences that would undermine their historical religion, language, customs, or politics.

But the description of the left as open and internationalist and the right as closed and nationalist is misleadingly simple. Nationalism has always been the most appealing element in right-wing doctrine. As such it has both seduced and been adopted by the left. Some leftists got caught up in it; others craftily tried to capture the political appeal of ethnicity by combining nationalist with their own populist or socialist doctrines. Before 1917, for example, the Russian and East European social-democratic movement was more riven by the nationalities question than by any other issue. Nationalist-socialist movements of various varieties, such as the Bundists, presented a challenge to antinationalists, such as the Bolsheviks. Out of this conflict emerged various views on the national question of which Lenin's are among the more interesting. Lenin berated the "reactionary" character of ethnic identity and at the same time recognized the intensity of its political grip. He understood that the Bolsheviks could not confront nationalism, but had to use it. The defense of national aspirations and of cultural autonomy for nondominant peoples became an expedient policy for the Bolsheviks. While privately contemptuous of ethnic identity, they saw it as expedient to stimulate the struggle of subordinated nationalities, in the expectation that the national sentiments of the latter would pit them against the dominant imperial powers. Thus the Bolsheviks gained in two ways. They purported to sympathize with popularly held sentiments, and they exacerbated the struggle of discontented peoples against state power. How little the Bolsheviks really cared about national sentiments became apparent when they acquired state power for themselves and they suppressed minority nationalist sentiments that challenged them.

If the basically right-wing sentiment of protection of ethnic identity has become so wound up in left-wing politics in the past, it is not surprising that the same thing is happening again today. The people who write indignantly about cultural imperialism and warn that direct satellite broadcasting can violate the cultural identity of peoples are sometimes traditionalist conservatives, but more often they are of the left: American new-leftists, Chilean radicals, Scandinavian social democrats, and so forth. It would be wrong to assume that they are engaged in a cynical Leninist manipulation of a popular slogan to actually implement its opposite. The people who are raising this issue today are generally sincere. It would be more appropriate to remark with astonishment on how widely people of the sincere left have been absorbed in classical doctrines of conservatism as a consequence of nationalism. Increasingly they find themselves pushed by the logic of their position to see themselves as more opposed to liberalism than to traditional culture, to assert that the free flow of information is a goal that must be reconsidered, to conclude that preservation of traditional ways is more important than a rapid rise of GNP, and to justify the use of state power to control the communications that reach the people. Their ideological predecessors fought to liberate the print media from state control, but increasingly people who call themselves men of the left find themselves advocating state monopoly control of the newer media. Thus a strange alliance puts conservative military regimes or theocratic oligarchies at one with nominal progressives in defense of censorship. Needless to say, the things they want censored, what they want controlled, and by whom are quite different. But they unite in advocating restrictions on broadcasting and other instrumentalities of the free flow of information.

Attacks on direct satellite broadcasting and other assertions in defense of national culture may thus come from any political direction and may serve as a means to any one of a large number of inconsistent political aims. The slogan of protection of national culture may be used to protect a local communications industry from stronger foreign competitors, e.g., protecting CBC in Canada against the U.S. networks. It may serve to restrict advertising so as to protect local businessmen from competition by large foreign firms. It may serve as a grounds for oppressing a minority culture that can be portrayed as antinational, especially if the minority has colleagues across the border, e.g., Asians in East Africa or Kurds in the Middle East. It can be used to combat the spread of a youth counterculture. It can be used to repress radical or participatory political ideas.

For example, it turns out that some of the support for the Soviet draft convention on direct broadcast satellites came from Third World countries whose conservative governments were more concerned about checking communists than about American propaganda. They saw the Soviet-sponsored convention as ironically becoming a protection against Soviet broadcasting.

Indeed, it will often be the case that what is described as protection of the national culture is rather the protection of the existing government. The Indo–Pakistan frontier, for example, is one of the few places in the world where cross-the-border TV penetration may become significant. India may acquire a TV satellite that could be received by a Pakistani who makes an investment of only several hundred dollars. Furthermore, the terrestrial transmitters that India is also establishing are located in a pattern that makes it hard not to conclude that there is an Indian intention to reach a Pakistani audience. Yet the Indian purpose is certainly not cultural evangelism. It seems more plausible that they want to use their cross-border capability to carry on psychological warfare in the event of renewed hostilities.

There is no doubt that foreign propaganda broadcasting can be, and is, effective under some conditions. One condition for effectiveness is that the recipient population does not trust its own domestic broadcasts. For example, during the recent Middle East War, Jordan started transmitting sober and relatively accurate telecasts in good Hebrew to Israel. Observers believe that that effort was quite effective because Israeli censorship was sufficiently severe to provide Israelis with an incentive to hear the other side.

The most successful example of the effectiveness of international broadcasting is, no doubt, the broadcasting of VOA, Radio Free Europe, and Radio Liberty to the Soviet Union and Eastern Europe (Pool, 1973). The information about world attitudes and trends provided by these broadcasts have made the evolution and persistence of the dissident movement for liberalization in those countries feasible. Youth learn about jazz, East Europeans learn what has been tried and permitted by the Soviets in other Warsaw Pact countries, intellectuals learn about current world debates, and Soviet citizens learn the real facts of the news through those broadcasts. As a result about one-sixth of the Soviet population (according to other research by this author) listens to foreign stations on an average day.

In contrast, only about 2% of the American public listen to shortwave broadcasts at all (Smith, 1969–1970). Rightly or wrongly, they are convinced that they are getting the essential facts via their own media. Indeed, very few families even have shortwave sets, in contrast to the half of Soviet families who do.

Thus the main determinant of attention to foreign media is the responsiveness of domestic media to the desires and interests of the public. The market place for ideas is not one in which imports flow easily. Other things being equal, consumers pick local products. The latter have many advantages which imports must overcome. (1) They are protected by barriers of language; people would rather see a film made in their own idiom than one with subtitles or even one that is dubbed. (2) They are protected by barriers of social support. Much of the enjoyment of media is in discussing them with one's friends. Reading this year's best seller is a social experience. Seeing the big game that is the subject of one's friends' conversation is a different experience than seeing one that none of them saw. Top TV shows or movies provide grist for conversation the next day, and that is much of their drawing power. (3) Local products are protected by barriers of culture. Domestic products portray characters eating the foods the people eat, wearing the clothes they wear, celebrating the events they celebrate, and gossiping about the celebrities they follow. Allusion is a large part of what art is about. Foreign works of art have jokes that are harder to get, stereotypes that do not ring a bell, situations that do not come from daily life.

In general, culture does not need protection. Culture is what people are already attached to. If the culture is satisfactory, if it is not itself already in the process of decomposition, if local media are doing their job of providing products that fit the culture, the audience will not look abroad.

TV in Viet Nam in the latter half of the 1960s provided an almost experimental example. The government of Viet Nam and its American allies decided that television could make a significant contribution to the conduct of the war. It could help the American troops feel at home. It could improve the quality of life and relieve the rural boredom for the population on the government side. A two-channel TV system was set up. One channel provided standard U.S. programming in English for the American troops. The other channel, programmed and produced by the Vietnamese in Vietnamese, featured traditional opera and similar indigenous material. In the villages, people watched the Vietnamese channel. At those hours when the Vietnamese channel went off the air but the American channel stayed on, instead of continuing to watch, *faut de mieux*, the audience would melt away from the village set. Not so in the cities. There were foreigners by the thousands; English signs and English-speaking customers, cars, bars, canned food, newspapers, and salaried jobs had already smashed the bowl of Vietnamese culture. Millions of Vietnamese turned by preference to the better produced, slicker American programs. Football games were popular. Batman won the rating race and became a popular folk hero. In short, the urban population already had acquired a new culture and new needs. Traditionalists deplored the fact and preferred not to admit it, but the Vietnamese TV channel—aimed deliberately at the rural population—was not serving the modernized Vietnamese as well as the U.S. channel.

The situation of urban Vietnamese is just the kind that those who argue for defense of culture against cultural imperialism have in mind. They point out that the indigenous society with its limited capabilities cannot compete with the attractive but artistically degraded products imported from abroad. But, as we can see in that example, the situation is far more complex than that. Whatever comparison of artistic quality there was, was on the side of the American product. Those members of the audience who were at all capable of understanding the U.S. channel turned to it rather than to the crude, quite coarse, and stereotyped local programming because, poor as it was, the American programs were better. Also, any opposition to that foreign programming material could hardly be described as defense of national culture; it would rather be a nostalgic effort to reassert a culture long since gone from the cities. The American programs attracted more or less educated, middle class, and modern sector employees because those programs related better to their culture than did the other channel. What one can legitimately criticize is that the alternatives were not rich enough. Had there been a third channel of indigenous but modernized urban-oriented material, it would certainly have drawn much audience away from the foreign product.

Thus, there is a case to be made, not so much for defense of national cultures by protectionist barriers to foreign materials, but rather for positive fostering of production capabilities to meet otherwise unmet needs. The building of studios, the establishment of training programs, the subsidization of arts makes sense, but protectionism in this, as in any market, is generally a way of stifling development and reducing the prospects of meeting the consumers' needs. People who like and want the kind of material that is available from abroad are barred from getting it. That does not create an incentive to producing equivalent, but more locally relevant, material at home. On the contrary, it eliminates the need to compete for the local audience. An open market for foreign imports, on the other hand, is likely to demonstrate the existence of an unmet demand, to offer models and a learning experience for domestic producers, and thus to result in a growth of local cultural expressions.

Let us illustrate by an American example. Hollywood has never been able to provide the American intellectual market (the 20 or 30 million of them) with sophisticated, thoughtful film or TV programs. It has not provided films for the art theatres or programs like *The Forsythe Saga* and *Masterpiece Theatre* for TV. The economics of the American film industry, with its featherbedding union contracts, residuals, weak noncommercial stations, etc., makes that sort of production very difficult indeed to finance. Foreign films for the art theatres and BBC for public television have filled the gap. Their success has demonstrated that there is an unmet need; it has been demonstrated in the first place that there is a market for such quality programs. Their success has also led to American imitation. The domestic product has a long way to go, but an increasing number of art films, and the appearance of programs like Papp's *Much Ado About Nothing* on regular TV, are signs of a trend.

The example of quality drama on public broadcasting is instructive in many ways. It is instructive, for one thing, because it shows that the barriers to indigenous production are not ones that beset just the developing countries. Indeed, contrary to the usual belief, large developing countries or groups of them are quite capable of producing the film and videotape they need. Filmmaking is a labor intensive, not a capital intensive, activity. It is expensive in the USA only because artificial monopoly structures, such as enormous rewards to talent, have been built into the industry. Noncommercial filmmakers, such as Richard Leacock, have demonstrated that high quality film can be produced cheaply. Indeed, American commercial filmmakers are increasingly coproducing films abroad, often in developing countries, so as to avoid monopoly charges. And India has proved that a poor country can build a major movie industry; Egypt has proved that a poor country can make a major broadcast effort; China has proved that a poor country can build a low cost system to communicate to the millions.

It is, of course, impossible for a small country (and most LDCs are small) to produce enough programs to fill the airwaves with a dozen or more hours a day of new original TV material 365 days a year, year after year. But that is just as true for Norway or Belgium as it is for Zanzibar or Honduras. The fact that it takes a market area of hundreds of millions of persons to support the enormous appetite of a TV system for new programs is indeed a severe limitation on TV's ability to reflect a single national culture. It can do that only within the less than 10 giant nations with populations of 100 million or more. Elsewhere, TV production will have to be a cooperative regional or other group activity with procedures for exchange between countries. Indeed, TV will be better if all countries engage in free exchange of the best products from wherever they are made—East or West, rich or poor. There is nothing in the economics of development or of video production that predestines which countries will succeed in the competition to produce widely desired and successful artistic material.

It may properly be asked why the U.S.A. has succeeded so preeminently up till now. There are probably three reasons. First, and least significant, is the fact that it was first into the business. Hollywood movies captured the market first and only later did other countries cut back the U.S. share. American TV covered its market first, and only later did Japan and some Western European countries achieve over 90% coverage. Second, the very large domestic market, with four networks serving 200 million people, provided the base for producing vast quantities of program material, from among which some is suitable for foreign syndication. Third, and most important, the American system, being predominantly commercial, is geared to producing what the public wants.

What the American public wants is not so very different from what other publics want. Cultural differences are important, and because that is our subject we have focused on them. But human universals are important too. Americans today are able to appreciate Aristophanes, the Ramayana, the I Ching, and the Bible. So too, the rock music that appeals to our youth appeals to youth in many countries. "Batman," "Star Trek," "I Love Lucy," or "Donald Duck" strike chords that give them their ratings here and strike the same chords with people in other countries. The American video and movie production system gives unusual priority to finding those popular chords. All producing countries compromise in various ways between the criterion of the market and criteria of what civil servants or other salaried intellectuals believe should be produced. The philosophical issue between their selection criteria is a profound one and every country compromises in some way. Even in China, producers worry about keeping the interest of their audience, though telling the people what they should be told certain has priority. Even in the U.S.A. some production is funded by foundations and by public broadcasting, thus allowing selected professionals to do their thing; but this plays a smaller part in the balance than elsewhere. It should be no surprise that in the country in which producers try hardest to produce what the public wants, they succeed. The Americanization of world culture so often commented on and often deplored might be better described as the discovery of what world cultural tastes actually are, and the adoption of those into the American media. If American pop culture is successful around the world—and it is—it is by a circular process. American commerce seeks to reflect world cultural tastes; the product in turn feeds back into the system and reinforces that which was already found popular.

To say that the export of mass media is giving the world public what it wants, though true, is not to deny the severity of the resulting problems. The problems are those of transition. By national culture, we refer to something that changes slowly. Mass media and popular culture are objects of fads in constant and rapid flux. That mismatch is much of the problem.

National cultures when they are lauded by their eulogists, are generally described as age-old traditions. To some degree, that is true. Every culture is the end product of thousands of years of history. But to a very large degree, the claims to a hoary past are mythology. Each generation sees its culture as that with which it grew up. Its hallowed values and traditions are those it learned in childhood. Many elements that it values as its culture were controversial foreign imports a generation or two before.

There are no isolated cultures in the world. Each is an accretion of imports and borrowings. When we look at the history of many of the things that we take to be most symbolic of cultural identity, we find that at some point they were a foreign intrusion. For example, peasant pottery is often symbolic of the quaint and unchanging ways of a preindustrial people. In Machiko in Japan and at Atitlan in Mexico, there are particularly beautiful folk arts of this kind. Yet in each case, it was a foreigner engaged in technical assistance some generations back who brought the art to the country to help the peasants modernize by acquiring a cottage craft for the cash market. In Japan it was an Englishman, in Atitlan, a Franciscan priest. The demand for cultural purity is but a demand to freeze this process of diffusion at some arbitrary present which happens to be the advocate's youth.

But one cannot view that demand to freeze change at one's youth with condescension. It is a normal, natural human impulse. Few of us learn very much once we are adults. There is nothing more painful than having to change one's values, habits, and style of life once one has reached the years of maturity. It happens to millions of people; we must respect their pain about it. There are refugees and immigrants; peasants who have lost their land; villagers who have moved to the city; workers in trades that have become obsolete; old residents of a neighborhood that has had an influx of migrants; members of an aristocracy or plutocracy or ethnic ruling group forced to accept the rise of equality of those who used to be their menials. Their unhappiness is one of the commonest and yet most poignant kinds of human tragedy.

It is out of men's resistance to this kind of change that their emotions become involved in the goal of preserving their culture as they came to know it early in life. It is because of the fact that men normally form a sense of identity only once in a lifetime that people become ardently attached to the symbols of that identity.

Mass media messages march to a different drummer. No biological fact slows their processes to the life cycle of a man. Their tempo is that of our technology in which change occurs with exponential acceleration. The time span of mass media fads grows shorter. The life of popular songs grows shorter. The time on top for a pop star grows shorter. The duration of news foci as measured by the crisis that gets the top headlines grows shorter.

The drum beat of new fads, new ideas, new styles every year brought forward by the mass media is an inevitable disharmony with the concept of a national culture, and its slow rate of change. Believers in free discourse cannot accept a policy for the mass media that subjects them to a censorship designed to prevent them from violating the norms of culture, but neither should humane men disregard the pain that rapid change imposes on men whose life cycle is no different than it was millenia ago.

IV. U.S. POLICY ALTERNATIVES

America faces a dilemma. We have a historical national commitment to the free flow of information. For both political and economic reasons, America favors openness of traffic among peoples. But we also sympathize with the desire of developing countries for autonomy and the right to live in their own style. Direct satellite broadcasting is not a matter of much importance to us, and we would like not to pick fights with friendly countries on such minor issues. But the principles and precedents at stake in this debate are important ones in other situations too. We would much prefer that the issue of human rights be fought out on such important matters as emigration from the U.S.S.R., where the reactionary character of closing a society is more obvious. But we are being compelled to debate the issue in a situation where the votes are not with us, where there are as of now, few vested interests on the side of freedom, nor even any deep commitment on our own part to the fight, and furthermore no reality testing available. The dangers cited by our critics are fantasies that can be painted as darkly as a Cassandra might wish, for there is no hard data to provide in refutation. Nonetheless, the debate is with us whether we like it or not. In the debate there are three basic postures available to this country. The first may be called the posture of accommodation. It says, "if you can't lick 'em, join 'em." That line would essentially adopt the views of defenders of the integrity of national cultures. The argument is:

1. The issue is of no importance to us anyhow.
2. The first amendment is a domestic matter; we do not try to impose our free speech standards on others.
3. The votes are on the other side; we cannot afford to be isolated in a small minority.
4. Furthermore, the opponents of cultural imperialism are right in wanting to protect their people from the commercialism, sex, and violence of our mass media.
5. Developing countries after all are very different from us; they need to use their scarce resources for serious development purposes and cannot afford the luxury of our consumerism and entertainment expenditure. Nor can they afford the instability of free speech.
6. No country will stand for alien propaganda; we do not like it either.
7. The balance of flows of information is so one-sided that we must help redress it; you cannot call it free flow if some peoples have much more access to the media than others.
8. People's concern about preserving their cultures is sincere. We cannot

disregard such genuine feelings. We must learn to listen.

Against that view the clearest counterposture is the one of firm libertarian principle expressed in Article 19 of the Universal Declaration of Human Rights:

> Everyone has the right to freedom of opinion and expression; this right includes freedom to hold opinions without interference and to seek, receive and impart information and ideas through any media and regardless of frontiers. (Adopted by General Assembly, December 10, 1948)

This approach refuses to concede to other governments our cooperation in trying to shackle what their peoples can see and hear. Such an approach is not only consonant with our traditions, it is also a realistic one for the U.S.A. to take, given its lead in satellite technology. International agreements in the present world system ratify established relations and practices; they lack the power to overturn them. While we would lose many votes, there is no realistic prospect of the nations of the world compelling us, the satellite launching nation, to enforce a convention that we decline to sign.

Thus, the second possible position could be called toughing it out. We can decide on the convergent basis of both our moral principles and power politics to refuse our assistance to any censorship proposals. If we do that, since the issue of direct satellite broadcasting will continue to be a hypothetical one, it will be in no one's urgent interest to press for actual action. And sooner or later, if forcefully and confidently presented, the arguments for free flow of ideas may get to many independent intellectuals. Governments in the past have rarely understood the arguments for freedom, and presumably rarely will, but that need not bother us.

The arguments against that approach, like all arguments against heavy handed use of power, point to the price one pays for failing to respect the deep and genuine feelings of other parties.

One therefore hopes that there might be a third or mixed position that can respond to the genuine national sensitivities aroused by satellite broadcasting, while at the same time not compromising our position against censorship of international broadcasts. One would also wish to find a posture that would support continued development of satellite communication. Such a posture would be one in which the U.S.A. takes a vigorous lead in making two-way satellite communication available to other countries and to international organizations for their own use.

Most—maybe all—satellite TV transmission will, we predict, be by redistribution rather than direct broadcasting, and most of that (in the absence of planned action) will be the same one-way flow from the U.S.A. and a few other advanced countries that we now see in the export of tapes and films. That is the true offense to national sensibilities, which, if not acted upon, will result in irrelevant obstructions to satellite development.

INTELSAT is a commercial common carrier, hopefully blind to the content of what it carries. It is not its business to remedy the situation. But it would be very much in the U.S. government's interest to subsidize a flow of communication by satellite from the developing countries to the rest of the world and also of communication by the U.N. AID, for example, should increasingly fund the placement of ground stations in poor countries and help with the creation of cooperative exchange activities for TV programs. The U.S. could propose, for example, that the U.N. establish a worldwide TV network that would distribute programs originated all over the world. There are many variants to this basic idea of helping develop the two-way flow of TV material by satellite.

Such cooperative measures need not be limited to TV communication. Since, as we have seen, direct satellite broadcasting is not the real issue, but only a surrogate for a series of complaints about the unfair balance of power in world communications, some of the useful reform measures may be ones that use satellites to distribute signals other than video. For example, there is a group at MIT working on an idea for a world packet data transmission system.

The idea of the packet data system is to narrow the gap in information resources between the industrialized countries and the LDCs. Today, a chasm separates the research situation in the West with such facilities as the Library of Congress, Weidner, the New York Public Library, the British Museum, the Moscow State Library, and so forth, from that in the LDCs, which create universities and research centers with libraries that would not satisfy a small college in this country. In the West, too, there is extensive publishing of data series, newsletters, reference bulletins, and periodicals that can be accessed directly or through libraries. It would take decades, at best, for the LDCs to catch up. Because of the computer, the gap will actually widen. Increasingly data is moving from hard copy form to machine readable data bases. In twenty years time, systems such as MEDLARS or the *New York Times* on-line information system will be widely used in this country. Given the sophisticated technology required for time-shared data networks with remote access, the developing countries will fall increasingly behind. But with satellite communications there is a solution. A worldwide packet data system could, we believe, make access to all these data bases available from anywhere in the world at a communications cost of less than a nickel per 100 words. Overnight the developing countries could close the information gap. A researcher in a university or planning office in any country could pick up his telephone and retrieve a fact from whatever data base he wishes anywhere in the world for the cost of a domestic telephone call. The world's great retrieval systems would become worldwide resources.

The first packet data network is the ARPA net which is now functioning and connecting about fifty university and DOD computers across the U.S.A.

and in England. Using low cost small computers called TIPS and IMPS as interfaces, users at any of the places on the net can use any of the computers on the net via special phone lines. The data packet transmission procedure that makes the system possible is now being adopted by several commercial companies. They are proposing to establish networks covering the U.S. and Europe, wherever the volume of business is adequate to pay for the equipment and service.

No commercial company would now find it worthwhile extending its net to cover the developing countries of the world. But the technology for doing that exists, thanks to INTELSAT and the ARPA net. The cost of the system would be in the low tens of millions if installed on a worldwide systematic plan. That is little, given its significance, even by the standards of present shrunken foreign aid efforts. Like communication systems generally, such a system would easily pay for itself once it reached comprehensive coverage scale. If installed on a small scale, in the way that the commercial investors are now willing to try to do on their own, it would pay only in a few heavy traffic locations that are in already industrialized places.

Lest I be accused of blue sky optimism, let me stress that what I am describing is an idea with many aspects still unstudied. Our study group has already identified a number of difficult problems. However, the difficulties are not in the satellite communications technology. The difficulties are language barriers, political resistances, agreement on data formats, and similar human factors. These are things that could be worked on cooperatively if the U.S. proposed to the LDCs to try to establish such a system and offered to underwrite the development effort and part of the cost.

That is the kind of progressive proposal for the use of satellites that will help the countries of the world see the value to themselves of satellite development.

Change is always a fearsome thing. People and nations are ambivalent about it. The fear of change is what is being expressed in impassioned defenses of national cultural integrity. But even those who raise that battle cry are ambivalent about change. In various rhetorical forms they will explain that they want some changes, if not others. They want "good" changes not "bad" changes, on the implicit assumption that people can agree on what is good and what is bad. They want progress but within their own cultural traditions. They want rising GNP but without alteration of religious and familiar values. It is easy and condescending to point out that that is impossible. Social change is inevitably painful and uncontrolled. In Ruth Benedict's vivid metaphor, one cannot change the bowl of culture without cracking it. But such hortatory generalizations will not set at rest the sincere fears and dismay of those who see treasured aspects of their cultures being swept away. To help ease the pain of change, we must enable those who are alarmed to also participate in the process in a way that will help them gain some of the values of respect and welfare that they are seeking. They must want change too. So those of us who wish to see progress in satellite communication must pay a small price in seeing to it that the satellites are useful to people in all countries, not just to us. We must make the satellites into channels for them to express their views to us, not just channels by which they receive. A UN-LDC world TV network and a worldwide packet data communications system would help achieve that goal.

SOME CONCLUSIONS*

For a telecommunications system to serve the less developed countries effectively as a bearer of technical knowledge, it must have certain characteristics. It must be cheap. It must also be reliable, relatively rugged, and not require highly sophisticated maintenance and operating personnel. It must operate even in the absence of an elaborate infrastructure of stable electric current, national microwave or cable networks, and smoothly functioning telephone service. Finally, it must link a developing country at its will to any possible sources of data, not just to ones in a favored metropole on which it is dependent.

These are not insoluble requirements. The first step was taken when widely dispersed cheap transistor radios gave rural populations the opportunity to hear their national voice, but also to hear world news and information from abroad. The second step, now under way, is the linking of all population centers for both TV and point-to-point stations. In the third step, now feasible but not yet undertaken, is the dissemination of computer terminals for text and data to all locations, to provide the functional equivalent of telephone communication at a much lower price and on a global basis; this also integrates developing areas into the most advanced information systems in the world.

That combination of technologies meets the requirements of ruggedness, maintainability and low cost. It also meets the political requirement of creating worldwide communication at the will of the user. Unlike cable and telephone networks and airline routes, which fan out from the old colonial metropole to its former colonies and dependencies, the radio and satellite systems described above allow any-point to any-point communication, and free the user to seek advice or information wherever he wishes.

Developing countries should insist on the freest possible access by telecommunications to the best available information resources from anywhere in

*This section is extracted from the author's, "The Influence of International Communication on Development," a paper presented at the International Conference on Communication Policy and Planning for Development, April 5–10, 1976, East–West Communication Institute, East–West Center, Honolulu, Hawaii.

the world. It is in their interest to oppose all restrictions on the free flow of information. Copyright, security restrictions, and commercial restrictions on the transfer of technical information, all check the progress of developing countries. Rapid transfer of technology is facilitated by the maximum possible flow of travel, messages, literature, and on-line interaction across the world's borders.

Dependence occurs whenever advanced countries possess know-how and techniques that developing countries are not able to acquire for themselves at will. Independence is therefore promoted by unrestricted free flow of information between countries, so that the developing country can acquire for itself whatever intellectual and cultural products it desires at the lowest possible price. The freer the flow of information, the wider the developing country's range of choice and the sooner it can acquire for itself the ability to produce the same sort of information of programming at home.

Protectionism in the intellectual and cultural field is, therefore, even more damaging to the country that practices it than it is in the field of material trade. In both fields a country pays a significant price for not doing those things in which it has a comparative advantage, but rather trying to do things at which it is inefficient. In physical trade, however, there may be certain self-perpetuating aspects to relying on imports. In things of the mind, however, the process of using a medium is also the process of learning to be its master. Protectionism in trade may facilitate learning to carry on an industry oneself; protectionism in regard to things of the mind, however, inhibits learning.

The conclusions here being presented are rarely accepted by governments, including the governments of underdeveloped countries. It should be no surprise that governments have an inherent bias toward controls, restrictions, and provincialism. The business of government, after all, is to govern; it is a rare government that is able to recognize when it is hurting its own people by its regulatory actions. It is a sad but undeniable fact that the largest part of all the oppression, brutality, and sadism in the world is done by governments. And the governments of the less developed countries suffer from underdevelopment too; on the average they are among the less enlightened in the world. So the fact that few developing states have encouraged or even allowed a free flow of information is no test of its value for them.

On the value to development of the free flow of information, the judgment of international organizations is likely to be no better than that of the governments that compose them and instruct their representatives to them. International organizations are likely to misinterpret the needs of the less developed countries, perceiving them through the distorting vision of government officials.

It is true that over a quarter of a century ago the United Nations, in Article 19 of the Universal Declaration of Human Rights, proclaimed that:

Everyone has the right to freedom of opinion and expression; this right includes freedom to hold opinions without interference and to seek, receive, and impart information and ideas through any media and regardless of frontiers.

The UN is unlikely to adopt such an insightful statement again in the near future.

While governments and international organizations are not prone to favor the interests of the less developed countries in stimulating a free flow of international information, there is fortunately a coincidence between the true interests of development and the ideological and moral predispositions of at least one important group in society. Scholars, scientists, practitioners of the intellectual arts tend to be among the strongest advocates of free flow. To liberal intellectuals the right to communicate is sacred; the doctrine of the free flow of information is a principle not to be compromised. Of course, there are always among intellectuals apologists of tyranny; there are always intellectuals on all sides of all questions. Nonetheless, the important point is that, just as governments whose business is to govern have a bias in favor of regulating, so communicators whose business is to communicate have a bias in favor of communicating freely.

The best hope, therefore, that progress will be made toward creating the global system of low cost and unfettered communication that the developing countries require in order to progress, comes from the ambitions and desires of the communicators themselves. Fortunately journalists wish to report what is happening in the world; radio and TV producers want to provide exciting and meaningful programs to large audiences; technologists wish to create global and efficient communications systems. As long as their professional ambition is fired by a perception of what an expanding communication system can mean to the people of the world, there is room for hope.

REFERENCES

Jones, N. C. (1967). "The Role of the United Nations in Communications Satellites." Unpublished dissertation, University of Missouri.

Lerner, D. (1958). "The Passing of Traditional Society: Modernizing the Middle East." Free Press, Glencoe, Illinois.

Nordenstreng, K., and Varis, T. (1974). "Television Traffic—A One-Way Street?" UNESCO, Paris. (Reports and Papers on Mass Communication, No. 70.)

Parry, A. (1960). "Russia's Rockets and Missiles." Doubleday, Garden City, New York.

Pool, I. de Sola. (1973). Communication in totalitarian societies. In "Handbook of Communication" (I. de Sola Pool, F. W. Frey, W. Schramm, N. Maccoby, and E. B. Parker, eds.), pp. 462–511. Rand McNally, Chicago, Illinois.

Smith, D. D. (1969–1970). America's short-wave audience: Twenty-five years later. Public Opinion Quarterly 33, 537–545.

8

Satellite Broadcasting, National Sovereignty, and Free Flow of Information

Edward W. Ploman

International Institute of Communications, London

Edward W. Ploman was born in Sweden and was educated at the University of Uppsala. He joined the Swedish Broadcasting Corporation in 1952 and was responsible for foreign language broadcasts, external services, from 1953 to 1957. Dr. Ploman was the Head of Eurovision, European Broadcasting Union, from 1959 to 1963 and was in the Radio and Visual Services Division of the Office of Public Information of the United Nations from 1963 to 1966. He was Director of International Relations for the Swedish Broadcasting Corporation from 1966 to 1971 and has been Executive Director of the International Institute of Communications since that date. Dr. Ploman has published books on broadcasting in Sweden and Germany. His *Broadcasting in Sweden* was published in 1976.

This chapter was written specifically for publication in this book.

The debate in the area of free flow of information often seems to erupt at the extreme poles of a wide spectrum expressed either in highly abstract, general legal principles or in equally extreme concrete terms focusing on a particular practical case. There are few instances of a discussion conducted over a period of time covering a range of aspects in the context of a defined problem area. This is one reason why the question of legal principles for satellite broadcasting is of specific interest.

Most obviously and immediately, the controversy surrounding the work on a legal regime for direct satellite broadcasting can be summarized in the key question of the relationship between and relative weight to be given to principles in the area of freedom of information and the free flow of communications, on the one hand, and on the other hand, to principles related to national sovereignty, noninterference, and the right of each country to evolve its own communications systems.

In concrete terms, the issues have been formulated through such questions as the following. Should any country have the right to undertake broadcasting of television programs via satellite directed to the audiences of other countries? Which existing rules of international law are applicable to this activity? Would new rules be required and, if so, at what level and of what kind? A key point has come to be expressed in terms of whether or not there should be a rule of prior agreement between a "sending" and a "receiving" state.

Differences of opinion start at the point of whether satellite broadcasting presents a problem at all. It has been maintained that the issue is a false problem or, at most, requires technical regulation but no politico-legal rules. At the other end of the scale, anxieties have been expressed in terms of an unregulated flood of satellite-born television programs that could only be undertaken by a few of the technically most advanced countries and that could impair cultural identity and media policy in the "receiving" countries.

Whatever opinion is held about the seriousness of these problems, the question of a legal regime for such broadcasts presents a number of significant features. In some respects it has come to serve as a catalyst for a number of international issues in the general area of international "information law."

In another perspective this question is relevant in terms of the response of the international community to a new technology and to the problems involved in having to deal with several branches of international law that show marked differences. Last, but not least, it lends itself well to a study of attitudes that are mostly taken for granted, but require reflective analysis if we are to advance beyond sterile confrontations in the area of an evolving international information order.

Before presenting an account of the background of the satellite broadcast issues, some general observations are in order.

At times, the debate on these issues has resembled a dialogue of the deaf or a series of disconnected monologues, without the parties in the debate really listening to what others have been saying. One result has been a tendency to impute ulterior motives or bad intentions to a party holding different views. In this context, the assumption will be the opposite: that the parties in the debate more often than not have genuinely stated their attitude and opinion with respect to issues that present themselves in new and unexpected forms.

There are in fact real problems in trying to establish a common universe of discourse. The discussion in this field tends to cluster around a number of expressions, each of which acts as a shorthand for a swarm of notions, concepts, and ideas that are still half-formed, in a constant process of change and a mixture of the old and the very new. Not only the expressions, but also their possible meanings, lack the clarity and the equilibrium of other notions and phrases that through years of use and reshaping have settled into a familiar form that is well understood.

Disagreements also arise from contrasting opinions, which in the final analysis depend on genuine philosophical differences, in the sense of different interpretations of reality. As has been shown by the debates in connection with the Helsinki and Belgrade conferences, certain basic differences of opinion suffer from the still unresolved dilemma of whether the chicken or the egg comes first: one side maintains that measures for security are a precondition for cooperation; the other side sees the sequence the other way around: cooperation leads to security. "The West believes that increased cooperation automatically leads to appeasement; the East considers that increased security leads gradually to improved cooperation" (Martelanc, 1977).

There is, furthermore, a need to distinguish between attitudes of a political nature and those conditioned by legal philosophy. Obviously, certain important issues or aspects of these issues are of a political nature and will have to be solved through juridico-political negotiation. In this respect, political and legal aspects are like the two sides of the same coin; the legal texts are often seen as no more than an expression of political attitudes. However, disagreements expressed in political terms may on closer analysis be shown to depend on differences in legal approaches.

Thus, "where the Anglo-American countries, for example, proceed pragmatically, formulating the rules of legal behaviour as they acquire experience, the civil law tradition tends to rely on the codification of rules in advance of action" (Laskin and Chayes, 1974). Since such attitudes are taken for granted and not openly discussed, it is perfectly understandable that from a civil law approach, the common-law-inspired reluctance to formulate rules in advance of the fact can be—and has been—interpreted as politically motivated prevarication or worse. The common law countries would then see the demands for early codification—natural for a civil law attitude—as equally awkward in terms of a, to them, rigid or artificial attitude.

Such rarely mentioned factors help to cast useful light on the issues discussed and the attitudes expressed by various countries.

For an analysis of the cluster of issues subsumed under the lable "free flow of information versus national sovereignty," in the context of legal principles for satellite broadcasting, it is necessary first to indicate the various contexts in which these discussions have taken place.

CONTEXT

The question of a legal regime for satellite broadcasting has been on the international agenda for almost ten years. It has been raised in a number of different institutions, of which the most important are the United Nations (UN) and the International Telecommunication Union (ITU). Thus, the question must be seen both in the context of international telecommunications regulation as evolved within the ITU, and in the context of the development of space law, as well as of "information law," in the UN. It is important to be aware of these various contexts since there are considerable differences in approach and procedures.

The issue of legal principles for direct broadcast satellites was taken up in the UN within the general context of the organization's involvement in outer space affairs and the development of space law.

It is important to remember that outer space questions were originally raised in the UN even before the launch of the first Sputnik, in connection with disarmament and control over atomic weapons. Following intensive negotiations concluded during the late 1950s, the treaty prohibiting nuclear weapons tests in the atmosphere, outer space, and under water was signed in 1963 by the U.K., U.S.A., and U.S.S.R.; it has since been signed by well over a hundred countries, with the notable exceptions of China and France. While certain outer space problems were related to the efforts to advance agreement on disarmament and prohibition of nuclear weapons, the question of the peaceful uses of outer space led to UN action as early as 1958. In December of that year the General Assembly adopted a resolution in which the Assembly recognizes "the common interest of mankind in outer space" (Resolution 1348 (XIII)). In this first outer space resolution a number of attitudes and concepts are expressed that were to serve as guidelines for the entire development of space law: the notion of a new dimension to man's existence, the possibility of practical benefits, the importance of international cooperation, and the intention of providing a framework that would avoid "the extension of present national rivalries into this new field." This aspect has conditioned much of the UN work, since the risks of an extension of great power or other national rivalry into outer space has been perceived as potentially catastrophic.

During the same period, the General Assembly established a committee on the Peaceful Uses of Outer Space which has become the focal point of the UN work in this field. For several years, the Committee experienced great difficulties due to disagreements between the two space powers. Finally, in 1961 an agreement was reached that implied that, contrary to normal practice in the UN, the Committee would work without voting, and according to a principle of consensus. While this in fact gives each member of the committee the right of veto, it has also meant that all of its recommendations to the General Assembly are unanimous and therefore carry great weight.

The Committee has worked through two subcommittees, one for scientific and technical questions, one for legal questions. Since, in practice outer space activities are carried out on a national or bilateral basis, the most important achievements in the UN waters have come through work in the legal field.

The first substantial achievement of the Committee was the elaboration of a

"Declaration of Legal Principles Governing the Activities of States in the Exploration and Use of Outer Space," which was adopted by the General Assembly in 1963. These principles were then used almost intact for the Outer Space Treaty of 1967 which is the basic international instrument in this field.

The Outer Space Treaty lays down general principles and concepts. It has been followed by work on agreements that cover special aspects, such as the rescue of astronauts and liability for damages caused by outer space activities. At present, three subjects are dealt with as high priority items: a treaty on the moon, legal principles for satellite broadcasting, and legal principles for remote sensing via satellites.

The Outer Space Treaty represents a milestone in the development of international law. It embodies a number of modern and, in certain respects, novel concepts. The emphasis is on internationalization of outer space. Outer space is declared open for exploration by all states without discrimination. National appropriation, even of celestial bodies, is ruled out. The general recognition of the interdependence of states and the introduction of a new subject of international law—mankind—goes even further.

This modern character of the Outer Space Treaty becomes very obvious in comparison with older international legal instruments. In the International Telecommunications Convention which, in its original version, dates back to 1865, the assumption is one of separate, totally independent states which agree—almost reluctantly, it seems—to cooperate in certain specifically defined areas.

Telecommunications law, as developed in the framework of the ITU, represents the second major branch of international law applicable to satellite broadcasting. This law presents a number of specific features compared to international law. International regulation of telecommunications is based on technical considerations rather than on general principles. The applicable instruments are drawn up, not by lawyers, but by technicians, often in painstaking technical detail. The telecommunications experts seem reasonably content with the regulations they have adopted, despite the fact that the regulatory framework for such matters as notification and registration of frequencies, or the international protection of frequency use, has reached an unusually high degree of complexity. According to one expert, "only a small band of initiates can find their way through the mass of clauses" (Berrada, 1972).

In many respects this system of international law-making has proved relatively successful. However, certain new problems have arisen that depend on the growing importance of telecommunications, the greater attention to social, political, and economic aspects in the formation of telecommunications policy, and, conversely, the need to consider telecommunications law in other contexts than the ITU, such as the UN in connection with the broadcast satellite issue.

These, then, are some of the main features of the background for the work on a legal regime for direct broadcast satellites.

Communications satellites had been mentioned in UN General Assembly resolutions since 1961, but only in very general terms. Satellite communications attracted more interest in connection with the negotiations for the establishment of Intelsat in the early 1960s. Again, the two space powers expressed opposing views. "U.S.A. characterized Intelsat as a model for international cooperation, the U.S.S.R. was of the opinion that Intelsat was against the international interest" (Ploman, 1974, p. 176). These discussions did, however, not lead to any action by the UN.

Since then, the interest has concentrated on the issue of satellite broadcasting. The possible implications of this new technology had been raised on various occasions in the early 1960s, and a proposal had also been made to include in the Outer Space Treaty a rule that would prohibit the use of direct broadcast satellites before international agreements had been concluded. This proposal was not retained, but it was decided to study the question.

Following an initiative by Canada and Sweden, the General Assembly agreed, in 1968, to set up a special Working Group on Direct Broadcast Satellites under the Outer Space Committee, in order to provide for a multidisciplinary forum "to study and report on the technical feasibility of communication by direct broadcast from satellites and the current and foreseeable developments in this field, including comparative user costs and other economic considerations as well as the implications of such developments in the social, cultural, legal and other areas" (Resolution 2453 B (XXIII)).

During the succeeding years, the Working Group became one of the focal points for the discussion of direct broadcast satellites. Soon the focus shifted from "the technical feasibility" to social, cultural, political, and legal questions. In the meantime, satellite questions were also discussed in UNESCO, where, in 1969, a conference of intergovernmental experts expressed similar differences of opinion as in the UN. In this context, demands were made for the protection of television transmissions via satellites, as well as for the protection of the public against such broadcasts.

More importantly, work on the allocation of frequencies for all kinds of space communications, and for technical and administrative regulation, was pursued in the ITU. At a conference in 1971 it proved possible to agree on important extensions of frequency ranges allocated for all kinds of space activities. Satellite broadcasting was included among the new space communication services for which frequencies were allocated, but only after agreement had been reached on rules for limiting the so-called spillover, that is, the unintentional radiation of a satellite signal into other countries. These rules, which include a concept of prior agreement, were laid down in the famous item 428 A of the ITU Radio Regulations, which came to play an important role in the following discussions. To press the issue somewhat, it could be said that countries were prepared to accept principles in the ITU context—in which technical problems can cover up for political issues—principles they were not ready to accept in the UN context.

At the present time, the UN Working Group, having finished its part of the work, it is the Legal Subcommittee which has the responsibility for framing a set of principles that can form the basis for international agreement.

Originally, both space powers had been reluctant to admit a discussion in the UN at all. In the course of the debate they came to occupy positions at the extremes of a wide scale of opinion.

In summary form, the U.S.A. position can be described as a minimalist and common-law-inspired attitude. If any principles should be adopted at all, they could possibly be given the form of a nonbinding declaration. They should be very general, be mainly mindful of principles of free flow and freedom of information, and could include a principle of prior consultation. A principle of prior consent by a "receiving country" has consistently been resisted. The U.S.S.R. position can be described as a maximalist, civil law conditioned position. Legal principles should be laid down in a binding treaty, which was originally proposed to include specific sanctions. Apart from a principle of prior consent, there should also be detailed content rules and provisions for measures concerning "illegal" broadcasts.

Intermediate positions—or rather positions that intend to go beyond the dichotomy represented by these two attitudes—have to a large extent clustered around a proposal made by Canada and Sweden. This proposal tries to satisfy the stated requirements of an international order, taking into account both the principle of sovereignty and the principle of the flow of communications, in the form of prior agreement to the establishment of direct broadcast satellite systems; it would leave further aspects for negotiation between the states concerned.

Through long and patient work, it has proved possible to achieve consensus on a number of principles. Negotiations are still going on with regard to the key issue of a principle on agreement between concerned states, prior to the establishment of a satellite system intended for television broadcasts to other countries. To a majority of countries such a provision is a prerequisite for any agreement; certain others find difficulties based on the concept of freedom of information. It should be noted, however, that, at a "technical" level, this principle has been adopted at the ITU World Administrative Radio Conference held in early 1977. This result has been used somewhat illogically by some countries as a reason for not pursuing the work in the UN, where these questions take on another complexion than in the ITU.

REFLECTIONS ON SELECTED ISSUES

To a large extent, the controversy surrounding the cluster of issues involved has been perceived and expressed in terms of free flow of information versus state sovereignty. It should be obvious that this formulation represents a potentially harmful simplification when used out of context. In the UN context, the discussion often proceeds through a sort of shorthand jargon, which not so much avoids analysis as accepts certain attitudes as given politically reality. The fact that this approach has certain advantages is proven by the undeniable progress in the UN work. However, much of the comment and debate outside the UN still shows a lack of reflection and analysis in terms of the different levels and dimensions of the complex problems involved.

The evolution of attitudes on the relevant issues and principles has been reflected in the UN documents and analyzed in various studies. Therefore, the following reflections will focus on certain aspects that are rarely, if ever, mentioned.

Some of these basic issues have already been mentioned, such as the opposition of genuine differences in "philosophical" and legal attitudes. An analysis of these complex and largely unexplored areas would go beyond the framework of these observations, which will concentrate on three related and interlocking aspects: (1) the difficulties arising from the legal technique used in the formulation of rules concerning freedom and free flow of information; (2) the contradictions in relevant principles as well as in the attitudes of states; and (3) the inadequacy of currently used concepts and principles.

1. The legal technique used when the relevant texts on freedom of information were formulated in the 1940s and 1950s starts from abstract and absolute "natural law" concepts. A good example is the famous Article 19 in the Universal Declaration of Human Rights: "Everyone has the right to freedom of opinion and expression; this right includes freedom to hold opinions without interference and to seek, receive and impart information and ideas through any media and regardless of frontiers." This provision is generally quoted without reference to Article 29 of the Declaration which states that the exercise of the rights and freedoms set out in the Declaration shall be subject "to such limitations as are determined by law solely for the purpose of securing the recognition and respect for the rights and freedom of others and of meeting the just requirements of morality, public order and the general welfare in society."

Thus the approach used implies a logically clear, but psychologically awkward, process: because of the high level, absolute abstractions are necessarily vague and therefore also "unreal," and they have to be complemented with a catalog of "exceptions," "restrictions," and "limitations." All these expressions carry a negative connotation, although in fact they correspond to current national practice—even in those countries that most vehemently defend the concept of freedom of information.

Since no country has applied—nor could apply—abstract "freedoms" in a vacuum, it would have been preferable and more conducive to international agreement to have made use of such concepts as conditions for the exercise of rights and freedoms, balanced against corresponding responsibilities. Experience shows that this is what actually happens at the national level, where lawmaking and public debate concerns the nature of the conditions for the exercise of these rights in difficult situations. In many countries the national practice, expressed not only in legislation, but also in media structures, professional codes of conduct, complaints procedures, and so forth, has reached a high degree of elaboration and sophistication. This is in contrast to the much more complex international situation, in which even information-wise countries seem content to reason in simplistic, unsophisticated terms already abandoned at home.

The difficulties encountered at the international level start with the interpretation of concepts that have been left undefined and vague. In the absence of even an only formal definition, it should be no surprise that interpretations can often be no more than "subjective," that is, in terms of national, cultural, or ideological assumptions.

Almost all expressions used in the quoted texts are of this nature: "expression," "seek, receive, and impart information," "due recognition," "just requirements," "morality," "public order," and "general welfare." In view of the political, social, and cultural variety in the world and the rapid changes in attitudes some of these expressions cannot be given an exact definition; perhaps it is wise not to try. There are, however, some expressions that present difficulties of another order. "Everyone" supposedly covers not only individuals but also organized groups, media institutions, and public authorities (including governments), as different categories of "communicators," who supposedly are free to seek, receive, and impart information. In this perspective, the wording of the provision in the Declaration appears—unfairly— somewhat absurd when seen in the context of the totally different functions and possibilities of the different "communicators." This difficulty is compounded by the expression "any media," when applied to these different categories of "communicators"; the envisaged freedoms have not and can never be the same. Thus, the complicated interplay between different kinds of communicators and media (or means of expression) has not been taken into account, which creates a series of difficulties with regard to both factual social situations and to the evolution of communications technology and systems.

"Freedom of information" now requires the same searching analysis as modern international relations theory has applied to the traditional notice of "state sovereignty." Neither of these concepts represents an absolute, static, indivisible reality. The reification of abstractions is as unacceptable in these areas as in others.

In the information field, the relativity of "freedom of information" is proven by national practice in those countries that give it a high priority. The "limitations" cover situations of the most varied kind, from the international commitment by states to regulate the use of radio frequencies to the conditions for the application of human rights.

2. Moving on to another aspect of current problems experienced in discussions about free flow of information and national sovereignty, a major dilemma can be perceived as a series of unresolved contradictions. These contradictions appear as different levels and in various guises. Contradictions are inherent in the principles supposed to order international relations and the behavior of states. At another level, comparative analysis of different branches of law reveals explicit contradictions. At still another level, states themselves can be seen to adopt contradictory attitudes in different contexts.

In this context, a few examples will have to suffice. Human rights are not generally discussed in relation to telecommunications law. It is, therefore, typical of the present confusion that such a question as control and licensing of radio stations is dealt with in totally different ways. Under the Universal Declaration such measures must be subsumed under admissible "limitations," whereas under the much older telecommunications law they represent an international obligation. Freedom of information and protection of copyright and neighboring rights are both hallowed concepts enshrined in the Universal Declaration. There is, understandably, a reluctance to admit that these two principles are not only complementary but also contradictory.

Such contradictions in international rules should not be surprising, since they correspond to similar contradictions at the national level, and states thus show clear contradictions in their behavior and practice. A number of European countries reacted very strongly against so-called pirate broadcasting—broadcasting done from outside their territories directed at audiences within their borders. The result was the adoption of a special agreement, under the auspices of the Council of Europe, against such "unauthorized" broadcasts. Many of the same countries have also introduced a proposal at the Law of the Sea Conference that would prohibit "pirate" broadcasting stations operating from the high seas. This would correspond to similar principles being adopted in the ITU context, which prohibit such broadcasting from either vessels or aircraft.

In the UN discussions on satellite broadcasting, many of these West European countries have opposed principles that in certain, if not all, respects are expressions of exactly the same attitude. Their opposition in the UN context against rules that imply prior agreement (or consent) to the establishment and use of satellite systems for broadcasting into other countries, has not prevented some of these countries from taking an opposite stand in the ITU context. There they refused to accept proposals (of discussions and results of the ITU World Administrative Radio Conference on satellite broadcasting held at the beginning of 1977) that would have made it possible for other countries to cover admittedly rather large areas of their own territories.

It is moot whether such contradictions should, or can be, explained in terms of guile, lack of coordination, or bureaucratic ineptitude. Whatever the reason, they are bound to happen in a field characterized by a lack of a generally accepted conceptual framework and by rapid change in both technical development and attitudes held.

3. Underlying these contradictions are most important and basic contradictions inherent in the present stage of international relations, as well as in the perceptions of these relations. It would not be possible, in this context, to give an account of the recent changes in the analysis of such concepts as "state," "sovereignty," and "international system," which traditionally have profoundly influenced foreign policy matters. In one perspective, these changes in analysis and attitude imply a criticism, at various levels, of traditional concepts which are seen as inadequate, inconsistent with experienced reality, and potentially damaging or harmful.

Thus, the traditional concept of an international system composed only of states characterized by total and equal independence, absolute and indivisible sovereignty, whose relations occur mainly in the form of competition and conflict, is being abandoned. In its place, a series of converging concepts is emerging. These new concepts stress the interdependence of states within a world system; a world or transnational society that includes "actors" other than the state, and relationships that exist both within and across boundaries; and less stress on the territorial dimension in favor of an "issue" dimension and on the heterogoneity of both states and other actors on the international stage. Since the traditional concepts were translated into such policies as defined by "collective security" and "balance of power," it is easy to grasp the importance of new concepts in this area.

The same is true in the field of communications and information and in applicable international law. Whatever the value of such concepts as freedom of information and free flow of information, they are no longer adequate in terms of present situations, needs, and perceptions. The elaboration of new concepts in this field has not yet gone as far as in the area of international relations. However, work is proceeding, as witnessed by the ongoing efforts to update and enrich the traditional context of "freedom of information" under the admittedly somewhat awkwardly formulated expressions "right to communicate," "balanced flow of information," and so on.

The reasons used for reappraisal of traditional concepts are easy to see. Neither satellite broadcasting nor the explosion of "free radios" in Italy fit traditional categories. In this perspective, those countries are proven right who, in the UN discussion on legal principles for satellite broadcasting, have insisted on transcending the dichotomy between the flow of information and national sovereignty. In an interdependant world there is a need for people everywhere to be informed; in a multicultural world there is also a requirement to respect decisions not to open broadcasting to advertising or pornography. International lawmaking must respond to the legal needs of present-day world society, and it must face the challenge.

REFERENCES

Berrada, A. (1972). "Frequencies for Broadcasting Satellites." International Broadcast Institute, London. (I.B.I. Monograph 2.)

Laskin, P. L., and Chayes, A. (1974). A brief history of the issues. *In* "Control of the Direct Broadcast Satellite: Values in Conflict," pp. 3–14. Aspen Institute Program on Communications and Society, Palo Alto, California.

Martelanc, T. (1977). The third basket in Helsinki and Belgrade. *InterMedia 5*, No. 5.

Ploman, E. W. (1974). "Kommunikation durch Satelliten." v. Hase und Koehler, Mainz, Germany.

Part 3

International Law: Codification of Fundamental Principles

Introduction

Kaarle Nordenstreng

Herbert I. Schiller

The preceding part of this volume, as well as such contributions to the debate around satellite broadcasting as contained in the Proceedings of the 1974 Airlie House Conference of the Aspen Institute (the source of Pool's chapter), provide ample evidence that international law is becoming a more and more important area of concern for both policy makers and scholars of international communication.

There are several reasons for this. First, there seems to be a trend toward legislative control of international communication in the world community, most notably within the framework of the United Nations and UNESCO, demonstrated by such work as the inventory compiled by Hilding Eek. As is the case in other areas of life, an increased international control in legislative terms may not mean increased restrictions on the flow of information between nations—rather, it may be a mere matter of codification, making explicit and institutionally recognized the practices and philosophies of the day. But it is also true that such practices and philosophies do change due not least to changes in the national and international balance of socioeconomic political forces, leading to struggles around the process of this codification. This, in fact, is exemplified by the case of direct satellite broadcasting and the earlier attempts to pass an international convention on the freedom of information.

Second, the legal codification of practices and principles often provides a crystallized picture of all problems involved, so that the very process of law-making may be seen as the first stage of scientific analysis. In fact, any student and scholar in the field of international communications should master at least the rudiments of what might be called "international communication law." The chapter by Leo Gross provides far more than this, and it is also an instructive lesson to those who so easily, and often carelessly, base their free flow positions on the famous Article 19 of the Universal Declaration of Human Rights.

Third, a legal approach to international communications serves as an important reminder that questions of (mass) communication cannot be separated from those of international relations in general. The late John B. Whitton's chapter concentrates only on some aspects of international communication, as conditioned by—and itself conditioning—interstate relations. But it also provides convincing evidence that even such a delicate sphere of international communication as propaganda has been traditionally bound by relatively well-established international norms.

The latest link between international communication (including hostile propaganda) and international relations was established in Helsinki in 1975, where the Final Act of the Conference on Security and Cooperation in Europe was signed. The significance of this document will be analyzed in more detail in the next part of this volume, but it deserves mention here. Helsinki has brought new emphasis to some principles of international relations that have significant consequences for the theory and practice of international communication, through national as well as international mass media.

An essential element in this overall political development is the recognition of the principle of nonintervention in the internal affairs of other states (listed sixth in the declaration on principles guiding relations between participating states in the Final Act of CSCE). The most general expression of this principle is to be found in "Sovereign equality, respect for the rights inherent in sovereignty," as it is formulated in the first principle of the Final Act, recognizing that the signatory states will "respect each other's right freely to choose and develop its political, social, economic and cultural systems as well as its right to determine its laws and regulations." (Note that this principle is nothing less than the argument used by advocates of the doctrine of prior consent, as pointed out by Signitzer; see the Introduction to Part 2.)

This certainly has consequences for the theory and practice of mass communication, for it affects the relations between friendly and adversary states. For instance, beaming of broadcasting via satellite directly from one country to the people of another country—an act that does not honor the latter state's "right freely to choose and develop its political, social, economic, and cultural systems"—is not in harmony with these principles, whereas it is perfectly acceptable to let information flow between countries, provided there is a consent for it between the peoples concerned, through their legitimate governments.

The era of Helsinki, in the sense that one should withdraw from direct interference, does not call only upon the mass media to respect the internal affairs of other countries. We must also take a serious look at the way that the mass media *within* each country are covering the world in time of peace, turning its attention to the problem of war propaganda and its control within a national sphere. In this connection, it should be noted that President Carter has signed the American Convention of Human Rights, stipulating, among other things that "Any propaganda for war and any advocacy of national, racial, or religious hatred . . . shall be considered as offenses punishable by law."

Naturally, the notions of war, racial, and other forms of propaganda are far from fixed concepts. Yet there is no reason to be cynical about their adequate definition. For instance, the concept of war propaganda was essentially clarified by the UN in 1974 by its definition of the term "aggression": "Aggression is the use of armed force by a State against the sovereignty, territorial integrity or political independence of another State . . ." (United Nations, 1975, p. 143).

Furthermore, as pointed out earlier, the legal control of unwanted information is nothing new. It has a long history. In the 1919 peace treaties, the early radio stations in Germany, Austria, Bulgaria, and Hungary were prohibited from broadcasting radio telegrams of a political, military, and naval nature. In 1936 a number of Latin American countries agreed to control their news broadcasts and political reports in order to guarantee their authenticity, and radio programs insulting to other states or offensive to the national feelings of their peoples were prohibited (Kolosov, 1973). Also, before World War II, the League of Nations passed an international convention to promote the use of broadcasting in the cause of peace, as is documented in the chapter by Eek.

The era of the Cold War, not so long past, did not respect the idea of a peaceful and cooperative approach to international communications. But in recent years the international community seems to be turning toward an approach of "peaceful coexistence," based on mutually acceptable principles. It is only logical, therefore, that principles and practices that have received considerable international support will be elaborated into "codes of conduct" to be adopted, administered, and sanctioned by the professional organizations in question—if not semigovernmental or even fully governmental bodies such as the United Nations. For instance, pressures toward more peaceful cooperation between nations (East–West) and toward a new international economic order (North–South), have triggered initiatives toward codifying the new demands into sets of "journalistic ethics," "codes of conduct for the TNOs," and so forth. (Cf. Hamelink, 1977, and Nordenstreng, 1976.)

That this is not an uncontroversial path is demonstrated by the case of the Draft Declaration under debate in UNESCO, as well as by attacks of the conventional western "free press" against UNESCO itself and against research institutions engaged in such analyses and codifications (like ILET in Mexico City).

However, it would be misleading to interpret this trend as an imposition of a "censorship mentality" upon libertarian traditions of mass communication. By and large, it is in close agreement with both Western and Eastern journalistic traditions that the audience is provided with an ever wider knowledge about other countries, as is declared in the Helsinki Final Act. In other words, the mass media, instead of promoting hostile propaganda, are supposed to inform the public about conditions in other societies in an accurate and a comprehensive manner.

REFERENCES

Hamelink, C. (1977). "Journalism: Ethical Principles in Code and Practice." (Paper presented at a seminar on International Communications and Third World Participation: A Conceptual and Practical Framework, Amsterdam, 5–8 September 1977, under the auspices of the Latin American Institute for Transnational Studies (ILET).)

Kolosov, Y. (1973). The mass media and international law. *International Affairs* (Moscow), (July), 53–58.

Nordenstreng, K. (1976). Detente and exchange of information between East and West. *Yearbook of Finnish Foreign Policy, 1975* (Finnish Institute of International Affairs, Helsinki), 57–65.

United Nations. General Assembly. (1975). "Resolutions Adopted by the General Assembly during Its Twenty-Ninth Session, 17 September–18 December 1974." United Nations, New York. (Official Records. Twenty-Ninth Session. Supplement No. 31 (A/9631).)

9

Principles Governing the Use of the Mass Media as Defined by the United Nations and UNESCO

Hilding Eek

University of Stockholm

Hilding Eek is Emeritus Professor of International Law at the University of Stockholm, Sweden. Dr. Eek was Chief of the Section for Freedom of Information at the United Nations Secretariat from 1948 to 1952, and has been a member of the Executive Council of UNESCO. He is the author of many books and papers on international law and freedom of information, including *Freedom of Information as a Project of International Legislation*.

This paper is an adaptation, in collaboration with Professor Kaarle Nordenstreng, of a working paper prepared for the UNESCO Secretariat as a basis for Document COM-75/CONF.201/4 (Paris, 3 December 1975) of the Intergovernmental Meeting of Experts to Prepare a Draft Declaration on Fundamental Principles Governing the Use of the Mass Media in Strengthening Peace and International Understanding and Combating War Propaganda, Racism, and Apartheid.

INTRODUCTION

The purpose of the present chapter is to give an outline of past work by the United Nations and its specialized agencies, particularly UNESCO, in protecting and promoting freedom of information and the free flow of information across national borders. It seems advisable, however, to explain at the outset that discussions both within the United Nations and UNESCO and outside these organizations, has been marked by controversies and differences of opinion. It is not easy to evaluate the problems involved, because on many occasions the controversial issues have not been clearly defined and distinguished.

In this respect the main difficulties seemingly relate to the fact that freedom of opinion and expression as a human right is supposed to be protected against interference by national public authorities. Therefore, the work toward the adoption of a convention on freedom of information has aimed at the acceptance by states of certain limitations of their legislative powers in the field. On the other hand, the purposes of the United Nations, as defined in Article 1 of the Charter, are not only to achieve international cooperation in promoting and encouraging respect for human rights and for fundamental freedoms, but also, as stated in the first paragraph of Article 1, to maintain international peace and security. To this end, organizations in the United Nations system have appealed to Member States to take action for the promotion of international understanding by various means, including those that counteract propaganda on behalf of war and hatred among nations. In addition, full freedom of information is not deemed acceptable if used against the efforts to protect fundamental human rights by combating activities such as racism and apartheid.

In tracing the history of the initiatives of the United Nations and UNESCO, this chapter deals with freedom of information on the basis of different aspects of, or approaches to, the problems involved that have marked the instruments adopted or drafted in the field by organizations of the United Nations and UNESCO. These different aspects or approaches may, for the purpose of the organization of this paper, be distinguished as follows:

1. Action to proclaim and protect freedom of opinion and expression as a fundamental human right.

2. Efforts to arrive at internationally accepted legal standards for the definition of freedom of information and to provide for the protection of that freedom by national legislation, particularly by a Convention on Freedom of Information.

3. Action aiming at the improvement of the status of the mass media and news personnel engaged in seeking and receiving information abroad or in imparting information across national frontiers.

4. Action aiming at the improvement of the performance of the mass media and their personnel, with emphasis particularly on the role of the mass media in strengthening peace and international understanding and in combating war propaganda, racism, and apartheid.

Connected with all these aspects are, of course, the work of the United Nations and of UNESCO that aims at facilitating the free flow of information and at removing obstacles thereto, both political and economic.

This chapter is organized along the lines indicated above; it does not list events or instruments on the basis of the organization within the United Nations system by which a certain action was taken. It should be noted, however, that, within the United Nations, questions concerning freedom of information have been generally addressed by the General Assembly and its committees, the Economic and Social Council, the Council's Commission on Human Rights, and its (now defunct) Sub-Commission on Freedom of Information and of the Press.

Of basic importance is the United Nations Conference on Freedom of Information, held in Geneva, Switzerland, 23 March–21 April, 1948. It seems to have been clear from the very early work of the United Nations, before the Universal Declaration of Human Rights was drafted, that a series of very complicated problems was involved in the promotion of freedom of information as one of the human rights. At its first session the General Assembly called on the Economic and Social Council to convoke a conference for the purpose of formulating its views concerning "the rights, obligations, and practices which should be included in the concept of freedom of information."

The Final Act of the Conference (E/CONF. 6/79) contains three draft conventions and 43 resolutions. The Conference forwarded the draft conventions to the Economic and Social Council. The conventions and some of the resolutions adopted by the Conference will be dealt with later in this chapter. The Final Act of the Conference, as well as the documents produced for it and submitted to it, indicate that Member States regarded the task of the Conference as being not only to seek to define the concept of freedom of information, but to lay down a long-term policy for the United Nations in the field of freedom of information.

FREEDOM OF INFORMATION IN THE CONTEXT OF FUNDAMENTAL HUMAN RIGHTS

The Charter of the United Nations

The Charter, which was signed on 26 June 1945 and which entered into force on 24 October 1945, states in Article 1 that the United Nations seek "to achieve international cooperation . . . in promoting and encouraging respect for human rights and for fundamental freedoms for all without distinction as to race, sex, language or religion." Article 55 of the Charter states that the United Nations shall promote "Universal respect for, and observance of human rights and fundamental freedoms" and Article 68 provides for the setting up of a Commission for the Promotion of Human Rights.

The Constitution of UNESCO

The UNESCO Constitution, adopted on 16 November 1945, touches upon the concept of freedom of information in the sixth preambular paragraph, which states that the

... Parties to this Constitution believing in full and equal opportunities for education for all, in the unrestricted pursuit of objective truth, and in the free exchange of ideas and knowledge, are agreed and determined to develop and to increase the means of communications between their peoples and to employ these means for the purposes of mutual understanding and a truer and more perfect knowledge of each other's lives.

The free flow of ideas is referred to more explicitly in Article 1 of the Constitution, defining, first, the overall purpose of the Organization to "contribute to peace and security by promoting. . . ." The second paragraph stipulates:

To realize this purpose the Organization will: (a) Collaborate in the work of advancing the mutual knowledge and understanding of peoples, through all means of mass communication and to that end recommend such international agreements as may be necessary to promote the free flow of ideas by word and image; . . . (c) Maintain, increase and diffuse knowledge . . . by encouraging cooperation among the nations in all branches of intellectual activity, including the international exchange of persons active in the fields of education, science and culture and the exchange of publications, objects of artistic and scientific interest and other materials of information; by initiating methods of international cooperation calculated to give the people of all countries access to the printed and published materials produced by any of them.

The Declaration of Human Rights

The first task of the Commission on Human Rights was to discuss the question of a draft Declaration of Human Rights. The Universal Declaration of Human Rights was adopted by the General Assembly of the United Nations on 10 December 1948 "as a common standard of achievement for all peoples and all nations." It is not a convention, but it purports to define human rights and fundamental freedoms that the Member States of the United Nations, by their adherence to the Charter, are bound to respect and observe.

Freedom of information is referred to in Article 19 of the Declaration, which reads as follows:

Everyone has the right to freedom of opinion and expression; this right includes freedom to hold opinions without interference and to seek, receive and impart information and ideas through any media and regardless of frontiers.

It may be noted that, while the Declaration deals with rights and freedoms belonging to "all human beings" (Article 1), confers these rights and freedoms on "everyone," and deals mainly with the safeguarding of the rule of law within countries, it also refers to some basic international aspects related to the achievement of a universal respect of the rule of law. This appears from Article 28, where it is said that "everyone is entitled to a social and *international* order in which the rights and freedom, set forth in the Declaration can be fully realized" (emphasis added). Moreover, the Preamble states in one of its paragraphs that "it is essential to promote the development of friendly relations between nations,'' and Article 29 (3) contains the following: "These rights and freedoms may in no case be exercised contrary to the purposes and principles of the United Nations.'' These purposes and principles are stated in the Preamble to and in Article 1 of the Charter.

The International Covenant on Civil and Political Rights

The Covenant, which is technically speaking a Convention, was unanimously adopted by the General Assembly of the United Nations on 18 December 1966. It entered into force on 23 March 1967, that is, three months after the date of the deposit with the Secretary-General of the United Nations of the thirty-fifth instrument of ratification or accession. By August 1977, forty-four states (not including the U.S.A.) had ratified the Covenant.

Freedom of information as a human right is dealt with in Articles 18, 19, and 20 of the Covenant. Article 18 states that "everyone shall have the right to freedom of thought, conscience and religion.'' After this introductory pronouncement, it deals primarily with freedom of religion. In Article 19, the above-quoted principle, laid down in Article 19 of the Universal Declaration, is elaborated. According to Paragraph 3 of the Article, the exercise of the rights with which the Article is concerned "carries with it special duties and responsibilities'' and may be subject to certain restrictions, "but these shall only be such as are provided by law and are necessary (a) for respect of the rights or reputations of others; (b) for the protection of national security or public order (*ordre public*), or of public health or morals.'' The requirement that restrictions be provided by law is evidently essential; legislation must, furthermore, in a state party to the Covenant, meet with some international standards relating to the "necessity'' of certain restrictions.

Article 20 of the Covenant reads as follows:

1. Any propaganda for war shall be prohibited by law.
2. Any advocacy of national, racial or religious hatred that constitutes incitement to discrimination, hostility, or violence shall be prohibited by law.

This Article puts upon the states, parties to the Covenant, the obligation to prohibit by law propaganda for war and any advocacy such as described in the Article. It seems clear that the legislation envisaged by the Covenant must be intended to apply not only to individuals, but also to mass media as corporate bodies. The law is supposed to give directives relating to the performance of all media of information, and in this respect the Covenant goes beyond simply providing for the protection of freedom of expression as an individual human right. Because of this, five of the countries that ratified the Covenant (Denmark, Finland, Norway, Sweden, and United Kingdom) have stated reservations with respect to this Article (Paragraph 1).

The International Convention of the Elimination of All Forms of Racial Discrimination

This Convention was adopted by the General Assembly of the United Nations on 21 December 1965. It entered into force on 4 January 1969.

By Article 3, states, parties to the Convention, condemn racial segregation and apartheid and undertake to prevent, prohibit, and eradicate all practices of this nature in territories under their jurisdiction. By Article 4, they condemn all propaganda and all organizations based on ideas or theories of superiority of one race or group of persons of one color or ethnic origin, or which attempt to justify or promote racial hatred and discrimination in any form. Too, they undertake to adopt immediate and positive measures designed to eradicate all incitement to such discrimination, and, to this end, "with due regard to the principles embodied in the Universal Declaration of Human Rights," they shall "declare an offence punishable by law all dissemination of ideas based on racial superiority or hatred," and make illegal and prohibit organizations that promote and incite racial discrimination and recognize participation in such organization or activities as an offense punishable by law.

Although these undertakings imply the duty to give, by law, directives to both individuals and media of information limiting their freedom, the human rights philosophy, which motivates the Convention as a whole, dictates the provisions in Article 5. By these provisions states undertake, inter alia, to guarantee the right of everyone, without distinction to race, color, or national or ethnic origin, to equality before the law, in the enjoyment of civil rights, including "the right to freedom of thought, conscience and religion" and "the right to freedom of opinion and expression."

The International Convention on the Suppression and Punishment of Crime of Apartheid

This Convention was adopted and opened for signature by the General Assembly on 30 November 1973 and became effective on 18 July 1976.

By Article 1, the states parties to the Convention declare that apartheid is a crime against humanity. In Article I and, more in detail, in Article 2 "the crime of apartheid" is defined.

According to Article II, criminal responsibility shall apply to "individuals, members of organizations and institutions and representatives of the State . . . whenever they commit, participate in, *directly incite* or conspire in the commission" of the acts defined in Article II (emphasis added). By Article IV, states parties to the Convention undertake, inter alia, "to adopt any legislative measures necessary to suppress as well as to prevent *any encouragement* of apartheid and similar segregationist policies or their manifestations and to punish persons guilty of that crime'' (emphasis added). Thus, the Convention puts upon contracting states the obligation to limit freedom of expression for the purpose of combating effectively the crime of apartheid.

ATTEMPTS TO DEFINE LEGAL STANDARDS FOR FREEDOM OF INFORMATION

This section will be concerned primarily with the draft Convention on Freedom of Information, its history, and the difficulties involved in reaching agreement on a final text. In addition to reviewing this legislative work, relevant international agreements reached within the framework of UNESCO will be mentioned.

The original draft Convention on Freedom of Information was submitted to the Geneva Conference on Freedom of Information, which met 23 March–21 April 1948. The work of the Conference was prepared by the Sub-Commission on Freedom of Information and of the Press, at that time a subcommission of the Commission on Human Rights. Among the documents adopted by the Sub-Commission was a basic paper entitled "Statement of the Rights, Obligations and Practices to be Included in the Concept of Freedom of Information." Although adopted in advance of the Conference, and regardless of the many events in the field that have occurred since the Conference, the statement still seems to deserve attention. It was adopted by the Sub-Commission at its second session, 19 January–3 February 1948.

Statement of the Rights, Obligations, and Practices to Be Included in the Concept of Freedom of Information

The statement lists virtually all of the issues that arise in this field. The right to freedom of information, the Statement reads, "carries with it duties and responsibilities." These are "so closely related" that their union justifies (1) "certain legal restrictions" and (2) "certain moral obligations of equal importance." As to the legal restrictions, the Statement observes that these should be imposed "only for causes clearly defined by law." Prior censorship of written and printed matter, the radio, and newsreels should not exist. The moral obligations are described in the following terms:

> The right to freedom of expression . . . confer upon all who enjoy it the moral obligation to tell the truth without prejudice and to spread knowledge without malicious intent, to facilitate the solution of the economic, social and humanitarian problems of the world as a whole through the free interchange of information bearing on such problems, to help promote human right and fundamental freedom without any arbitrary discrimination, to help maintain peace and security, and to counteract the persistent spreading of false or distorted reports which provoke hatred or prejudice against States, persons or groups of different

race, language, religion or philosophical conviction, confuse the peoples of the world, aggravate relations between nations, or otherwise threaten and destroy the fruits of the common victorious struggle of nations against the Nazi, Fascist, and Japanese aggressions during the last World War.

One paragraph of the Statement offers suggestions as to the precautions required "to prevent the media of information from becoming instruments of exploitation of public opinion, whether in the service of governments, financial interests or other private bodies." It was stated that experience showed "that dangers arise when the media of information are in the hands of monopolies or quasi-monopolies, either public or private."

The Conference did not act on the Statement by trying to adopt or suggest a text of "the concept of freedom of information." The Statement is, however, reflected in Resolutions 1, 2, 3, and 4 of the Final Act of the Conference, under the heading "General Principles," presaging the complex, ideological pattern that characterized the subsequent history of freedom of information in the United Nations.

The History of the Draft Convention

The 1948 United Nations Conference on Freedom of Information prepared, as already stated, three draft conventions. The third was the Draft Convention on Freedom of Information, intended to define freedom of information as a legal right, carrying with it duties and responsibilities and subject to certain limitations. The Draft Convention originated from a proposal made at Geneva by the United Kingdom delegation.

The Final Act of the Conference was considered by the Economic and Social Council at its seventh session (July–August 1948). The Council transmitted the three draft conventions recommended by the Conference to the General Assembly. While some action was taken by both the Council and the General Assembly on two of the draft conventions, the General Assembly— after having tried to revise the first articles of the Geneva Draft Convention on Freedom of Information during the second part of its third session (April–March 1949)—decided to postpone the question. At its fifth regular session (1950) the General Assembly decided to set up an ad hoc Committee to prepare a Draft Convention on Freedom of Information, taking into account the work already done. The ad hoc Committee met early in 1951 and drafted a Preamble and 19 articles of a Convention. The Committee's report (A/AC.42/7) was transmitted to the General Assembly at its sixth regular session (1951–1952), but action was postponed until the 1953 regular session. The item appeared on the agenda of the General Assembly at the regular sessions in most of the following years.

However, in the course of the regular sessions in 1959, 1960, and 1961, the Third Committee of the General Assembly succeeded in adopting the texts of the Preamble and of Articles 1–4 of the 1951 Draft Convention. As adopted by the Third Committee, the Draft Convention deals with freedom of information in Article I, in these terms:

(a) Each Contracting State shall undertake to respect and protect the right of every person to have at his disposal diverse sources of information;

(b) Each Contracting State shall secure to its own nationals, and to such of the nationals of every other Contracting State as are lawfully within its territory, freedom to gather, receive and impart without governmental interference, save as provided in Article 2, and regardless of frontiers, information and opinions orally, in writing or in print, in the form of art or by duly licensed visual or auditory devices;

(c) No Contracting State shall regulate or control the use or availability of any of the means of communication referred to in the preceding paragraph in any manner discriminating against any of its own nationals or of such of the nationals of any other Contracting State as are lawfully within its territory on political grounds or on the basis of their race, sex, language or religion.

Article 2 of this Draft Convention deals with permissible restrictions on freedom of information. The main difficulties that have arisen in connection with the Draft relate to the wording of this Article. As adopted by the Third Committee at the fifteenth session of the General Assembly, the Article reads as follows:

1. The exercise of the freedoms referred to in Article 1 carries with it duties and responsibilities. It may, however, be subject only to such necessary restrictions as are clearly defined by law and applied in accordance with the law in respect of: national security and public order (*ordre public*); systematic dissemination of false reports harmful to friendly relations among nations and of expressions inciting to war or to national, racial or religious hatred; attacks on founders of religions; incitement to violence and crime; public health and morals; the rights, honour and reputation of others; and the fair administration of justice.

2. The restrictions specified in the preceding paragraph shall not be deemed to justify the imposition by any State of prior censorship on news, comments and political opinions and may not be used as grounds for restricting the right to criticize the government.

Article 2 has been understood to reserve to the contracting states the *right* to retain or introduce in their national legislation certain limitations on the exercise of freedom of information as defined in Article 1 of the Draft Convention. In other words, by being a party to the Convention, a state would not *assume the obligation* to introduce in its legislation any such provisions; a contracting state may in its discretion *abstain* from limiting freedom of information to the extent permitted by Article 2.

In countries, however, where freedom of the press and of expression in general is based on constitutional texts or other legislation that does not accept as permissible such restrictions as mentioned in Article 2 of the Draft Convention, there are serious political obstacles for the adoption of the standards laid down by the Draft Convention. Within such countries, journalists and media of information tend to describe Article 2 as "suggestive"; it is supposed to lower the standards of freedom of information already secured by law. As a project in the field of the unification of national legislation concerning information activities, the Draft has also met the problems of different national legal techniques such as appear whenever uniform law is considered, even where political or ideological differences are absent.

The preamble of this Draft Convention, as adopted by the Third Committee, also includes formulations of principal importance. In addition to recalling freedom of information as a fundamental human right, the preamble notes, inter alia:

> Free interchange of accurate, objective and comprehensive information and of opinions, both in the national and international spheres, is essential to the causes of democracy and peace and for the achievement of political, social, cultural and economic progress.

> Freedom of information implies respect for the right of everyone to form opinion through the fullest possible knowledge of the facts.

> In order to achieve these aims the media of information should be free from pressure of dictation but that these media, by virtue of their power for influencing public opinion, bear to the peoples of the world a great responsibility, and have the duty to respect the truth and to promote understanding among nations.

The difficulties met in seeking general agreement on the text of a basic Convention on Freedom of Information have been the reasons for the adoption of some other procedures. The Economic and Social Council, at its twenty-seventh session (1959), considered that a United Nations *Declaration on Freedom of Information* could be a further step in promoting freedom of information. The question was dealt with at the twenty-eighth and the twenty-ninth sessions of the Council which, at the twenty-ninth session (1960), adopted a Draft Declaration and transmitted it to the General Assembly for its consideration. The consideration of this draft is, along with the Draft Convention, still on the agenda of the General Assembly.

Another means of keeping the question of freedom of information alive within the United Nations program has been the preparation of reports on developments in the field of freedom of information. At its fourteenth session (May–August, 1952), the Economic and Social Council appointed Mr. Salvador P. Lopez (Philippines) as Rapporteur on matters relating to freedom of information. In 1953 Mr. Lopez submitted to the Council a "Report on Contemporary Problems and Developments, with Recommendations for Practical Action" (E/2426). It included a recommendation to the General Assembly to proceed with a detailed consideration of the Draft Convention. Mr. Lopez also stated that, while difficulties confronting the adoption of a Convention on Freedom of Information were not insuperable, there was merit in the suggestion that the United Nations consider the possibility of drafting and adopting a Declaration on Freedom of Information.

In 1954, Mr. Lopez submitted a supplementary report of freedom of information to the Economic and Social Council (E/2426/Add. 1–5). By Resolution 718 (XXVII) of the Council, the Secretary-General of the United Nations was requested to prepare a substantive report for submission to the Council in 1961 on developments in the field of information since 1954. The task was entrusted by the Secretary-General to a consultant (Dr. Hilding Eek of Sweden), and his report was submitted to the Council in 1961 (E/3443).

Agreements within UNESCO

In 1948, at its third session, held in Beirut, the UNESCO General Conference adopted the *Agreement for Facilitating the International Circulation of Visual and Auditory Materials of an Educational, Scientific and Cultural Character* ("Beirut Agreement"). This instrument states in its preamble that the contracting parties are convinced that in facilitating the international circulation of the materials covered, "the free flow of ideas by word and image will be promoted and the mutual understanding of peoples thereby encouraged, in conformity with the aims of the United Nations Educational, Scientific and Cultural Organizations." To promote the free flow of information, the Agreement grants to the materials covered exemption from all customs duties and from all quantitative restrictions, as well as from certain internal fees and other charges and the waiver of import licences. In 1977 the Agreement is being adopted by twenty-eight contracting states.

In 1950, at its fifth session in Florence, the General Conference adopted the *Agreement on the Importation of Educational, Scientific and Cultural Material* ("Florence Agreement"), designed to ease, as mentioned in the preamble, "the free exchange of ideas and knowledge." The preamble recalls some of the terms, referred to above, of the Constitution of UNESCO, and subsequently states that "these aims will be effectively furthered by any international agreement facilitating the free flow of books, publications and educational, scientific and cultural materials."

Accordingly, the Agreement exempts from customs duties and certain other importation charges, a wide range of objects, including books, and works of art; in addition, the Agreement grants the necessary licenses and foreign exchange for the importation of some categories of materials, notably books for libraries. In 1977 the agreement is being adopted by sixty-nine countries.

INSTRUMENTS RELATING TO NEWS AND JOURNALISTS

The Gathering and International Transmission of News

One of the draft conventions prepared by the 1948 Geneva Conference on Freedom of Information was based on a proposal made by the Delegation of the United States of America, entitled "Draft Convention on the Gathering and International Transmission of News." The original draft was concerned with the protection of foreign correspondents and their access to news, as well as with their access to transmission facilities and with the egress from the territories of contracting states of all news material of correspondents and agencies of other contracting states without censorship, editing, or delay. The General Assembly decided, however, at its third session, to merge this Draft Convention with the Geneva Convention Concerning the Institution of an International Right of Correction (see below), into one statement: The Convention on the International Transmission of News, and the Right of Correction. However, the General Assembly decided at that time not to open the amalgamated Convention for signature. But later, in 1952, the General Assembly adopted a separate Convention on the International Right of Correction, to be reviewed below.

By this action, those articles of the amalgamated text relating to the international transmission of news remained approved but not opened for signature. These articles deal with the protection of foreign correspondents and with their free access to transmission facilities and with the egress from the territories of contracting states of all news material of correspondents and agencies of other contracting states without censorship, editing, or delay. Such questions have also been considered by the Economic and Social Council. In 1951, the Council appealed to governments, in Resolution 387B(XIII), to safeguard the right of correspondents freely and faithfully to gather and transmit news. In 1954, by its Resolution 522C(XVII), the Council transmitted to states, members, and nonmembers of the United Nations two studies relating to the status and work of foreign correspondents, with a request that states consider the possibility of implementing the administrative measures contemplated in these studies.

Another question concerning news personnel working abroad has been dealt with by the General Assembly in recent years. It concerns the protection of journalists engaged in dangerous missions in areas of armed conflict. A Draft Convention on the subject was submitted to the General Assembly by the Secretary-General in 1973 but has been referred to later sessions.

The Convention on the International Right of Correction

The Press Acts of many countries, particularly in Western Europe, often include provisions for a right of reply or correction. The right is construed as a safeguard of every man's freedom, but it evidently also creates a liability on newspapers or the media, which may, by law, be required to provide space or time for the publication of replies or corrections. The right of reply was discussed at the 1948 Conference in Geneva in two contexts. In its consideration of Article 17 of the Draft Covenant on Human Rights, the Conference took note of a paragraph of draft Article 17, which said that a state may establish, on reasonable terms, a right of reply or similar corrective remedy. Second, the Conference adopted the text of a Draft Convention concerning the Institution of an International Right of Correction, originally proposed by the Delegation of France.

The Convention was adopted by the General Assembly at its seventh session on 16 December 1952 and entered into force on 24 August 1962, when six signatory states had deposited their instruments of ratification or accession. In August 1977 the Convention had been ratified by ten states.

The Convention does not impose any obligations on news media or newspeople directly. Its provisions concern the relations between states. It provides, in Article 1, that in cases in which a contracting state alleges that news reports likely to injure its relations with other states—transmitted from one country to another country by a correspondent or by news agencies and disseminated abroad—are false or distorted, it may submit its version of the facts (called "communiqué") to the contracting states within whose territories such reports have been published. Any government of a contracting state receiving such a communiqué shall make it available to the news enterprises functioning within its territory. Under Article 4 of the Convention, the Secretary-General of the United Nations is to give appropriate publicity to the communiqué.

The Draft International Code of Ethics for Information Personnel

An international code of ethics for information personnel was drafted by the Sub-Commission of Freedom of Information and of the Press, which began this work at its fourth session in 1950 and ended it at its fifth and last session in 1952. At its fourteenth session (1952), the Economic and Social Council asked the Secretary-General to transmit the Draft International Code of Ethics to information enterprises and professional organizations for such action as they might deem appropriate. This indicated at the same time that the United Nations might be prepared to cooperate in arrangements for an international professional conference to complete work on the code. The General Assembly, however, at its ninth session (1954), in Resolution 838(IX), decided to take no further action in regard to the organization of an international conference to prepare the final text of a code of ethics, and it requested the Secretary General to transmit the text of the Draft to the enterprises and associations with which he had been in communication regarding the matter, for their information and for such action as they might deem proper.

National Sovereignty, Evelyn Parentela, tape 904 The text of the Draft International Code of Ethics contains one article (Article IV) that deals with reports and comments on foreign countries. It reads as follows:

It is the duty of those who describe and comment upon events relating to a foreign country to acquire the necessary knowledge of such country which will enable them to report and comment accurately and fairly thereon.

Article III, Paragraph 3 of the Draft International Code of Ethics states inter alia, that "if charges against reputation or moral character are made" (against individuals), "opportunity should be given for reply." However, no "right of reply" to be invoked by a government is laid down in the Draft Code.

THE PERFORMANCE OF THE MASS MEDIA WITH PARTICULAR REFERENCE TO PROMOTION OF PEACE AND INTERNATIONAL UNDERSTANDING: RESOLUTIONS, DECLARATIONS, AND CONVENTIONS

Decisions by organizations of the United Nations and by UNESCO use different titles, indicating different status of authority and purpose. It seems reasonable, therefore, in a paper dealing with a variety of such decisions or "instruments" (as they are generally called), to comment briefly on the terms used.

Although all decisions are based on, or explain, a policy, it may be correct to say that the purpose of a mere *resolution* is mainly to state a policy, which, further on in the work of the organization, may develop into an international instrument of higher dignity. An example is given by the Final Act of the 1948 Conference on Freedom of Information in Geneva, in which a set of resolutions was adopted as a basis of work to be carried on, thereafter, by organs of the United Nations and its specialized agencies. A resolution is not, under international law, binding upon a state whose delegation has voted for it. It does not contain clauses that are compulsory with respect to further action by such a state. But a resolution, if adopted by a great majority of states, will carry considerable weight. Moreover, its convincing force and possibility of leading to further action are enhanced when it is followed by further resolutions along the same lines.

A *convention*, the text of which has been adopted by, for instance, the General Assembly of the United Nations or the General Conference of UNESCO, or an intergovernmental conference, is meant to be binding after ratification or accession by states as soon as it, according to its own provisions, has entered into force. The rules on international law, relating to conventions or other international instruments meant to be binding, have developed through what, in Article 38 of the Statute of International Court of Justice, is called "international custom, as evidence of general practice accepted by law" and were recently codified in the 1969 Vienna Convention on the Law of Treaties.

The authority of a *declaration* as more important than a resolution, though not a convention or treaty, had been discussed in recent years both within organs of the United Nations and in literature in the field of international law. It seems to be generally understood today that a declaration carries more weight than a resolution; it means more than a simple statement of policy. Therefore, the term "declaration" is chosen for statements of principles, close to those adopted by a convention, though not regulated by the law of treaties.

At the request in 1962 of the United Nations Commission on Human Rights, the Legal Office of the United Nations Secreteriat presented a Memorandum to the Commission in which the Legal Office explained that in United Nations practice a declaration is a formal and solemn instrument, suitable for rare occasions when principles of great and lasting importance are being enunciated. The Memorandum also stated that a declaration is adopted by resolution by a United Nations organization. As such, it could not be binding upon member states in the sense that a treaty is binding upon the parties to it purely by the device of terming it a declaration rather than a recommendation. However, in view of the greater solemnity and significance of a "declaration," it might be considered to impart, on the part of the organization adopting it, a strong expectation that members of the international community would abide by it. "Consequently," the statement said, "in so far as the expectation is gradually justified by State practice, a declaration may by custom become recognized as laying down rules binding upon the States."

Policy decisions of organizations within the United Nations, aiming at appealing to the mass media to assist in the promotion of international understanding include resolutions calling for positive action with respect to activities in the field of educational, scientific, and cultural cooperation. Also included are resolutions condemning propaganda regarded as harmful for the preservation and further development of friendly relations between the peoples of the world. The first significant instrument of this kind had already been adopted under the auspices of the League of Nations.

The International Convention Concerning the Use of Broadcasting in the Cause of Peace

This Convention was adopted in Geneva on 23 September 1936. In his opening address to the Inter-Governmental Conference for the adoption of the Convention, the President, Mr. Arnold Raestad of Norway, stated that political broadcasting had "enormous potentialities as a means of fomenting international discord." He explained this point of view in the following words:

> Broadcasts have no material substance, and therefore cannot be stopped at the frontiers; they can be directed towards any point in space; the political effects may be extensive and immediate, but they are not easy to foresee or to control or canalise at need. The underly-

ing ideas of the draft convention are somewhat similar to those that induce governments to renounce the use of certain means of destruction, which, though indubitably effective, cannot be limited in their action to the real objective" (Tomlinson, 1938, p. 229).

The Convention entered into force on April 2, 1938 and is now deposited with the United Nations.

By this Convention the parties undertake, inter alia, to prohibit the broadcasting of transmissions of such character as to incite to acts incompatible with the international order or the security of another contracting party. They also undertake to supervise transmissions originating within their territories with a view to preventing them from constituting an incitement to war or to acts likely to lead thereto.

By Resolution 841 (IX) of 17 December 1954, the General Assembly requested states parties to the Convention to declare whether they wished to transfer to the United Nations the functions performed under the terms of the Convention by the League of Nations. It then asked the Secretary-General to prepare for this purpose a draft protocol and to include in it new articles that would provide that each state party should refrain from radio broadcasts involving unfair attacks or slander against other people anywhere, and also that each state party should not interfere with the reception within its territory of foreign radio broadcasts. Such protocol was prepared by the Secretary-General and circulated to the states parties, but no final action has yet been taken.

Resolutions of the General Assembly of the United Nations

At its first session, the General Assembly, in Resolution 59(I) of 14 December 1946, declared *freedom information* "a fundamental human right," and "the touchstone of all freedoms to which the United Nations is consecrated" and "an essential factor in any serious effort to promote the peace and progress of the world." Accordingly, the General Assembly called upon the Economic and Social Council to convoke a conference for the purpose of formulating its views concerning "the rights, obligations and practices which should be included in the concept of freedom of information." It was upon this resolution that the United Nations Conference of Freedom of Information was held in Geneva.

The Resolution 110 (II), which was adopted unanimously by the General Assembly at its second session, on 3 November 1947, concerns *"Measures to be taken against propaganda and the inciters of a new war."* The Resolution, after recalling that the Charter "calls for the promotion of universal respect for, and observance of, fundamental freedoms which include freedom of expression," condemns "all forms of propaganda . . . which is either designed or likely to provoke or encourage any threat to the peace, breach of the peace, or act of aggression." In the same Resolution, the General Assembly requested the government of each member state to take appropriate steps within its constitutional limits.

(a) to promote, by all means of publicity and propaganda available to them, friendly relations among nations based upon the purposes and principles of the Charter;

(b) to encourage the dissemination of all information designed to give expression to the undoubted desire of all peoples for peace"

The General Assembly also decided to refer this resolution to the forthcoming Conference of Freedom of Information.

At its same (second) session in 1947, the General Assembly adopted another Resolution that should also be mentioned. This resolution concerned *false or distorted reports likely to injure friendly relations between States*. The Resolution invited governments to study such measures as might be taken on the national plane to combat such reports and transmit to the Geneva Conference the results of their studies.

It should be noted that the United Nations Conference on Freedom of Information unanimously adopted two resolutions relating to the need for counteracting false or distorted reports, which undermine friendly relations between states, and to war propaganda. The first of these (Resolution No. 2) endorsed the two previous resolutions of the General Assembly and declared contrary to the purposes of the United Nations "the spreading of false and distorted reports" and "propaganda which is either designed or likely to provoke or encourage any threat to the peace, breach of the peace, or act of aggression." It also declared that such reports and such propaganda "constitute a problem of the first importance calling for urgent corrective action on the national and international planes." In its resolutions the Conference also emphasized the moral obligation of the press and other agencies of information to seek the truth and report the facts (Resolution 1) and recommended that the governments of countries in which media of information disseminate racial and national hatred should

encourage, in consultation with organizations of journalists, suitable and effective non-legislative measures against the dissemination of such hatred and prejudice, and take, within their constitutional limits, appropriate measures to encourage the dissemination of information promoting friendly relations between races and nations based upon the purposes and principles of the United Nations.

Furthermore, at its seventh regular session (1952), the General Assembly recommended "that United Nations bodies studying the problems of freedom of information should consider appropriate measures for *avoiding the harm done to international understanding by the dissemination of false and distorted information*." In his report (1953), the Rapporteur on Freedom of information remarked about this resolution that it was "the latest in a series of resolutions adopted by various organs of the United Nations on this subject." He added the following comment:

It is significant that all the resolutions of the General Assembly and the Geneva Conference condemning propaganda for war and false and distorted reports were adopted without negative vote, showing that the existence of the evil and the need to combat it are generally recognized. However, there is considerable disagreement on the practical measures which should be taken to counteract such propaganda reports, with the result that positive action in the field has been slow.

Here one should also note the work performed by the Third Committee in drafting the Convention on Freedom of Information (see above).

Resolutions of the General Conference of UNESCO

The General Conference of UNESCO has on several occasions passed resolutions pertaining to the task of this organization to *promote peace and international understanding*. For example, a resolution at the sixteenth session of the General Conference 1970:

> Deeming that information media should play an important part in furthering international understanding and cooperation in the interest of peace and human welfare; *affirms* the inadmissibility of using information media for propaganda on behalf of war, racialism and hatred among nations; and *invites* all states to take the necessary steps, including legislative measures, to encourage, the use of information media against propaganda on behalf of war, racialism and hatred among nations, and to provide Unesco with information on the subject.

The resolution also invited the Director-General of UNESCO to submit to the General Conference, at its seventeenth session, a report on existing legislation and measures taken by member states to encourage the *use of information media against propaganda on behalf of war, racialism, and hatred among nations* (Document 17 C/77 and Add.). At its seventeenth session (1972), the General Conference requested the Director-General

> to prepare and to submit to the General Conference at its eighteenth session a draft declaration concerning the fundamental principles governing the use of mass media with a view to strengthening peace and international understanding and combating war propaganda, racialism and apartheid.

This Draft Declaration was submitted to the General Conference at its eighteenth session in 1974, where it was decided to arrange a Meeting of Governmental Experts to further elaborate this Draft Declaration so as to have a final draft for the nineteenth session of the General Conference. However, this session in Nairobi in November 1976 did not reach an agreement on the issue, and the item was further postponed until the twentieth session in 1978.

At the eighteenth session of the General Conference the Director-General also submitted a report, entitled "Suggestions to Member States on Measures to Promote the Free Flow of Information and International Exchanges" (Document 18 C/90), which surveys the present situation in the field of communication and lists measures Member States might take to facilitate the flow of information and to encourage international exchanges. The measures suggested may be described as those aiming at the promotion of international understanding by positive measures, as opposed to those that aim at the prevention of actions by mass media that endanger international understanding. The report, however, in Paragraph 3 of its introduction, notes the following:

> The advent of global communication has naturally led to increasing concern with the content of what is being transmitted. In a world of crisis and change, the very instantaneity of modern means of transmission impels those concerned with the mass media to exercise a sense of responsibility commensurate with the vast audiences they command.

The Declaration of the Principles of International Cultural Cooperation

This Declaration was unanimously adopted by the General Conference of Unesco at its fourteenth session, on 4 November 1966, the twentieth anniversary of the foundation of the Organization. The Declaration was proclaimed "to the end that governments, authorities, organizations, associations and institutions responsible for cultural activities may constantly be guided by these principles." Its purpose is to advance "through the educational, scientific and cultural relations of the peoples of the world, the objectives of peace and welfare that are defined in the Charter of the United Nations."

Article I states that "each culture has a dignity and value which must be respected and preserved" and that "every people has the right and the duty to develop its culture." Article IV proclaims that "the aims of international cultural cooperation . . . shall be to spread knowledge . . . and . . . to enable everyone to have access to knowledge. . . ." Article VI affirms that "international cooperation, while promoting the enrichment of all cultures . . . shall respect the distinctive character of each." Article VII adds that "broad dissemination of ideas and knowledge, based on the freest exchange and discussion, is essential to creative activity, the pursuit of truth and the development of personality." Article VIII lays down the principle that "cultural cooperation shall be carried on for the mutual benefit of all nations" and that exchanges shall take place "in a spirit of broad reciprocity."

In this Declaration a large place is assigned to the mass media. Articles IX and VII of the Declaration are of special interest. Under Article IX cultural cooperation "shall contribute to the establishment of stable, long-term relations between peoples, which should be subjected as little as possible to the strains which may arise in international life." Paragraph 2 of Article VII reads as follows:

> In cultural cooperation, stress shall be laid on ideas and values conducive to the creation of a climate of friendship and peace. Any mark of hostility in attitudes and in expression of opinion shall be avoided. Every effort shall be made, in presenting and disseminating information, to ensure its authenticity.

The Declaration of Guiding Principles on the Use of Satellite Broadcasting for the Free Flow of Information, the Spread of Education, and Greater Cultural Exchange

This Declaration was proclaimed by the General Conference of UNESCO at its seventeenth session, on 15 November 1972.

The Declaration deals, in general, with mutual relations between countries in the development of satellite broadcasting, as based on the principles and rules of international law, particularly the Charter of the United Nations and the Outer Space Treaty (Article I).

Article III of this Declaration states that "the benefits of satellite broadcasting should be available to all countries without discrimination and regardless of their degree of development." Article IV affirms that "satellite broadcasting provides a new means of disseminating knowledge and promoting better understanding among peoples," and Article V goes on to say that "the objective of satellite broadcasting for the free flow of information is to ensure the widest possible dissemination, among the peoples of the world, of news of all countries, developed and developing alike." Article VII adds that "cultural programmes . . . should respect the distinctive character, the value and the dignity of each," and Article IX refers to "the principle of freedom of information."

In the preamble of this Declaration, the General Conference of UNESCO refers to the United Nations General Assembly Resolution 110(II) of 3 November 1947, condemning propaganda designed or likely to provoke or encourage any threat to the peace, breach of the peace, or act of aggression.

Paragraph 2 of Article IV of the Declaration states that the fulfillment of the potentialities of satellite broadcasting "requires that account be taken of the needs and rights of audiences, as well as the objectives of peace, friendship and cooperation between peoples, and of economic, social and cultural progress."

The second paragraph of Article V sets forth the following principle:

Satellite broadcasting, making possible instantaneous world-wide dissemination of news, requires that every effort be made to ensure the factual accuracy of the information reaching the public. News broadcasts shall identify the body which assumes responsibility for the news programme as a whole, attributing where appropriate particular news items to their source.

United Nations Instruments Concerning Direct Broadcasting Satellites

In 1963, the General Assembly unanimously adopted a resolution originally proposed by the Delegation of the U.S.S.R., entitled "Declaration of Legal

Principles Governing the Activities of States in the Exploration and Use of Outer Space.'' While this Declaration does not specify the new forms of mass communication facilitated by satellites beaming transmissions directly to home receivers, it does take account of the General Assembly Resolution 110(II) of 1947 and declares that it is also applicable to outer space.

Similarly, reference is made to the same General Assembly Resolution in the Treaty on Principles Governing the Activities of States in the Exploration and Use of Outer Space, including the moon and other celestial bodies. This so-called "Outer Space Treaty" was unanimously adopted in December 1966, and it entered into force on 10 October 1967. Like the earlier Declaration, the Treaty does not explicitly cover the use of satellites in mass communication, except in its preamble:

> Taking account of United Nations General Assembly Resolution 110(II) of 3 November 1947, which condemned propaganda designed or likely to provoke or encourage any threat to the peace, breach of the peace or act of aggression, and considering that the aforementioned resolution is applicable to outer space.

At the time of adoption of this Treaty, the United Nations Committee on the Peaceful Uses of Outer Space was given the mandate, by the General Assembly Resolution 2260 (XXII) 1967, to study the technical feasibility of direct broadcasting satellites and their implications. This task, carried out in 1969–74 within a special working group on direct broadcasting satellites, has, among other things, included consideration of program material and its compatibility with principles such as that covered by General Assembly Resolution 110 (II). Furthermore, the principle of freedom of information has been subjected, in this connection, to a new political and legislative deliberation, particularly with reference to the so-called "prior consent" issue—that is, whether or not transmissions over a direct broadcasting satellite from one country to another should take place only with the deliberate consent of the receiving State. The present chapter will not review the work carried out within the framework of the Outer Space Committee in greater detail (see, e.g., Signitzer, 1976).

In reference to the work performed by the Outer Space Committee, on direct broadcasting satellites, the General Assembly has passed Resolutions 2733 A (XXV) in 1970 and 2916 (XXVII) in 1972, stressing the potential of this technology for international understanding and a wider dissemination of information, but also urging the prevention of its use for transmission of programs promoting war, hatred, apartheid, and colonialism. Accordingly, the Legal Sub-Committee of the Outer Space Committee, in drafting a Convention on this matter, as called upon by the Resolution 2916 (XXVII), has formulated, in its fifteenth session (3–28 May 1976), the relevant purposes and objectives, by declaring that international activities in this field "should be carried out in a manner compatible with the development of mutual understanding and the strengthening of friendly relations and cooperation among all States and peoples in the interest of maintaining international peace and security."

REFERENCES

Eek, H. (1953). "Freedom of Information as a Project of International Legislation." Lundequistska Bokhandeln, Uppsala, Sweden.

Signitzer, B. (1976). "Regulation of Direct Broadcasting from Satellites: The U.N. Involvement." Praeger, New York.

Tomlinson, J. D. (1938). "The International Control of Radio-Communications." Journal de Genève, Geneva, Switzerland.

10

Some International Law Aspects of the Freedom of Information and the Right to Communicate

Leo Gross

Tufts University

Leo Gross is Professor Emeritus of International Law, The Fletcher School of Law and Diplomacy, Tufts University. He has been a Professor at the Fletcher School since 1944 and has held visiting professorships in universities in all parts of the world. Professor Gross has written papers and books on international law, the United Nations, and international cooperation and peace. He is the editor of *International Law in the Twentieth Century* and of *The Future of the International Court of Justice*. A volume of essays, *The Relevance of International Law* (Karl W. Deutsch and Stanley Hoffman, eds.), was published in his honor in 1968.

This contribution was commissioned and is copyrighted by the Edward R. Murrow Center of the Fletcher School of Law and Diplomacy, Tufts University, for its Conference on "The Third World and Press Freedom," May 11–13, 1977, Time-Life Building, New York. It is printed with permission of the author and the copyright holder.

This paper is intended to provide an overview of the legal framework—that is, the principles and rules of international law which may be applicable to the freedom of information, the "free flow" of information, and its postulated evolution from a "one-way" flow to a "balanced" or "two-way" flow in the name of the right to communicate. In the first part some observations will be made on the nature and basic principles of international law, which, although familiar to international lawyers, may provide useful background material for nonlawyers who are interested in the flow of information through the medium of newspapers, radio, or television. Next, the question will be examined whether the freedom of information and its ancillary "rights" are based on principles or rules of international law binding upon States. Finally, it may be helpful to indicate whether, in the absence of any such specific principles or rules concerning the media of information, there are any rules in neighboring areas, such as air and space law, which may be applicable to the flow of information across national boundaries.

I

International law has traditionally been perceived as regulating relations between States. While this has been, and still is, correct in the sense that States have the capacity to make and unmake international law, it has also been true that, at least in its modern era—which is usually traced to the Peace of Westphalia (1648)—international law has been concerned with individuals. Freedom of religion is a long-standing concern going back to that Peace. Increasingly, with the onset of the industrial revolution and the rapid increase in the movement of persons and goods across national boundaries, international law was the medium through which States attempted to facilitate such transnational activities. It could not be otherwise, since States have exclusive authority only within their territory. If transactions going beyond the territory of a State are to be regulated at all, the cooperation of two or more States is required. This is also true with respect to activities within the territory of a State, which are intended to produce, or which in fact *do* produce, an effect in the territory of another State. Thus, international law develops with, and depends on, the consent of two or more States and takes the form of a bilateral or multilateral treaty that usually requires ratification. This is called conventional international law. However, there is also customary international law, which emerges from the practice of states and their acceptance of such practice as binding.* The origin and evolution of customary international law has never been explained satisfactorily. While it may be a matter of controversy whether a certain principle or rule is or is not part of customary in-

---

*In a recent judgment (North Sea Continental Shelf, Judgement of February 20, 1969, I.C.J. *Reports*, 1969) the International Court of Justice emphasized these two requirements by stating that mere acts are not sufficient to establish a rule of customary international law. "For in order to achieve this result" said the Court,

> two conditions must be fulfilled. Not only must the acts concerned amount to a settled practice, but they must also be such, or be carried out in such a way, as to be evidence of a belief that this practice is rendered obligatory by the existence of a rule of law requiring it. The need for such a belief, i.e., the existence of a subjective element, is implicit in the very notion of the *opinio juris sive necessitatis*. The States concerned must therefore feel that they are conforming to what amounts to a legal obligation. The frequency, or even habitual character of the acts is not in itself enough. There are many international acts, e.g., in the field of ceremonial and protocol, which are performed almost invariably, but which are motivated only by considerations of courtesy, convenience or tradition, and not by any sense of legal duty. (p. 3, at 44, para. 77)

ternational law, there is no doubt that a body of customary international law exists. Thus, in the case of a dispute submitted to the International Court of Justice, the Court, "whose function is to decide in accordance with international law such disputes as are submitted to it," is directed to apply international conventions and "international custom, as evidence of a general practice accepted as law."*

It is important to bear in mind that since international law depends upon the consent or practice of two or more States,† the agreement of the States concerned is necessary in order to determine the meaning of a written or unwritten (customary) principle or rule and its applicability in a given situation. By common agreement, this function may be conferred by the States at variance on a tribunal of arbitration or the International Court of Justice, which renders a binding decision. Just as the rules require common consent for their creation, so they require common consent for their interpretation and application. Of course, States do hold views—sometimes very firm views—about their own rights and obligations and those of other States, but such views must be taken for what they are: views of interested parties. As such, they have no binding force for other States, they are autointerpretations. Before a tribunal or the Court they become allegations as to the facts and the law and are treated as such. However, it should be noted that resort to a tribunal or the Court is the exception and that States prefer to seek settlement of disputed facts or principles by diplomatic negotiations or to postpone solutions or, in some cases, to resort to unilateral action that may aggravate or stalemate the dispute.‡

*Article 38(1)b of the Statute of the Court, which is an integral part of the Charter of the United Nations. The Court is also directed to apply "the general principles of law recognized by civilized nations" and, as subsidiary means, the teachings "of the most highly qualified publicists of the various nations."

†This aspect of international law was formulated in the *Lotus* case, decided in 1927 by the Permanent Court of International Justice, the predecessor of the present Court, as follows (Publications of the *P.C.I.J.*, Ser. A, No. 10)

> International law governs relations between independent States. The rules of law binding upon States therefore emanate from their own free will as expressed in conventions or by usages generally accepted as expressing principles of law and established in order to regulate the relations between these coexisting independent communities or with a view to the achievement of common aims. Restrictions upon the independence of States cannot therefore be presumed. (p. 18)

‡Sir Gerald Fitzmaurice (1973) provides an explanation that seems very persuasive. Drawing upon his experience as legal adviser, he concludes that "apart from the natural reluctance to litigate felt by almost everyone, governments prefer to deal with disputes by political means rather than by submission to adjudication, and fight shy of the *commitment* involved by going to law: they dislike the loss of control that is entailed over the future of the case, the outcome of which they can no longer influence politically once it is before a court of law, since this will depend upon legal considerations with which they do not find themselves at home" (p. 279). It may well be that this fear of losing control is the most important psychological factor in determining the justiciability of disputes in the *subjective* sense (Gross, 1977, p. 210).

One of the characteristics of States in modern international law is their independence or sovereignty. This term has been much debated and frequently misunderstood. But as defined by a distinguished jurist (Separate Opinion of Judge Anzilotti in the Austro-German Customs Union case (1931), Publications of the *Permanent Court of International Justice*, Series A/B, No. 41, p. 57), sovereignty means "that the State has over it no other authority than that of international law." States, though sovereign, are not above the law but are bound by it.* This may seem like a truism, but in the rhetoric of states one frequently encounters the mistaken notion that the limitations that international law inevitably imposes upon States are somehow contrary to, or incompatible with, their sovereignty. But compliance with the law is inseparable from the very notion of international law. Thus the Charter of the United Nations, which declares, in Paragraph 1 of Article 2, that "the Organization is based on the principle of the sovereign equality of all its Members," also declares in Paragraph 2:

> All Members, in order to ensure to all of them the rights and benefits resulting from membership, shall fulfill in good faith the obligations assumed by them in accordance with the present Charter.

The duty to fulfill obligations in good faith applies, of course, not merely to the Charter but to all conventional and customary international law. The 1969 Vienna Convention on the Law of Treaties incorporates in Article 26 the customary rule of international law of *pacta sunt servanda*: "Every treaty in force is binding upon the parties to it and must be performed by them in good faith."

In the same vein, Section X of the Declaration on Principles Guiding Relations between Participating States in the Final Act of the 1975 Helsinki Conference on Security and Co-Operation in Europe, provides:

> The participating States will fulfill in good faith their obligations under international law, both those obligations arising from the generally recognized principles and rules of international law and those obligations arising from treaties or other agreements, in conformity with international law, to which they are parties.
>
> In exercising their sovereign rights, including the right to determine their laws and regulations, they will conform with their legal obligations under international law; they will furthermore pay due regard to and implement the provisions in the Final Act of the Conference on Security and Co-Operation in Europe. (Conference on Security and Co-Operation in Europe, p. 82)

---

*In a document prepared for the General Assembly by the International Law Commission (Draft Declaration on Rights and Duties of States, Article 14, GA Res. 375(IV), of Dec. 6, 1949, Annex), established by the Assembly for the progressive development and codification of international law, this point was formulated as follows: "Every State has the duty to conduct its relations with other States in accordance with international law and with the principle that the sovereignty of each State is subject to the supremacy of international law." Although the Assembly did not adopt the Draft Declaration, it deemed it "a notable and substantial contribution towards the progressive development of international law and its codification" and, as such, commended it "to the continuing attention of Member States and jurists of all nations."

It may be both useful and necessary to refer to two additional basic principles that may have a bearing on the freedom of information and the right to communicate. It is generally accepted that States may not invoke provisions of their internal law as justification for their failure to perform their obligations under treaties or under customary international law. This principle is incorporated in Article 27 of the 1969 Vienna Convention on the Law of Treaties with a qualification, which is not material here. The principle hardly needs elaboration or justification. Were it otherwise it would always be open to States to escape their obligations under international law by the simple act of changing their constitution or amending their legislation. This would spell the end of international law and usher in an era of anarchy. It is, therefore, of vital importance for all States who prefer international order to international anarchy to act in accordance with the "generally accepted principle of international law that in the relations between Powers who are contracting Parties to a treaty, the provisions of municipal law cannot prevail over those of the treaty" (The Greco-Bulgarian "Communities" case, Advisory Opinion of the *P.C.I.J.*, 1930. Publications of the *P.C.I.J.*, Series B, No. 17, p. 32).

The other principle of equal importance is known as domestic jurisdiction. In the absence of applicable principles or rules of customary and conventional international law, States are free to exercise their sovereignty within their territory. As the Permanent Court of International Justice stated in the *Lotus* case, cited above, "restrictions upon the independence of States cannot . . . be presumed." The principle of domestic jurisdiction is reinforced by the principle of nonintervention, which found expression in too many instruments to be examined here, including the Final Act of the Helsinki Conference (Conference on Security and Co-Operation in Europe, 1975). It provides in Section VI:

> The participating States will refrain from any intervention, direct or indirect, individual or collective, in the internal or external affairs falling within the domestic jurisdiction of another participating State, regardless of their mutual relations. . . . Accordingly, they will, *inter alia*, refrain from direct or indirect assistance to terrorist activities, or to subversive or other activities directed toward the violent overthrow of the regime of another participating State. (p. 80)

It is not clear what is meant by "external affairs falling within the domestic jurisdiction." (For a recent study of domestic jurisdiction, see Watson, 1977.)

It is a frequent error, in the rhetoric of Governments and jurists, to refer to domestic jurisdiction as "inherent" or "indivisible" or "inalienable." There is nothing inherent or indivisible about it. On the contrary, it is a relative principle. As the development of conventional law demonstrates, the area of domestic jurisdiction has been dramatically reduced. Suffice it to recall matters of security and finance, economics and communications, health and sanitation, and finally of human rights, which have become matters of international concern and regulation by treaty and even, as some argue with respect to human rights, by customary international law. The Permanent Court of International Justice, in a landmark case (Tunis-Morocco Nationality Decrees case, Advisory Opinion 1923, *P.C.I.J.*, Series B, No. 4, p. 24), correctly stated the principle saying:

> The question whether a matter is or is not solely within the jurisdiction of a State is an essentially relative question; it depends upon the development of international relations.

What is or is not within the domestic, that is, discretionary, jurisdiction,* depends not merely upon the state of development of international relations, but upon the States concerned. Thus, two or more States may enter into an agreement concerning freedom of the press, the gathering and transmission of news through specified media, or the admission or exchange of radio or television broadcasts. Between parties to such an agreement, these matters are no longer within their respective domestic jurisdiction. But the same matters remain within the domestic jurisdiction of States that have assumed no commitments in relation to other States. In short, it is not the nature of the subject matter that is decisive for answering the question whether it is or is not within domestic jurisdiction, but rather the existence or absence of treaty commitments or of a principle or rule of customary law. It may not be amiss to emphasize, since there is some confusion on this point, that in the absence of an obligation derived from customary or conventional international law, the State is "sole judge," even though the subject matter is of concern to other States or of international concern. It is always open to States to enter into agreements that serve their mutual interests. If there is no principle or rule by which a State binds itself in relation to another State, it may admit or exclude reporters or radio or television broadcasts as it may exclude any aliens or books or newspapers or raw materials or manufactured goods.

It may be noted that there were periods in the development of international relations when freedom of persons and goods prevailed in a substantial part of the world. In such time periods it was not only a fact of international life but one that was regarded as mutually beneficial. But, increasingly, laissez faire gave way to assertions of control and regulations, to what may be called "dirigisme." This has certainly been so since the end of World War I, and has become dominant since World War II, in spite of the unprecedented interdependence between the States and peoples of the world. The freedoms that were once taken for granted have become part and parcel of a continuing bargaining process between pairs of States, between groups of States, and between all States in the international system.

In this process, international organizations play a vital part. They offer a

---

*In the same case, the Court held that the clause in Article 15(8) of the Covenant of the League of Nations concerning matters "solely within the domestic jurisdiction" relates to "certain matters which, though they may very closely concern the interests of more than one State, are not, in principle, regulated by international law. As regards such matters, each State is sole judge."

convenient forum for large-scale conferences. This is particularly true of the United Nations and, in matters of culture and education, UNESCO. When deliberations in the United Nations or in UNESCO yield a convention or a treaty, such a convention or treaty will become binding on the States that sign and ratify or accept them in the usual way. But, on occasion, as a first step to a treaty, such as the 1967 Outer Space Treaty, the organization concerned merely adopts, by the requisite majority or unanimously, a resolution or declaration. The question then arises whether such resolutions or declarations are binding on members generally or on those who voted for them. There is also the question whether resolutions, such as the 1948 Universal Declaration of Human Rights, are or have become part of customary international law and therefore binding on all States. This question is of fundamental importance, as Article 19 of the Universal Declaration proclaims the freedom of information and, perhaps, even the right to communicate, and is regarded as the legal basis for the "free flow" of information through all media and across national boundaries.

II

In the current debate about freedom of information, Article 19 of the 1948 Universal Declaration of Human Rights occupies a central place. It states:

> Everyone has the right to freedom of opinion and expression; this right includes freedom to hold opinions without interference and to seek, receive and impart information and ideas through any media and regardless of frontiers.

Read in its ordinary meaning, this clause establishes one world for the purpose of receiving and imparting information as an individual right. It is clear from the text that there was no intent here to promote a one-way flow of information. On the contrary, flow in all directions and regardless of frontiers was the aim. That the flow of information has become one-sided in some parts of the world, and in relations between a number of States, is not due to Article 19 but to other factors that are well known. Article 19 was not designed to generate information, but merely to ensure its unobstructed flow in accordance with the law of the sending and receiving States. The latter condition, laid down in Article 29 of the Declaration,* is frequently overlooked,

---

*Article 29 reads as follows:

(1) Everyone has duties to the community in which alone the free and full development of his personality is possible.

(2) In the exercise of his rights and freedoms, everyone shall be subject only to such limitations as are determined by law solely for the purpose of securing due recognition and respect for the rights and freedoms of others and of meeting the just requirements of morality, public order and the general welfare in a democratic society.

(3) These rights and freedoms may in no case be exercised contrary to the purposes and principles of the United Nations.

but it is as much a part of the Declaration as is Article 19. This is not surprising, considering that the text of the Preamble proclaims the Declaration as "a common standard of achievement" and that the rights and freedoms enumerated in the Declaration should be secured "by their universal and effective recognition and observance" among the peoples of the Member States. Thus, the States are to provide for these freedoms, including Article 19, and the individuals enjoy them in virtue of, and within the limits of, national constitutions, laws, and legal traditions.

But did the Declaration impose a legal obligation on the States to adopt its rights and freedoms into their legal systems? If it did not, or if the States failed to enact implementing legislation, can individuals claim these rights directly from the Declaration? The latter question can be answered in the negative, although there were some cases in which it was invoked in a domestic court. But, in principle, such resolutions or declarations are not self-executing, and Article 29 (cited above) would support this conclusion.

The former question has been much debated in the literature, and the Declaration has often been described as binding in the discussions in the United Nations and elsewhere. Much has been made of the fact that the 1948 Declaration was recited in countless subsequent resolutions of the General Assembly. It has also been pointed out that it was adopted in the constitutions and the legislation of many States. Obviously this argument can equally well be turned around: the adoptions would indicate that the States concerned considered them necessary in order to make the Declaration applicable within their territories. It has also been argued that the Declaration implements the general provisions of the UN Charter that are binding on Members. This argument begs the question: do the provisions of the Charter relating to human rights

---

In a recent Soviet textbook, *International Space Law*, edited by A. S. Piradov, (1976), the following view on Article 19 is to be found:

> For over a quarter of a century legal scholars have now been arguing as to whether there is a universally recognised principle of the freedom of information in international law. The main argument of those who claim that there is such a principle is the fact that some declarations and conventions on protecting human rights contain provisions concerning the right of everyone freely "to seek, receive and impart information and ideas through any media and regardless of frontiers."
>
> These provisions, however, have a different meaning than that attributed to them by some legal experts and diplomats. To begin with, human rights are not in the full sense of the word international. The rights of citizens are regulated by the legislation of every state on a sovereign basis and independently of any external authority. Acts of international law relating to human rights merely imply the acceptance by states of certain general principles, which are to be reflected in their national legislation. The degree to which these general principles are taken into account and the form this takes can vary according to national, historical and other features. Article 28 of the Universal Declaration of Human Rights states that "everyone is entitled to a social and international order in which the rights and freedoms set forth in this Declaration can be fully realised." Obviously only each state itself can ensure a proper social order on its territory, and this applies to the mass media too. (p. 190)

impose obligations or are they, particularly Article 55, merely statements of objectives and purposes for achievement of which the Members, in Article 56, "pledge themselves to take joint and separate action in cooperation with the Organization"? The text supports an affirmative response to the latter.

Moreover, the Charter does not confer a legislative function or competence on the General Assembly. Apart from resolutions relating to the internal functions of the Organization, like admission of States to membership, adoption of the budget, and some similar matters, resolutions, even when they are called declarations in order to underscore their significance, are recommendations which do not bind the Members legally.

The General Assembly recently had occasion to discuss the question whether its resolutions are a distinct source of law which the International Court of Justice should apply in appropriate cases. The Assembly gave what appears to be a clearly evasive answer. It recognized in the Preamble of Resolution 3232(XXIX) of November 12, 1974:

> that the development of international law may be reflected inter alia, by declarations and resolutions of the General Assembly which may to that extent be taken into consideration by the International Court of Justice.

No doubt this is possible, but there must first be a development of international law in the usual way, that is, practice and the conviction that this has become legally binding. As the International Court of Justice pointed out in the *Continental Shelf* case, these two conditions must be satisfied. (See footnote on p. 196.)

Similar views were expressed as early as 1962 in a Memorandum of the Office of Legal Affairs of the UN Secretariat* and quite recently by Eric Suy, the Legal Counsel and Undersecretary-General of the United Nations.† It is

---

*In this Memorandum (U.N. Doc. E/CN.4/L.610, April 2, 1962), it was stated that a declaration "may impart, on behalf of the organ adopting it, a strong expectation that Members of the international community will abide by it. Consequently, insofar as the expectation is gradually justified by State practice, a declaration may by custom become recognized as laying down rules binding upon States" (pp. 1–2).

†In a letter to the *New York Times,* dated March 22, 1977, he wrote (Suy, 1977): "While it is clear that a General Assembly declaration does not have the force of law by the mere fact of adoption, it is possible that in the course of time such a declaration, if it reflects the legal conviction of states, may acquire the force of customary international law through state practice." Mr. Suy's letter was a written response to a letter by the former director of the Human Rights Division in the UN Secretariat, Mr. John P. Humphrey, in which he stated (Humphrey, 1977): "Whatever the intention of its authors may have been at the time, this declaration (of human rights) has, in the opinion of the most competent lawyers who have studied the matter, now become (insofar as the norms enunciated in it are justifiable) part of the customary law of nations and is therefore binding on all states, whether they voted for it or not." In support of Mr. Humphrey and disagreeing with Mr. Suy, Mr. K. Venkata Raman wrote to the *Times* (Raman, 1977): "The legal authority of the Universal Declaration rests in its relation to the U.N. Charter, which, as President Carter has rightly pointed out, is legally binding on every member government of the United Nations." For a more elaborate argument along these lines, see Buergenthal (1974) and Lee (1972). The concept of the "right to communicate" was formulated by Jean D'Arcy (1969) and has subsequently been expanded upon by writers such as Harms and Richstad (1975).

reasonably certain that the Universal Declaration has not yet become part of customary international law.

The 1948 Declaration was intended as the first stage in the process of formulating an obligatory international bill of rights. This process was completed in 1966 by the adoption of two instruments: the International Covenant on Economic, Social and Cultural Rights and the International Covenant on Civil and Political Rights, to which is attached an Optional Protocol. These Covenants and the Protocol entered into force on January 3, 1976 and on March 23, 1976, respectively. As of April 1977, forty-two States have become bound by the Economic Rights Covenant and thirty-nine States by the Civil and Political Rights Covenant and Protocol. The Optional Protocol has been ratified by thirteen States and three States, Denmark, Norway, and Sweden, made declarations under Article 41 of the Civil and Political Rights Covenant. Spain ratified both covenants (UN Press Release, W/812, April 29, 1977, p. 2).

The Protocol contains provisions for examining "communications from individuals claiming to be victims of violations of any of the rights set forth in the Covenant." Such communications and comments from the governments alleged to have committed violations will be considered by the Human Rights Committee established pursuant to Article 28 of the Civil and Political Rights Covenant. The Committee is to report on its activities to the General Assembly through the ECOSOC. The oversight provisions under this Protocol do not go very far, and their effectiveness remains to be tested. This Covenant also opens the way to State-to-State complaints for those parties to it that have made a declaration under Article 41. Such complaints are to be considered by the Human Rights Committee which will endeavor to resolve the matter. In case no solution is reached, the Committee may, pursuant to Article 42, and with the prior consent of the States Parties, establish a Conciliation Commission. The Commission shall seek a solution, but if no solution is reached, the Commission shall make a report. This shall include the findings on all questions of fact and the Commission's views "on the possibilities of an amicable solution of the matter" (Article 42, para. 7(c)). It is then open to the parties to accept the contents of the report. The effectiveness of this procedure is yet to be tested.

The Covenant on Economic, Social and Cultural Rights is generally considered the "softer" of the two Covenants for two reasons. First, it lacks any enforcement procedure whatsoever, and, second, it formulates rights that are to be secured by the action of the States Parties. However, in the current discussion on freedom of information, Article 15 should not be overlooked:

Article 15

1. The States Parties to the present Covenant recognize the right of everyone:
    (a) To take part in cultural life;
    (b) To enjoy the benefits of scientific progress and its applications;
    (c) To benefit from the protection of the moral and material interests resulting from

any scientific, literary or artistic production of which he is the author.

2. The steps to be taken by the States Parties to the present Covenant to achieve the full realization of this right shall include those necessary for the conservation, the development and the diffusion of science and culture.

3. The States Parties to the present Covenant undertake to respect the freedom indispensable for scientific research and creative activity.

4. The States Parties to the present Covenant recognize the benefits to be derived from the encouragement and development of international contacts and co-operation in the scientific and cultural fields.

The content of Articles 19 and 29 of the Universal Declaration, in a somewhat modified form, appear in Article 19 of the Civil and Political Rights Covenant, and this article includes some of the content of Article 29 of the Universal Declaration cited above. Article 20 of the Covenant is also relevant, as it appears to qualify the right to freedom of information laid down in Article 19. The text of these two articles is as follows:

Article 19

1. Everyone shall have the right to hold opinions without interference.

2. Everyone shall have the right to freedom of expression; this right shall include freedom to seek, receive and impart information and ideas of all kinds, regardless of frontiers, either orally, in writing or in print, in the form of art, or through any other media of his choice.

3. The exercise of the rights provided for in paragraph 2 of this Article carries with it special duties and responsibilities. It may therefore be subject to certain restrictions, but these shall only be such as are provided by law and are necessary:

    (a) For respect of the rights or reputations of others;

    (b) For the protection of national security or of public order (ordre public), or of public health or morals.

Article 20

1. Any propaganda for war shall be prohibited by law.

2. Any advocacy of national, racial or religious hatred that constitutes incitement to discrimination, hostility or violence shall be prohibited by law.

Two observations are in order. First, the right to freedom of information has now become part of a legally binding treaty for States that have, or will become, parties to the Covenant. Second, like Article 19 of the Universal Declaration, it offers a legal basis for a two-way flow of information. On the other hand, it is to be noted that it establishes the right for individuals, and it is not clear how far, if at all, it confers rights upon the *media themselves*; and also the net of possible legal restrictions (Article 19, para. 3(b) and Article 20) is cast very wide. The fact that a State, like the U.S.S.R., which has not been regarded in the West as a champion of the right to freedom of information, has become a party to the Covenant, may indicate its belief that it can live comfortably with Article 19. On the other hand, this fact may also be seen as a token of willingness to bring the Soviet Union closer to the basic requirements of the right to freedom of information.

Clearly, if nothing else, Article 19 offers a legal basis for promoting the freedom of information on the international plane. How useful it will prove to be depends on the number of States that ratify or accede to the Covenant. If the United States takes the freedom of information and other rights seriously and desires to play a significant role in their application, it must ratify the Covenant and Protocol and also make the optional declaration under Article 41 of the former. President Carter signed the two Covenants on behalf of the United States on October 5, 1977 (*New York Times,* October 6, 1977, p. A2).

The 1966 Civil and Political Covenant was in the works for nearly two decades and does not reflect the emerging concern with one-, two-, or multiple-way flow of information in its wider sense. Notably absent is a specific reference to what is called the "right to communicate." It has already been suggested that this right may conveniently be seen as included in the formulation given to the right to freedom of information in Article 19 of the Covenant.

It is interesting to note that the right to communicate is also absent from the more recent Final Act of the Helskinki Conference. To be sure, there is nothing in the "Third Basket" that could be construed as an endorsement of the one-way flow of information. Nor is there anything that could be construed as an endorsement of the two-way flow. Like the 1948 Universal Declaration the "Third Basket" is a statement of aims and objectives, and as such it lacks the specificity normally associated with legal prescriptions. There is, however, no doubt that Parts 2 and 3 entitled "Information" and "Co-operation and Exchanges in the Field of Culture," respectively, are imbued with the spirit of mutuality and mutual agreement. They offer some guidance for the future collaboration between States represented at the Helsinki Conference, as well as between States in all parts of the world.

III

The proposition that has been basic to the argument presented so far is that, in principle, States are sovereign under international law. The area of their discretionary jurisdiction depends upon the development of customary and conventional international law. A State does not have to prove that it is free to act in certain matters, but it has to prove that there are no limitations placed upon its freedom to act either by customary international law or by conventions to which it is a party. It is important to recall that a State's view on its legal rights or obligations is not conclusive. Freedom to receive and impart information across national boundaries, even if it were established as a principle of customary international law, would still be subject to State regulation. It has been admitted that the limitations imposed by international law upon a State's regulatory authority are ill defined (see Buergenthal, 1974, pp. 83–84)—so that, in practice, the freedom may be reduced to the vanishing point.

Without pretending at a detailed analysis, some general observations may be suggested, especially with respect to radio and television broadcasts.

It has already been said that States are sovereign over their territory. It has to be added now that States are also sovereign in the air space above their territory and their territorial waters.* This principle was first forumulated by the Paris Convention for the Regulation of Aerial Navigation of October 13, 1919. It provides that "every State has complete and exclusive sovereignty in the air space above its territory and territorial waters." The principle was restated in the Chicago Convention on International Civil Aviation of 1944 as follows:

Article 1

The contracting States recognize that every State has complete and exclusive sovereignty over the airspace above its territory.

Article 2

For the purposes of this Convention the territory of a State shall be deemed to be the land areas and territorial waters adjacent thereto under the sovereignty, suzerainty, protection or mandate of such State.

The effect of these principles has been summed up in a leading treatise (Oppenheim, 1955) as follows:

The principle of exclusive sovereignty in the air space for the subjacent State, which has received general approval in connection with aerial navigation, enables that State to prohibit the disturbance of the air space over its territory by means of Herzian waves caused for the purpose of wireless communication and emanating from a foreign source. (p. 529)

But this principle has been limited by several telecommunication conventions and by radio regulations of a general and regional character.

Controversies have arisen over the right of a State to "jam" broadcasts emanating from other countries.† The United States Department of State con-

---

*There is a good deal of controversy about the extent of territorial waters. They range from three to twelve miles and more. The Third Law of the Sea Conference, in progress since 1974, may produce an agreement on this matter.

†"Jamming" has been defined as "the deliberate use of interfering radio signals from one or more transmitters to garble legitimate emissions from other transmitters in order to make them unintelligible at reception" (letter by Assistant Chief of Telecommunications Policy Staff (Lebel), Department of State, of August 30, 1950. 13 Whiteman, *Digest of International Law*, p. 1030). In its Draft Convention of 1972 (see p. 213), the Soviet Union included Article IX, worded as follows:

1. Any State Party to this Convention may employ the means at its disposal to counteract illegal television broadcasting of which it is the object, not only in its own territory but also in outer space and other areas beyond the limits of the national jurisdiction of any State.

2. States Parties to this Convention agree to give every assistance in stopping illegal television broadcasting.

sidered the jamming of the Voice of America "unlawful" as such, because it is claimed to be contrary to Article 44 of the Atlantic City Telecommunications Convention of 1947 (Article 48 of the 1965 Montreux Convention) and Article 3 of the Radio Regulations, which prohibit "harmful interference" to radio services of Members. However, referring to the U.S.S.R. jamming, the Department stated that "an additional factor enters into the problem, namely, the nature and the extent of the right of a sovereign government to prevent the broadcasting into its territory of information which, for reasons of its own, that government deems harmful to its national interest." The Department of State went on to say (see Whiteman, cited in fn.†, p. 207):

> On this question there appears to exist no specific or formal limitations under international law to the action which a sovereign government can take.
>
> Where a government resorts to jamming of incoming radio signals to prevent such "harmful" information from reaching its territory, it is theoretically confined in that process to the use of signals which will cause no harmful interference *outside its territory*. I use the expression "theoretically confined" because it is obviously not possible technically to generate a radio signal which will completely blanket incoming radio broadcasts up to a point coinciding exactly with the national boundaries, and yet will have no appreciable effect immediately beyond that point. But it is possible to limit the geographical range of the jamming radiations to a fairly well defined distance beyond the borders, while accomplishing the desired purpose within the national territory. (pp. 1031–32)

It is unnecessary for the purpose of this paper to examine the technical provisions of the Radio Regulations on "unnecessary transmission" and "harmful interference." It is sufficient to note the admission that there are no "formal limitations" on the action a sovereign government may take against transmissions it deems to constitute "unnecessary transmission" and "harmful interference" or just plain propaganda. It may well be that further technological progress will enable jamming to be carried out by a State in a "theoretically confined" area, that is, within the confines of its territory. In any event, the U.S. was not required to accept the Soviet view on the matter any more than the Soviet Union was required to accept as correct the U.S. view.

In this particular case, the United States found ample support in the United Nations. First, the ECOSOC Sub-Committee on Freedom of Information, then ECOSOC, and finally the General Assembly adopted resolutions in which mention was made of General Assembly Resolution 59(I),* Article 19 of the

---

*This resolution, adopted on December 14, 1946, called for the convocation of a conference on freedom of information. The Preamble, however, is still of interest and is as follows:

THE GENERAL ASSEMBLY,
WHEREAS   .

Freedom of information is a fundamental human right and is the touchstone of all the freedoms to which the United Nations is consecrated;

Freedom of information implies the right to gather, transmit and publish news anywhere and everywhere without fetters. As such it is an essential factor in any serious effort to promote the peace and progress of the world;

1948 Universal Declaration, and Article 44 of the Atlantic City Telecommunications Convention. General Assembly resolution 424(V) of December 14, 1950 continued as follows:

> *Considering* that the duly authorized radio operating agencies in some countries are deliberately interfering with the reception by the people of those countries of certain radio signals originating beyond their territories, and bearing in mind the discussion which took place in the Economic and Social Council and in the Sub-Commission on Freedom of Information and of the Press on this subject,
>
> *Considering* that peace among nations rests on the goodwill of all peoples and governments and that tolerance and understanding are prerequisites for establishing goodwill in the international field,
>
> 1. *Adopts* the declaration of the Economic and Social Council contained in its resolution 306 B (XI) of 9 August 1950 to the effect that this type of interference constitutes a violation of the accepted principles of freedom of information;
>
> 2. *Condemns* measures of this nature as a denial of the right of all persons to be fully informed concerning news, opinions and ideas regardless of frontiers;
>
> 3. *Invites* the governments of all Member States to refrain from such interference with the right of their peoples to freedom of information;
>
> 4. *Invites* all governments to refrain from radio broadcasts that would mean unfair attacks or slanders against other peoples anywhere and in so doing to conform strictly to an ethical conduct in the interest of world peace by reporting facts truly and objectively;
>
> 5. *Invites* also Member States to give every possible facility so that their peoples may know objectively the activities of the United Nations in promoting peace and, in particular, to facilitate the reception and transmission of the United Nations official broadcasts.*

This vigorous endorsement of the principles of freedom of information is somewhat qualified by Paragraph 4. Who is to judge the contents of the broadcasts? "Unfair attacks or slanders" and "ethical conduct" are rather broad concepts lacking objective definitions. And, as suggested above, General Assembly resolutions do not make law. Moreover, the Assembly, marching to a different drummer, adopted in 1972 Resolution 2916(XXVII) which is greatly more restrictive.† Be that as it may, the attempt to base the illegal-

---

Freedom of information requires as an indispensable element the willingness and capacity to employ its privileges without abuse. It requires as a basic discipline the moral obligation to seek the facts without prejudice and to spread knowledge without malicious intent;

Understanding and co-operation among nations are impossible without an alert and sound world opinion, which, in turn, is wholly dependent upon freedom of information;

*Jens Evensen (1965) commented on this resolution as follows: "Such allegations may admittedly be commendable de lege ferenda; but to maintain that these views express prevailing rules of international law, is probably not tenable" (p. 560). Similar views were expressed more explicitly by O'Connell (1965): "There is no duty on a State not to resort to *jamming of radio* broadcasts from other States. Sometimes the right to jam is explained as an act of self-defense, but it is preferable to treat it as an act of sovereignty, unless there is some treaty requirement favorable to free transmisssion . . . . Various United Nations organs have condemned the practice but this is not law-creative" (p. 331). Views of several writers on the subject will be found in Whiteman, *Digest of International Law,* pp. 265–271.

† See p. 213.

ity of jamming on, and to derive support for the free flow of information into the territory of another State without its consent from, telecommunication conventions does not appear persuasive. In the first place, these conventions are designed to ensure the enjoyment of radio broadcasts *within* a State's territory. Second, the reliance on the prohibition of harmful interference which pervades applicable conventions begs the question, for this principle, as defined in Article 35 of the 1973 Telecommunication Convention of Madrid-Torremolinos, protects only States which themselves "operate in accordance with the provisions of the Radio Regulations."*

The most recent area of international regulation is outer space. This will be briefly examined in order to determine whether the space law provides a new basis for freedom or free flow of information irrespective of state sovereignty and the right of excluding harmful or undesirable messages.

The Treaty on Principles Governing the Activities of States in the Exploration and Use of Outer Space, Including the Moon and Other Celestial Bodies, was adopted by General Assembly Resolution 2222(XXI) on January 25, 1967. Unlike the conventions on air discussed above, the Space Treaty proclaims the freedom of outer space in Article 1(2): "Outer space, including the Moon and other celestial bodies, shall be free for exploration and use by all States without discrimination of any kind, on a basis of equality and in accordance with international law, and there shall be free access to all areas of celestial bodies." Although there is no provision in the Space Treaty relating directly to the current controversy about satellite broadcasting, the reference to international law in Article 1 is probably significant. Of potential significance are several other provisions in Articles 3, 6, and 9.

Article 3 stipulates a duty for States Parties that the use of outer space shall be carried out "in accordance with international law, including the Charter of the United Nations, in the interest of maintaining peace and security and promoting international co-operation and understanding."

Article 6 stipulates the international responsibility of States Parties for the activities carried out "by governmental agencies or by non-governmental entities, and for assuring that national activities are carried out in conformity with the provisions set forth in the present Treaty." The activities of non-governmental entities "in outer space . . . shall require authorization and continuing supervision by the appropriate State Party to the Treaty."

Article 9 requires that all activities in outer space shall be conducted "with due regard to the corresponding interests of all other States Parties to the

---

*Annex 2 of this Convention defines "harmful interference" as "any emission, radiation or induction which endangers the functioning of a radio navigation service or of any safety service, or seriously degrades, obstructs or repeatedly interrupts a radio communication service operating in accordance with the Radio Regulations." In Article 19 of the Convention, Members reserve the right to stop any private telegram and "to cut off any other private telecommunications which appear dangerous to the security of the State or contrary to their laws, to public order or to decency."

Treaty." It then goes on to lay down the requirement of consultation in case of harmful interference in these words:

If a State Party to the Treaty has reason to believe that an activity or experiment planned by it or its nationals in outer space, including the moon and other celestial bodies, would cause potentially harmful interference with activities of other States Parties in the peaceful exploration and use of outer space, including the moon and other celestial bodies, it shall undertake appropriate international consultations before proceeding with any such activity or experiment. A State Party to the Treaty which has reason to believe that an activity or experiment planned by another State Party in outer space, including the moon and other celestial bodies, would cause potentially harmful interference with activities in the peaceful exploration and use of outer space, including the moon and other celestial bodies, may request consultation concerning the activity or experiment.

The provision for consultations does not ensure that agreement will be reached, but if none is reached, the States concerned will act in accordance with their own conception of their rights and obligations. It must, of course, be clearly understood that such autointerpretations have no binding force.

The references to international law and the Charter of the United Nations may include both formal and substantive principles. Insofar as the content of television or radio transmission is concerned, it is well to recall that, under international law, States have the right of self-determination. Pursuant to it, the States are free to adopt political, economic, social, and cultural policies and systems of their own choosing. This is expressly incorporated in Article 1(1) of both International Covenants of 1966.* The right of self-determination of States is not to be confused with the controversial right to self-determination of peoples.

The principle of freedom of outer space like the freedom of the high seas has its limits. Just as the freedom of the high seas ends where the territorial sea begins, so freedom of outer space ends where the territorial air space begins. But whereas there is a right of innocent passage through the territorial sea there is no such right through territorial air space. The right of innocent passage does not include, apart from some exceptions, the right for ships to enter ports without the consent of the territorial State. Similarly the use of outer space for satellite broadcasting does not include the right to enter the territorial air space or the territory of the subjacent State. If it is conceded, as in the present submission it must be, that a State may exclude radio transmissions, then it must also be conceded that it may exclude television broadcasts. It is always open to States to negotiate agreements for opening up access to their territories for radio and for television broadcasts. Some States have done so. Other States have not opposed it, but without any sense of legal obliga-

---

*The text is as follows: "All peoples have the right of self-determination. By virtue of that right they freely determine their political status and freely pursue their economic, social and cultural development." It would have been more appropriate to say that "states" have this right, as international law deals with states and not peoples.

tion. There is as yet no general agreement on the subject.

However, the usual procedure of preparing the ground for a binding treaty on satellite broadcasting through nonbinding resolutions has been under way for several years. Without any pretense at comprehensiveness, one or two resolutions will be mentioned. One is the "Declaration of Guiding Principles on the Use of Satellite Broadcasting for the Free Flow of Information, the Spread of Education and Greater Cultural Exchange" adopted on November 15, 1972, by the General Conference of UNESCO. (UNESCO: General Conference, 17th sess., Paris, 17 Oct.–21 Nov., 1972, Vol. I Resolutions and Recommendations, pp. 67–69.)

The 1972 UNESCO Declaration, while recognizing in Article V "the free flow of information" as the objective for satellite broadcasting and the principle of freedom of information in Article IX, also calls for respect for "the sovereignty and equality of all States." It contains suggestions for greater attention to the culture and degree of development of different countries. Article VI stresses "the right" of each country, "to decide on the content of the educational programmes broadcast by satellite to its people." Article IX(1), not surprisingly, spells out the requirement of consent:

> In order to further the objectives set out in the preceding articles, it is necessary that States, taking into account the principle of freedom of information, reach or promote prior agreements concerning satellite broadcasting to the population of countries other than the country of origin of the transmission.

This may be utterly unacceptable to advocates of "freedom of trade" and freedom of competition, but it is merely an application to new technology of a well-settled principle of international law. As noted earlier, since World War I there has been a trend away from free trade toward protectionism and, at most, "freer trade." Protectionism has frequently been justified in terms of the need to protect "infant industries." Today, cultural protectionism may similarly be supported by developing countries in terms of the perceived need to protect "infant cultures." Saying this is not necessarily approving it. It is certainly arguable that all States and peoples stand to gain from a balanced multilevel exchange of programs that respects national susceptibilities, perhaps even idiosyncracies.*

In the United Nations, the Soviet Union on August 9, 1972, introduced a "Draft Convention on Principles Governing the Use by States of Artificial Earth Satellites for Direct Television Broadcasting" (Doc. A/8771. GAOR: 27th sess., Agenda items 28, 29 and 37, Annexes, pp. 1–5). The outcome of

---

*The case for "cultural protectionism" is examined and rejected by Hargrove (1974). The current demands for the protection of the steel, television, shoe, and garment industries in the United States come inevitably to mind.

the debate was Resolution 2916(XXVII) of November 9, 1972, which noted the draft convention and, in its operative part, requested the Committee on the Peaceful Uses of Outer Space to undertake the elaboration of principles for a convention on direct television broadcasting.* In the Preamble, the General Assembly expressed its belief that such broadcasting "must be based on the principles of mutual respect for sovereignty, non-interference in domestic affairs, equality, co-operation and mutual benefit." It also considered that satellite broadcasting "could raise significant problems connected with the need to ensure the free flow of communications on a basis of strict respect for the sovereign rights of States." In this connection it is important to note that Article IX of the Soviet Draft Convention extended the protective principle from the air to outer space in providing:

1. Any State Party to this Convention may employ the means at its disposal to counteract illegal television broadcasting of which it is the object, not only in its own territory but also in outer space and other areas beyond the limits of the national jurisdiction of any State.
2. States Parties to this Convention agree to give every assistance in stopping illegal television broadcasting. Under Article V of the proposed Soviet Convention direct television broadcasting would be illegal if carried out without the consent of the State concerned. Any transmission of television broadcasts would also be illegal if contrary to substantive limitations on content which are indicated in broadly inclusive terms in Article IV and VI.

The United States, which cast the only negative vote against the resolution, insisted in the debate that the resolution "does not put sufficient emphasis on the central importance of the free flow of information and ideas in the modern world," and that "in actual practice the sovereignty of States and the unimpeded flow of information and ideas should complement rather than conflict with one another" (GAOR: 27th sess., Plenary, 2081st mtg., Nov. 9, 1972, p. 5).

The most recent document in this series is the "Draft Declaration of Fundamental Principles Governing the Use of the Mass Media in Strengthening Peace and International Understanding and in Combating War, Propaganda, Racism and Apartheid" submitted to the UNESCO General Conference at its Nineteenth Session in Nairobi in 1976 (Enclosure IV 19C, 19C/91, 1 July 1976). The consideration of this draft declaration was postponed. It is a politicized draft, including pronouncements and cross-references to highly objectionable resolutions of the General Assembly of the United Nations. Its emphasis is particularly strong on national sovereignty, noninterference, "the existing disequilibrium in the circulation of information" from developing countries, and the achievement of "a balanced exchange of information" (Ar-

*A legal unit of the Committee met in New York in March/April 1977. U.N. Press Release WS/806, 18 March 1977, p. 6, and WS/810, 15 April 1977, p. 4.

ticle IV). It also would make it a duty for mass media to promote the realization "of a new international economic order" (Article VII). It calls on "professional organizations in the field of mass communication to define and promote standards of professional ethics on a national and international level" (Article XI). Finally, it declares in Article XII: "States are responsible for the activities in the international sphere of all mass media under their jurisdiction."

Obviously this declaration, even if adopted, would have no binding force (see Opening Address by Mr. John E. Fobes, Deputy Director-General of UNESCO, Annex II, Appendix 1, p. 3 of the document cited), and it may be possible that it is ultra vires the competence of UNESCO. However, while in some parts the draft declaration may reflect, albeit in a somewhat exaggerated form, the principles of international law discussed above, it is indicative of a strong tendency in the direction of "dirigisme," or state control. The principle of State responsibility is well known in international law, and the Space Treaty incorporates it in Article 6, but only with reference to activities by nongovernmental entities. The proposed Article XII would extend it to activities of all media, notably the press, an extension that is bound to meet with strong opposition of the proponents of the free press. The intended objective of the draft declaration may well be the controlled flow of controlled information. States are free to choose the sociopolitical system under which they wish to live, but there is no reason why States attached to the principles of freedom of thought and of expression and the free flow of information should participate in attempts to subvert them. In this context, the following statement by Piradov (1976) is of interest:

> This leads to the conclusion that in international relations there does not exist—and cannot be established in the present circumstances—any universally recognised principle of the freedom of mass information. This being so, the problem of the freedom of information requires a new approach, with due consideration for the changes that have taken place in international law over the past 25 years. It appears that the international community requires not so much the adoption of a covenant on the freedom of information as criteria defining the rights and obligations of states in the process of their use of the international mass media.
>
> The specific features of direct TV broadcasting require the framing of special legal rules to give more precise definition to the rights and obligations of states in this sphere of activities.
>
> The most important legal aspects of direct TV broadcasting are, in our view, agreement to ban direct TV broadcasts for foreign populations without the explicit consent of the governments of the states concerned; an unconditional ban on the use of direct TV broadcasts for the propaganda of war, militarism, racism, and other ideas condemned by international law, or for interference in the internal affairs of states; recognition of the international responsibility of states for the contents of direct TV broadcasts conducted either by governmental or nongovernmental organisations; the solution of the problems involved in the possible unpremeditated emergence of direct TV broadcast signals beyond the boundaries of the states co-operating in this field; the allocation of sections of the synchronous equatorial (geostationary) orbit, most convenient for deploying broadcasting satellites, and

an unconditional ban on the use of subliminal techniques in direct TV broadcasting. (pp. 192ff.)

It is not the purpose of this paper to discuss ways and means for promoting a balanced flow of information on which there is an ample literature. It may well be, as suggested earlier, that a case can be made for protecting "infant industries" in the field of press, radio, and television. Perhaps a more sustained effort in this direction will be made when it is realized that "protectionism" in its widest sense is not at all incompatible with existing customary international law, although, insofar as real goods are concerned, a host of bilateral and multilateral agreements among compatible States have smoothed the rough edges of national sovereignty. It has often been said that national sovereignty is the greatest obstacle to progress. But the radical alternative, a world state, is still beyond the horizon. Thus, there are only palliatives to think about, and one of them is to try to work within the system. Radicals of all States have rejected this approach as unacceptable. But, for responsible governments, there is no other.

REFERENCES

Buergenthal, T. (1974). The right to receive information across national boundaries. *In* "Control of the Direct Broadcast Satellite: Values in Conflict." (Aspen Institute Program on Communications and Society, in Association with the Office of External Research, Department of State), pp. 73–84. Aspen Institute Program on Communications and Society, Palo Alto, California.

Conference on Security and Co-Operation in Europe. (1975). "Conference on Security and Co-Operation in Europe, Final Act, Helsinki, 1975." U.S. Government Printing Office, Washington, D.C. (Department of State Publication 8826, General Foreign Policy Series 298.)

D'Arcy, J. (1969). Direct broadcast satellites and the right to communicate. *EBU Review* No. 118B, 14f.

Evensen, J. (1965). Aspects of international law relating to modern radio communications. *In* Hague Academy of International Law, "Recueil des Cours," Vol. II, pp. 471–583. Sijthoff, Leyden, The Netherlands.

Fitzmaurice, G. (1973). "The Future of Public International Law and of the International Legal System in the Circumstances of Today." Special Report, Livre du Centenaire 1873–1973, pp. 196–328. Institut de Droit International.

Fitzmaurice, G. (1976). Enlargement of the contentious jurisdiction of the court. *In* "The Future of the International Court of Justice" (L. Gross, ed.) pp. 461–498. Oceana Publications, Dobbs Ferry, New York.

Gross, L. (1953). States as organs of international law and the problem of autointerpretation. *In* "Law and Politics in the World Community." (G. A. Lipsky, ed.), pp. 59–88. University of California Press, Berkeley, California.

Gross, L. (1977). On the justiciability of international disputes. *In* "A Tribute to Hans Morgenthau." (K. Thompson and R. J. Myers, eds.). New Republic Book Company, Washington, D.C.

Hargrove, J. L. (1974). International law and the case for cultural protectionism. *In* "Control of the Direct Broadcast Satellite: Values in Conflict." (Aspen Institute Program on Communications and Society, in Association with the Office of External Research, Department of State), pp. 85–96. Aspen Institute Program on Communications and Society, Palo Alto, California.

Harms, L. S., and Richstad, J. (1975). Human rights, major communications issues, communication policies and planning—and the right to communicate. *In* "The Global Context for the Formation of Domestic Communications Policy," pp. 55–62. International Broadcast Institute, London.

Humphrey, J. P. (1977). Human rights: The "weak" U.N. Covenant. *New York Times* March 20, p. E16.

Lee, L. T. (1972). Law, human rights and population: A strategy for action. *Virginia Journal of International Law 12*, 309–325.

O'Connell, D. P. (1965). "International Law," Vol. I. Oceana Publications, Dobbs Ferry, New York.

Oppenheim, L. (1955). "International Law" (H. Lauterpacht, ed.), Vol. I, 8th ed. McKay, New York.

Piradov, A. S., ed. (1976). "International Space Law." Progress Publishing, Moscow.

Raman, K. V. (1977). World human rights: The binding declaration. *New York Times* April 7, p. A24.

Suy, E. (1977). A powerful influence. *New York Times*, April 1, p. A28.

Watson, J. S. (1977). Autointerpretation, competence, and the continuing validity of Article 2(7) of the Charter. *American Journal of International Law 71*, 60–84.

11

Hostile International Propaganda and International Law

John B. Whitton

Princeton University

Before his recent death, **John B. Whitton** had been Professor Emeritus of International Law at Princeton University, where he had taught politics and international law for thirty-three years. He founded the Princeton Listening Center for the Study of Political Broadcasting in 1939 and was the author of many papers on propaganda and international law. Dr. Whitton was also the author of a book entitled, *Propaganda and International Law*, and the coauthor of *Propaganda: Toward Disarmament in the War of Words*.

This paper was first published in 1971 and is reprinted from "Hostile International Propaganda and International Law," by John B. Whitton in *The Annals of The American Academy of Political and Social Science,* Volume 398. © 1971, by The American Academy of Political and Social Science. All rights reserved.

Given the decentralized nature of the international community, compliance with international norms related to propaganda is today largely voluntary, except when precarious and highly unreliable measures of retaliation and self-help can be utilized. In this situation, interpretation of the law is too often subjective and self-serving. States, great and small, eschew proposals for effective limitations on international communication because they hold propaganda to be a valuable weapon of power. In fact, for the small state, ideological warfare may be its only weapon in the absence of other capabilities, military, economic, and diplomatic. Soviet Russia counts heavily on propaganda to spread communism; the West employs it in retaliation and self-defense. Moscow claims to favor rules against war propaganda, but not if the conflict in question is an "anti-colonial war" or for one of "liberation" as she defines these terms. Free states, in principle, support measures against hostile propaganda, but resist proposed controls, both legal and administrative, for fear of encroaching on sacred principles of freedom of speech and of the press. If, in some ideal world, agencies for the interpretation of the norms here considered did exist, the judges thereof would be hard put to differentiate between education, information, and propaganda, or to trace the frontier between persuasion and coercion, or for that matter between fair comment and impermissible defamation. In our real world such agencies do not exist, although in this matter the United Nations and the Organization of American States have great potentialities—unfortunately not yet realized. Hence, too often what on our side is accepted as a statement of the facts concerning social and political conditions in a given country will be keenly resented there as false and slanderous. Given the presence of intolerable violations of human rights for which a country is responsible, such ''propaganda'' really amounts to disciplinary/corrective action and even, *faute de mieux*, has the elements of valuable international legislation (Falk, 1968, pp. 354–68; Murty, 1968, pp. 174–76).

These difficulties, which can only be suggested here, present a grave challenge to the students of world law and international organization. Until some progress is made in resolving them, the existing rules and principles governing international communication cannot be expected to moderate the dangers of propaganda. These norms will now be discussed.

SUBVERSIVE PROPAGANDA

> Our armies are at your frontiers. They bring war to tyrants, liberty to citizens. Take a stand! May the Belgian lion wake up! People of Belgium, we vow to make you free!
> (Sorel, 1885–1904, Vol. 2, p. 217; Vol. 4, p. 164)

In this early appeal for revolt, issued in 1792 by the French revolutionary forces, the nature and purpose of subversive propaganda are clearly evident. We refer to communications directed from one country to another with the hope of causing in the target state a movement to overthrow the existing political order. Of all categories of hostile propaganda, this has been the most frequent, the most deeply feared and resented, and the greatest cause of friction and retaliation—from diplomatic protest to actual warfare.

There are three main categories of this ''ideological warfare,'' although they may at times overlap.

First, certain communications are designed to spread a new, revolutionary ideology and form of government by inciting foreign peoples to revolt and to replace their governing elite by one similar to that of the communicator. The subversive appeals of the French Revolutionists, of which we have just given an example, spread resentment and fear throughout Europe and led to numerous protests. Undoubtedly the greatest apparatus for subversive intrigue and communication has been that organized by Soviet Russia, which has been active throughout Europe and the entire world, directed and carried out not only in Moscow but in all the satellite countries (Barghoorn, 1964). Castro's appeals by press, radio, and agents to other American countries are another example.

A second category of subversive propaganda is what can be called *liberation propaganda*. Here the ideological element is lacking, but a new element, irrendentism, may be equally impassioned and violent. For example, Cavour's appeals to the "unredeemed" Italian territories played an important role in his successful drive for the unification of Italy (Matter, 1925–27, Vol. 3, p. 35). Since World War II, American propaganda over Radio Free Europe has been considered by many as encouraging Hungary, for example, to liberate itself from the Soviet yoke (Holt, 1958). Washington would prefer to treat these programs as mere information, but Moscow has attacked them as subversive and illegal.

Another type of subversion through communication is not motivated by an ideology, nor aimed directly at liberating a captive people yearning for independence. In this category the communicator uses disruptive techniques as a means of weakening or dividing a people marked for conquest, or to gain prestige, influence, or power in the grim game of international politics. Thus, Hitler used both radio and underground agents to sap the strength of Czechoslovakia as a prelude to Munich, a power play masked as a type of irrendentism directed toward the Sudetenland (Childs and Whitton, 1942, pp. 1–108; Kris and Speier, 1944). Many of the virulent appeals exchanged by Arab rulers since World War II, while subversive in aim, were really designed to serve some ambitious plan nourished in the mind of an aggressive ruler.

Subversive appeals for revolt originating in a foreign state have long been considered by governing elites to be disruptive and thus dangerous, and have been resisted, even by forceful action; but they have also been held to be illegal. Thus, Vattel (1916) wrote in the eighteenth century: ". . . it is unlawful for Nations to do any act tending to create trouble to another state, to stir up discord, to corrupt its citizens, to alienate its allies . . ." (Bk. 2, Chap. 1, Sec. 18). But a specific norm proscribing incitement by ideological appeals to rebellion did not evolve until the French Revolution, to become firmly established in the course of the nineteenth century. It developed as a product of power politics, notably out of the various incidents of attempted subversion by great powers affecting small states marked out as spheres of influence or even for conquest. (Martin, 1958, pp. 172–198). Subversive propaganda was later of extreme importance as a factor in the immediate origins of the First World War, when Serbia directed irredentist appeals to Bosnia and Herzegovina (Martin, 1958, p. 174, 249). Since World War II there have been many cases of subversion followed by the invocation of norms to condemn and outlaw it.

Thus, the term "propaganda," a rarity in nineteenth century manuals of international law, now occupies a place in all full treatments of the law of nations and has been considered worthy of analysis in a number of specialized articles and several books.*

As hostile, especially subversive, propaganda was used more and more frequently, and as states expended more and more money and effort on it as one of the instrumentalities of power, it was inevitable that it should attract serious study by law-makers. Not only was its illegality acknowledged, but the reasons underlying the rules became clear. It was seen that when a government sends disruptive appeals to a foreign people, this is an act in violation of a sacred principle of the law of nations universally acknowledged, namely, the right of a state to sovereign independence, free from foreign coercion. In the language of the traditional statement of the fundamental rights of states, such acts violate the right of a state to exist (Oppenheim, 1955, vol. 1, p. 259; Marty, 1968, p. 11).

Another consideration that substantiates the illegality of subversive communication is its identification as a form of illegal intervention. The international rules against intervention are also based on the right of each state to be free from coercion—in other words, on its right to sovereign independence. By considering subversive propaganda as a form of illegal intervention, the norm is strengthened, as there are numerous precedents to uphold the illegality of intervention. Fauchille (1921–26) considers subversion to be "intervention de propagande," (Vol. 1, Sec. 300) while Thomas and Thomas (1956), in their book on intervention, write that efforts in one state to "change a government" (p. 276) in another nation engage the responsibility of the state, if the communicator is a governmental agency or a political party which in reality is the government, or any other institution or organization directed and financed by the state. But, as discussed later, if the subversive appeals are the work of individuals or private groups, including the independent press, the degree of responsibility of the government is controversial and could be established only in the most extreme cases.

That subversive propaganda is illegal is borne out by another consideration: the view that it is a type of aggression, and thus within the rules that proscribe aggressive war. It is claimed that subversion is not only a violation of the sacred rights of sovereignty, but is basically an act of war, for it may lead to retaliation and violence, even to war itself. Also, it may so weaken the victim of the subversive maneuvers as to tempt an enemy to attack it, especially if the latter is supporting the insurgents (Wright, 1948). Such a view is substantiated by the many efforts by UN agencies and learned writers to include subversion within the official definition of aggression, a goal still un-

*For bibliography of the international law of propaganda, see Whitton and Larson (1963, pp. 55–56, 277–295). Four books on the subject as a whole have appeared in this order: Martin (1958), Whitton and Larson (1963), Havighurst (1967), and Murty (1968).

achieved. Thus, the General Assembly in its Peace Through Deeds Resolution (1950) recognized that the "fomenting of civil strife in the interests of a foreign power" is a pattern of aggression (Resolution 380(V), Nov. 17, 1950). Also, in the Draft Code of Offenses Against the Peace and Security of Mankind, Article 2(5) declares activities calculated to "foment strife in another state" to be a crime against the peace and security of mankind (Article 2(5), *Yearbook of the United Nations*, 1952, p. 842).

Finally, the norm outlawing subversive propaganda among the nations seems firmly established as a rule of customary international law. In this matter, it is most significant that, during the many diplomatic incidents involving charges of offensive communications of this category, with the inevitable protests that followed, the existence of the rule itself is never denied. The guilty state finds plenty of excuses for the communication complained of—denial that the offensive words had ever been uttered, claim that they were justified retaliation, reprisal, or self-defense, or that the communicator was not under the legal control of the state—but the rule itself is not challenged (Whitton and Larson, 1963, pp. 97–99). One could also cite as persuasive authority numerous treaties, bilateral and multilateral, some in draft and others signed and ratified, that obligate the parties to refrain from subversive messages across state lines (Martin, 1958, pp. 62–108). Furthermore, at the War Crimes trials at Nuremberg, several Nazi leaders were charged with making subversive appeals to Czechs and Austrians, and it was clear that the tribunal considered such incitement to be contrary to international law (Martin, 1958, pp. 143–149). It is significant, too, that numerous resolutions have been voted in the United Nations and the Organization of American States condemning subversive ideological warfare as illegal and a danger to peace (Whitton and Larson, 1963, pp. 101–102). Thus, despite frequent violations, it is clear, from a review of customary international law, the writings of publicists, the relevant treaties in this matter, and the decisions at Nuremberg—supported by pertinent analogies to domestic laws everywhere—that the act of engaging in subversive propaganda, except when within the limits prescribed by precedent and principle, is contrary to the law of nations.

DEFAMATORY PROPAGANDA

A second category of hostile international communications that has given rise to many diplomatic incidents, some of the greatest gravity, is what is called *defamatory propaganda*. This refers to words, written or spoken, or pictorial representations such as drawings or photographs, that tend to degrade, revile, or insult foreign states, their institutions, leaders, and people. Considered particularly serious are offensive references to resident diplomats. Sometimes defamatory propaganda overlaps with either subversive or warmongering communications. For instance, the government of State A, in an effort to arouse its citizenry for an aggressive war on State B, may spread scurrilous reports concerning the leaders of the latter country. Or an elite of one country, striving through ideological warfare to incite the people of another country to revolt, may fill the local and foreign press with false reports of scandalous conduct by the king or prime minister. Hitler, with Goebbels and other Nazi leaders, was guilty of both categories of ideological attack (Kris and Speier, 1944; Childs and Whitton, 1942).

Numerous illustrations of such hostile communications are available from earliest times. In 1787, Lord Gordon was convicted in England of defaming Marie Antoinette, and a few years later in the same country one Peltier was found guilty of libeling Napoleon (Whitton and Larson, p. 105). In this century there have been frequent charges and countercharges of this character. In fact, more such incidents have occurred during the height of the Cold War than at any time in history. During the thirties, likewise a period of extreme international tension, the situation was so bad in this respect that Lauterpacht, one of the leading international law authorities of our time, believed that the conditions "must be regarded as exceptional and as evidencing a suspension, in this matter, of the operation of an accepted rule of international law in the relations of states" (Oppenheim, 1937, vol. 1, p. 231). This unprecedented degree of mutual vilification is explainable in part by the international situation, but also by two new factors: (1) the discovery by governing elites of the value of invective as a weapon of power, and (2) the invention of amazingly efficient and effective methods for the transmission of "news" across frontiers, especially the radio.

Wright stated the traditional norm in this matter: "International law clearly forbids the higher officials of a state to indulge in uncomplimentary or insulting comments upon the personality of another state or its rulers" (Wright, 1938, p. 528). Such comments, even by lesser leaders or by independent newspapers and radio chains, have likewise been the object of diplomatic protest. Traditionally, an apology is due if the norm has been violated. This rule is based on general principles of law supported by analogies drawn from domestic laws of libel, slander, and group libel. It is deduced from a long series of precedents dating from the eighteenth century.

One reason for the rule against international defamation is the fact that it may lead to disputes and conflict, and is thus a serious danger to peace. Some domestic laws in this matter explicitly reflect this principle, proscribing verbal attacks on foreign leaders that are calculated to involve the state in conflict with other nations (Martin, 1958, pp. 132–36). So far as defamation of foreign heads of state is concerned, the duty to refrain therefrom is based on the traditional right of a sovereign to the respect of other sovereigns. The resident diplomat has always been entitled to special status in domestic and international law, including the right to demand protection for both his person and his property. This is not only because he represents his sovereign, but also because of the general recognition that without such special status he would be unable effectively to perform his functions as a diplomat. Such status is universally accorded on a basis of reciprocity (Oppenheim, 1955, vol. 1, pp. 787–88).

How meticulously these rules are observed will depend largely on both the relations between the parties concerned and the general international situation. Between friendly states, this problem rarely arises, and if some over-zealous patriot happens to utter words disparaging to a foreign leader, the latter may simply ignore the incident—often the best way to handle the matter. The British sovereign did not pay too much attention to the threat by the Mayor of Chicago to give him a punch in the nose. But if the slanderous statement is considered a serious matter—especially if based on false information—the incident can be closed through appropriate apology or a published retraction. Here is an excellent opportunity for the utilization of the International Right of Reply, a creation of the United Nations under a treaty actually in force between a number of nations (Whitton, 1950).

Often the exchange of charges and insults—for instance, between Communist China and Soviet Russia or between the Arab states in recent years—is a reflection of the strained relations that exist between the parties concerned. If this ill-feeling diminishes—for instance, through the settlement of the underlying dispute—the verbal compaign may ease or fade away. A complicating situation occurs when inhuman conditions exist in a certain country—notably, grave violations of human rights. In such a situation, critical reports in the foreign press may be justified when all other methods, national and international, have proved fruitless to bring about necessary reforms.

Much thought and effort, both official and unofficial, has been devoted to the question of the publication of defamatory—especially false—news by the independent press and radio of a country. The East and West disagree on how to handle such situations, the former favoring rigid controls and severe criminal statutes, the latter resolutely opposing such sanctions as inconsistent with traditional doctrines of freedom of speech and press. All are agreed that the publication of false news should be prohibited, but there is wide discord over the best method to accomplish this end. Extreme proposals have been made on both sides of the controversy; Soviet Russia would throw journalists in jail, British authorities have maintained that ''the best antidote for propaganda is more propaganda'' (Whitton and Larson, 1963, pp. 176, 241).

Despite the many violations of traditional norms that have occurred in this matter, and despite the present confusion over just what rules do actually exist, it must not be forgotten that defamatory attacks on leaders and other public men, and even those disparaging foreign peoples, still do elicit diplomatic protests, and such protests are supported by claims that a breach of international law has been committed.

PROPAGANDA FOR WAR

War propaganda refers to direct attempts, at times by organized and concerted pressures of an ideological nature, to shape the minds of the masses of a particular nation in the direction of transnational conflict by force of arms or other methods of forceful coercion. Such pressures include propaganda designed to persuade and incite armed insurgents to overthrow a foreign regime with which the communicator is technically at peace. The latter act is discussed above in the treatment of subversive propaganda.

This "warmongering" or "indirect aggression" occurs in several categories which may at times overlap. First, the home population may be urged by impassioned patriotic appeals to embark on a war of aggression, or support one already in progress. This was done in Germany and Japan by governmental media prior to and during World War II. Second, the incitement may be addressed to a foreign people and its leaders, advocating war against a third state; thus, Nasser tried to persuade certain Arab states to destroy Israel. Third, a campaign of divisive and subversive propaganda may be undertaken in a foreign country in an effort to confuse and weaken a regime marked for conquest.

Another distinction turns on the identity of the communicator. This may be the government itself (for instance, through a "Bureau of Information"), a semigovernmental agency or political party over which the government has some control, or, finally, a medium with a status of complete independence. As for the first two cases, the responsibility of the state for an aggressive communication is clear. But the duty of a state with respect to communications by the independent press and radio is controversial.

Numerous instances of incitement to war by press, radio, and television have occurred in troubled areas. Any steady watcher of the media since World War II could easily assemble a vast dossier containing reports of such incidents. For example, King Saud, according to *The New York Times* (Jan. 4, 1954), made this declaration:

> The Arab nations should sacrifice up to 10 million of their 50 million people if necessary, to wipe out Israel. . . . Israel to the Arab world is like a cancer to the human body and the only remedy is to uproot it just like a cancer.

When William Randolph Hearst was campaigning for a declaration of war by the United States on Spain, and dispatched Frederick Remington to Cuba in search of atrocity stories capable of inflaming the American public against Spain, he sent the artist this famous telegram: "You furnish the pictures and I'll furnish the war!" (Winkler, 1955, pp. 95–6). This, however, is a case of agitation by an individual, a matter discussed later.

It is only in the twentieth century that jurists have begun to assert that propaganda for war is illegal. This is understandable, since before the League of Nations, the Briand–Kellogg Pact (Pact of Paris), and the Charter of the UN, to declare war was considered one of the sovereign rights of every state—for a good reason, a bad reason, or none at all. But when aggressive war became illegal, it was only natural that ideological pressures to that end should be considered illegal as well.

A major factor in this development was the recognition that incitement to conflict constitutes a grave menace to peace. The intended victim may be impelled to take measures of self-defense. The weak state, like Czechoslovakia confronting Hitler, may, of course, find itself the helpless victim of invasion and conquest.

War propaganda is held to be illegal by virtue of the general principle of law recognized by all nations declaring that incitement to crime is itself a criminal offense. The Common Law is typical in this respect (Clark and Marshall, 1958):

> Solicitation is a distinct common law misdemeanor in which the act forbidden consists of the accused person's parole or written efforts to activate another to commit a criminal offense. (p. 194)

Hence, since a war of aggression is now declared illegal, propaganda as incitement to commit this offense also constitutes a violation of the law of nations.

The war crimes trials in Germany and Japan following World War II stand as a precedent, not only for the rule that aggressive war is a crime but also for the norm against ideological aggression. Professor Murty (1968), after an exhaustive study of the war crimes trials, concludes:

> The above trials, the provisions of the charters constituting the tribunals, and the world community response which at least the Nuremberg judgment has received, lead us reasonably to expect that in future trials for crimes against peace . . . the use of the ideological instrument to further plans of aggression by violence will be regarded as wrongful. (p. 151)

He goes on to suggest that any person will be guilty of a crime against the peace if, possessing power to shape or influence the policies of his state for purposes of aggression, he personally participates in the operation of the ideological strategy.

Support for the outlawing of war propaganda as a grave danger to peace, as well as for a definition of aggression to include the crime of war propaganda has come from both the League of Nations and the United Nations.

Under the League of Nations, the Preliminary Draft of the General Convention to Improve the Means of Preventing War declared ''there are circumstances in which aggressive propaganda against a foreign power may take such offensive forms and assume such a threatening character as to constitute a real danger to peace'' (League of Nations, *VII Political* (1931), Doc. A.14.1931, VII.8, pp. 32, 43). A legal committee in 1932 strongly recommended the prohibition of war propaganda.* One article in the 1936 Convention Concerning the Use of Broadcasting in the Cause of Peace bound the parties "to insure that their transmissions do not constitute an incitement to war, or to acts likely to lead to war." (See Krause, 1960, for a summary and analysis of this treaty.) This treaty was ratified by a few states, and was renewed later under the United Nations. The latter body has made significant efforts along these lines. The General Assembly in 1947 condemned "all forms of propaganda, in whatever country conducted, which is either designed or likely to provoke or encourage any threat to the peace, breach of the peace, or act of aggression" (UN General Assembly Resolution 110 (II), *Yearbook of the United Nations, 1947–48*, pp. 91–93). The great United Nations conference of 1948 on Freedom of Information and of the Press by an overwhelming majority solemnly condemned all war propaganda (Whitton, 1949, p. 75). This was reconfirmed in 1950 by another General Assembly resolution (*Yearbook of the United Nations, 1951*, pp. 203–204). The United Nations draft Covenant on Civil and Political Rights (1966) obligates the parties to prohibit all war propaganda as well as any advocacy of national, racial or religious hatred that constitutes incitement to discrimination, hostility, or violence (Murty, 1968, p. 4). Here is ample evidence of the concern in the international community with respect to the dangers of aggressive communications.

PRIVATE PROPAGANDA

When governments or their agencies commit acts of hostile international propaganda, it appears from the foregoing review that a considerable body of norms already exists that may be invoked in diplomatic exchanges or by appropriate world organizations. But when the problem concerns acts of individuals—independent subjects at law—the force of existing law is controversial. Here we deal with newspapers, radio chains, and publishers who are free from governmental control, and even private individuals who may in speech or writing defame foreign states, their leaders, peoples, and institutions, promote rebel movements abroad—for instance, the American press supporting the Irish rebellion—or even engage in warmongering.

In general, it appears that governments have been inclined, in the absence of a treaty, to deny responsibility for the acts of individuals in other than very exceptional circumstances. But while the legal duties of the parties involved are not always clear, their moral obligations surely are. A tremendous amount

---

*Referring to the Legal Committee of the abortive League of Nations Conference for the Reduction and Limitation of Armaments. (League of Nations, *IX Disarmament* (1933), 1935, 1–4, p. 702.

of international misunderstanding—notably, the persistence of long-standing clichés and stereotypes that disparage foreign peoples, and the creation, escalation, and perpetuation of nationalistic feelings of superiority and even hatred—can be laid at the door of the private media. In this respect, school books have come in for especially strong criticism. But essential reforms in this area must be sought, not so much in new regulations and better laws as in long-term endeavors such as that already carried on in this field by the UN and its branch, UNESCO, as well as by governments and even the media themselves in certain countries.

The best known cases of offensive communication by independent individuals have concerned subversive propaganda. Two irreconcilable schools of thought have dominated the field here, the "broad responsibility" school and the "narrow responsibility" school. It is significant, however, that both schools agree that the state is not responsible if the subversive propaganda by its residents does not exceed mere moral support of a foreign uprising. Both schools agree also that the responsibility of the state is engaged if residents are found guilty of overt acts of direct aid to a foreign insurrection. States must exercise due diligence to prevent the launching of military action from their territories against another state (Murty, 1968, p. 105). Hence if in State A a group gives overt and active aid to rebels in State B, the target state would have solid grounds for protest and may expect State A to make amends if a newspaper in State A campaigns in favor of such a group—for instance, calling for recruits or financial contributions (Whitton and Larson, 1963, p. 140). Many conflicts have arisen, also, over agitation by political refugees. This was a consequence of the many revolutions in the nineteenth century, causing refugees in great numbers to become exiles abroad and from there to agitate and intrigue against the new regime in their homeland (Martin, 1958, pp. 130, 174; Van Dyke, 1940, pp. 58–73). The same kind of propaganda goes on today. From the time of the French Revolution, states have imposed regulations on resident refugees to meet this situation, even resorting to expulsion (Whitton and Larson, 1963, pp. 104, 139, 143–44). Here the line between mere moral support and active assistance may be difficult to determine, and the policy adopted by the particular asylum state toward resident refugees will depend on its peculiar situation in the international setup. A major consideration is whether there is a desire to maintain peaceful relations with the protesting state. Weak or exposed states, in order to avoid controversy, will be inclined to take firm measures, while strong states, especially those with liberal traditions, may tolerate all but the most flagrant cases of refugee propaganda with foreign repercussions.

Coming now to the subject of defamatory propaganda by individuals, attacks by individuals on resident diplomats have traditionally been considered unlawful; they have led to diplomatic protests and called for appropriate remedies, usually an apology and even the punishment of the offender (Whitton and Larson, 1963, pp. 148–49). This follows from the well-established duty of protection owed all accredited diplomats. Also, a large number of states accord protection to foreign sovereigns and heads of states from libel and slander; but whether a firm rule of international law has developed in this matter is controversial. The same is true of comments by individuals derogatory to the state itself, its constitution and policies, although such comments may be very dangerous to the course of peaceful international relations. One may observe great flexibility in the attitudes of governments in this area. Some governments take strong measures, through the executive or the courts, or both, to discourage such communications when they are of a nature to involve the nation in international controversy (Martin, 1958, p. 174). It is worth noting that there are several available remedies to meet this situation, and the state of the commentator may insist that the target state, before appealing to the government for redress, should first exhaust available local remedies—for instance, an action in the courts.* Even the United States, one of the most liberal in this area, has on occasion expressed regret for such remarks, written or spoken, considered objectionable by foreign states. But this country has persistently refused to accept any proposal, by treaty or otherwise, likely to compromise the right of free speech.

As for propaganda for war, some authors maintain that states are bound to take necessary preventive measures to assure that the nation does not become involved in a war of aggression, and that under this principle the state is obliged to intervene to suppress war propaganda (Martin 1958, pp. 132–6). More than 25 states provide in their domestic laws for the prosecution of individuals who have been urging the nation to make war against a foreign nation (Martin, 1958, pp. 132–6). Some authors have gone so far as to maintain that war propaganda by an individual should constitute a crime in international law, akin to piracy, over which any state could assume jurisdiction (Pella, 1929, pp. 174–9; Whitton and Larson, 1936, pp. 158–9, 170–1). It must be admitted, however, that effective war propaganda without government involvement would be a rarity. Even in the case of the Nazis, the guilty parties were not independent agents, but a part of the establishment. But if, in some future conflict, one can imagine a state having been found guilty of waging a war of aggression, an independent radio or newspaper might theoretically be prosecuted at the war crimes trial for having waged a long and persistent campaign to arouse the nation, both leaders and peoples, to embark on that war. Of course, the main thrust here would be to hold the government responsible for not exercising due diligence with respect to such media, and, more likely, for having encouraged or even supported the alleged independent communicators found guilty of war mongering.

---

*See Van Dyke (1940), pp. 69–70. He concludes that "protection of resident foreign diplomats from libel is so generally afforded by municipal law as to indicate a response to a requirement of international law."

REFERENCES

Barghoorn, F. C. (1964). "Soviet Foreign Propaganda." Princeton University Press, Princeton, New Jersey.

Childs, H. L., and Whitton, J. B. (1942). "Propaganda by Short Wave." Princeton University Press, Princeton, New Jersey.

Clark, W. L., and Marshall, W. L. (1958). "A Treatise on the Law of Crimes." 6th ed., revised by M. F. Wingersky. Callaghan, Chicago, Illinois.

Falk, R. A. (1968). "Legal Order in a Violent World." Princeton University Press, Princeton, New Jersey.

Fauchille, P. (1921–1926). "Traité de Droit International Public." Rousseau, Paris.

Havighurst, C. C., ed. (1967). "International Control of Propaganda." Oceana Publications, Dobbs Ferry, New York.

Holt, R. T. (1958). "Radio Free Europe." University of Minnesota Press, Minneapolis, Minnesota.

Krause, G. B. (1960). Der Rundfunkfriedenspakt von 1936. *Jahrbuch für Internationales Recht* 9, 35–57.

Kris, E., and Speier, H. (1944). "German Radio Propaganda." Oxford University Press, London.

Martin, L. J. (1958). "International Propaganda, Its Legal and Diplomatic Control." University of Minnesota Press, Minneapolis, Minnesota.

Matter, P. (1925–1927). "Cavour et l'Unité Italienne, 1848–1856." F. Alcan, Paris.

Murty, B. S. (1968). "Propaganda and World Public Order." Yale University Press, New Haven, Connecticut.

Oppenheim, L. F. L. (1937). "International Law." 5th ed. Longmans, Green, London.

Oppenheim, L. F. L. (1955). "International Law." 8th ed., ed. by H. Lauterpacht. McKay, New York.

Pella, V. (1929). Un nouveau délit: La propaganda pour la guerre d'aggression. *Revue de Droit International 3*, 174–179.

Sorel, A. (1885–1904). "L'Europe et la Révolution Française." E. Plon-Nourrit, Paris.

Thomas, A. V. W., and Thomas, A. J., Jr. (1956). "Non-Intervention, the Law and Its Import in the Americas." Southern Methodist University Press, Dallas, Texas.

Van Dyke, V. (1940). The responsibility of States for international propaganda. *American Journal of International Law 34*, 58–73.

Vattel, E. de. (1916). "The Law of Nations." Trans. by C. G. Fenwick, Carnegie Institution, Washington, D.C.

Whitton, J. B. (1949). United Nations Conference on Freedom of Information and the Movement Against International Propaganda. *American Journal of International Law 43*, 73–87.

Whitton, J. B. (1950). An international right of reply? *American Journal of International Law 44*, 141–145.

Whitton, J. B., and Larson, A. (1963). "Propaganda: Toward Disarmament in the War of Words." Oceana Publications, Dobbs Ferry, New York.

Winkler, J. K. (1955). "William Randolph Hearst: A New Appraisal." Hastings House, New York.

Wright, Q. (1938). The denunciation of treaty violators. *American Journal of International Law 32*, 526–535.

Wright, Q. (1948). The crime of "war mongering." *American Journal of International Law 42*, 128–136.

Part 4

International Communication in Transition: The New Global Balance

Introduction

Kaarle Nordenstreng

Herbert I. Schiller

Underlying the perspective in this book is the recognition of the massive shift in the global relation of forces that has been taking place over the last few decades. This new alignment of power, still in process, challenges social science theory no less than international diplomacy. The subjects examined in the preceding sections of the book (communication law, direct satellite broadcasting, and national development) may be viewed therefore as some of the sectors in which these fundamental and historically-determined social developments can be witnessed.

An in-depth analysis of this global phenomenon in all its dimensions, including relations between socialism and capitalism (East–West) and industrial and underdeveloped countries (North–South), necessarily would demand consideration of some of the most basic problems of social science. An analysis of this order and magnitude would challenge as well the contemporary assumptions of communication research, thus demonstrating that this particular field of social science is organically bound to a general theory of society (cf. Pietilä, 1977). Though a thorough analysis of such profound questions falls outside the scope of this volume, the need for such an undertaking should not be overlooked. Thus, it is far from sufficient for example, to observe the occurrence of "media imperialism," without relating this idea to the general socioeconomico-political conditions that have determined historically the course of imperialism (cf. Tunstall, 1977). What is needed to complement such media-bound explanations is an examination of the roots and nature of imperialism, viewed in a holistic way. Actually such analyses constitute, by now, a whole tradition, dating back to the beginning of this century (see, e.g., Hobson, 1938; Lenin, 1970).

Seen against these larger frameworks, the concluding section of this book sets itself a relatively modest task: it presents some evidence of the impact of the overall change in the global balance on the informational sector.

It is significant to note the dramatic increase in attention over the past few years these matters have received. International communication—implicitly or explicitly connected to international relations in general—has suddenly become a momentous issue, not only in scholarly circles but also in national and international policy making.

An indication of the centrality and seriousness with which current international communication questions are viewed by at least some influential Western groupings is apparent in the statement of the President of Radio Free Europe and Radio Liberty (Mickelson, 1977). He writes:

> The Soviet Union is leading a concerted international campaign with the enthusiastic support of a large number of Third World countries to put the dead hand of the bureaucrat at the throttle of the worldwide communications transmissions systems. The campaign has already mobilized such support that we are now approaching a crisis in international communications, perhaps more serious than anything we have seen since the Second World War. The campaign is evident in two separate movements. . . . The most overt of these two movements is the Soviet Union's direct attempt to impose the theory of complete state sovereignty over all forms of communication. The second is the less obvious but possibly more dangerous concept of mobilizing Third World countries support for this theory. By using such catch phrases as "development support communications" and "communications imperialism" they mask the bald drive for governmental control by appealing to the defense of indigenous interest and culture against the historic "dominance" of the West. (p. 315)

These developments have been reflected also, and not surprisingly, within the United Nations and UNESCO (Harley, 1977):

> At the 19th General Conference of UNESCO this past November (1976) at Nairobi, there were two and a half days of heated debate on the international role of the media. Spokesmen for the Third World deplored the West's overwhelming dominance of the world's news and assailed its global news agencies for assorted sins of omission and commission. They called for a drastic rebalancing of the free flow of information as part of the new economic order. The Socialist countries maintained that the press must be a part of the social system, devoting its efforts to social progress and the achievement of national goals and aspirations. Spokesmen for the West, on the other hand, maintained that the press must be free and independent of government, that it should not be used to further state policy, and that the way to establish a more effective press in the Third World was certainly not through greater government control. . . . The issues of free-versus-controlled and Third-World-versus-Western press are not new. They have been raised again and again in international forums. (p. S9532)

Although the hegemonic tone of the Western "consciousness industry" suggests an opposite reading of the situation, in fact, the centers of world capitalism have been forced onto the defensive globally with respect to informational issues. This helps to explain the well-publicized campaigns in the West against the "new international information order," with attacks directed against "Soviet-sponsored resolutions" in UNESCO, the cooperation among the nonindustrialized nations for a "decolonization of information," and the controversies surrounding the "third basket" of Helsinki. Actually, these efforts have not tried to conceal that what is at issue is an overall process—one that concerns the vital interests of the Western market system, under pressure from an uneasy coalition of socialist and developing countries, and the actively struggling national liberation movements. See, e.g., Sussman, 1977; and for a more academic analysis with the same perspective see Kintner, 1977.)

Despite the dilemma the demand for a "new world information order" presents to the Western system of communications domination, at least the more observable deficiencies of the existing order cannot be denied (Read, 1977):

> While the Soviet position is unacceptable to us, and any suggestion that the principle of free flow of information be redefined is troublesome, we nonetheless must recognize that the international flow of mass communication is imbalanced and the United States is the major source of origination. This phenomenon, coupled with other vast and varied U.S. international involvements, gives credence to the notion that a world culture imprinted "made-in-America" exists today. (pp. 33–4)

And, although there is an apparent interest in "understanding" the informational complaints of the underdeveloped countries, it is also clear that the Western industrialized countries are not about to make major concessions that might weaken their dominating positions in international information structures. Thus, for instance, Western countries, who agreed at the 19th General Conference of UNESCO to "support the efforts of the developing countries which are seeking to establish and strengthen their own information and communication systems in line with their needs," have refused to make normative references to the *contents* of the mass media. The obvious aim of such tactics of "repressive tolerance" is to adjust to the heavy pressure for modifications in the control system while avoiding substantive change. Still, the demand for a new information order can only sharpen the contradictions and intensify the ideological struggle.

From another point of view, the changing global balance of forces encourages a reevaluation of the philosophies that determine the way we think about mass communications—the so-called "theories of the press" (see Siebert, Petersen, and Schramm, 1956). The Hutchins Commission on the Freedom of the Press was, at its time (1946), an indispensable effort to adjust libertarian press philosophies to the process of monopolization of American mass communication; similarly, the new international order seems now to be pointing to new philosophical notions of the press, both nationally and internationally. For example, the Colombo Summit Meeting of the Non-Aligned Countries endorsed a declaration in August 1976, stating among other things, that "In a situation where the means of information are dominated and monopolized by a few, freedom of information really comes to mean the freedom of these few who propagate information in the manner of their choosing and the virtual denial to the rest of the right to inform and be informed objectively and accurately." (See, e.g., *Communicator*, 1976, p. 20, and Schiller, 1978.)

This passage rejects the libertarian doctrine of the press on three different counts. First, it suggests that laissez faire freedom leads to monopolization. Second, it reminds us how inadequate it is to guarantee abstractly the right to freedom of information without also insuring in material terms that this right will be implemented. And third, information transmitted by the media is assigned an explicit content criterion—it should be objective and accurate.

The foregoing notwithstanding, the changes recommended in the information order to date have been quite modest. If examined objectively, the proposals and positions of the socialist and nonaligned countries are far from sweeping. Consider, for example, the following passage from the Declaration of San José of July 1976 (UNESCO, 1976):

> The representatives of the governments of the States of Latin America and the Caribbean . . . hereby declare . . . that communication policies should contribute to knowledge, understanding, friendship, cooperation and integration of peoples through a process of identification of common goals and needs, respecting national sovereignties and the international legal principles of non-intervention in the affairs of States as well as the cultural and political plurality of societies and individuals, with a view to achieving world solidarity and peace. (p. 24)

Hardly revolutionary, the Declaration does little more than state the obvious and confirms some internationally valid principles. And yet the meeting at which this statement was agreed upon was harshly criticized by the representatives of the U.S. media and their Latin American followers. (See, e.g., Capriles, 1977, and Salinas, 1977.) A similar reception greeted the UNESCO draft declaration of fundamental principles governing the use of the mass media. Yet what the attacks prove is not so much some sinister tendency of UNESCO to erode freedom as the power of the Western media to define exclusively the terms of the debate in their own interest.

The contributions that follow cast some light on the new global balance from three different angles. The editors' article concerns itself with the East–West dimension. It claims that, contrary to the familiar argument created by Western press coverage of the "third basket" of the Helsinki Final Act, the lessening of the Cold War means much more than the exportation of Western conceptions of "free flow" and "human rights" to the Eastern hemisphere. It is suggested that the Helsinki Accords in fact contain a new philosophical notion of freedom of information—one that is more balanced and in line with the interests of the developing and socialist countries than that traditionally advocated by Western liberalism.

The article by Rosenblum emphasizes the North–South dimension and reveals the concerns of Western media professionals—particularly within transnational news agencies—caught in the middle of the demands for a new global balance.

Finally, Trans Van Dinh's contribution documents the emergence of the new informational demands of the nonaligned countries—the source of much of the current crisis in international communications.

REFERENCES

Capriles, O. (1977). "Actions and Reactions to Communication Policies within the Framework of UNESCO." Paper presented at the ILET Seminar International Communications and Third World Participation: A Conceptual and Practical Framework, Amsterdam, September 5–8, 1977.

Communicator. (1976). *11* (No. 2–3). Indian Institute of Mass Communication, New Delhi.

Harley, W. G. (1977). International Operations Subcommittee of the Senate Committee on Foreign Relations. Statement by William G. Harley. *Congressional Record 123* (No. 101), S9532–S9534.

Hobson, J. A. (1902). "Imperialism." G. Allen and Unwin, London.

Kintner, W. R. (1977). A program for America: Freedom and foreign policy. *Orbis 21*, 139–156.

Lenin, V. I. (1970). "Imperialism, The Highest Stage of Capitalism, A Popular Outline." Progress Publishers, Moscow.

Mickelson, S. (1977). The free flow of information; to come close to the truth. (Speech delivered before the City Club of Cleveland, Ohio, January 21, 1977.) *Vital Speeches of the Day 43*, 314–317.

Pietilä, V. (1977). "On the Scientific Status and Position of Communication Research." Institute of Journalism and Mass Communication, University of Tampere, Tampere, Finland. (Reports No. 35.)

Read, W. H. (1977). U.S. private media abroad (an updated chapter of a previously unpublished Library of Congress Congressional Research Service Study prepared for the Foreign Relations Committee of the U.S. Senate, as part of a study of the United States Information Agency). *In* U.S. Congress. Senate. Committee on Foreign Relations. Subcommittee on International Operations. "The Role and Control of International Communications and Information," pp. 1–35. U.S. Government Printing Office, Washington, D.C. (Committee Print.)

Salinas, R. (1977). "News Agencies and the New Information Order." Institute of Journalism and Mass Communication, University of Tampere, Tampere, Finland. (Reports No. 39.)

Schiller, H. I. (1978). Decolonization of information. *Latin American Perspectives* (Winter) 35–48.

Siebert, F. S., Peterson, T., and Schramm, W. (1956). "Four Theories of the Press." University of Illinois Press, Urbana, Illinois.

Sussman, L. R. (1977). The "march" through the world's mass media. *Orbis 20*, 857–879.

Tunstall, J. (1977). "The Media are American." Columbia University Press, New York.

UNESCO. (1976). "Intergovernmental Conference on Communication Policies in Latin America and the Caribbean. Final Report. San José (Costa Rica), 12–21 July 1976." UNESCO, Paris. (COM/MD/38.)

12
Helsinki: The New Equation

Kaarle Nordenstreng
University of Tampere

Herbert I. Schiller
University of California, San Diego

This paper was first published in *Journal of Communication*, Volume 26, Winter 1976, and is included in this volume by permission of *Journal of Communication*.

For three sunny days, from 30 July until 1 August 1975, the capital of Finland was a scene of deliberations unthinkable even a few years ago. Heads of state from thirty-three European nations and the United States and Canada gathered in Helsinki's Finlandia Hall to review and sign a document, produced jointly and reflecting the consensus of all parties, calling for peaceful relations between countries and increased international cooperation in practically all fields—from commerce and industry to culture and communication.

In general political terms, capitalism and socialism agreed in Helsinki that peaceful negotiations rather than war and violence should be the parameters in the development of their relations and the means by which to settle their mutual relations.

But peaceful coexistence between different social systems, made possible by political detente, has not suddenly turned earlier adversaries with conflicting interests to friends with only parallel interests. By now it is a widely accepted notion that detente does not eliminate the so-called "ideological struggle": capitalism and socialism continue to compete with each other. However, the trend is from "brutal" antagonisms to more subtle forms, which set a particularly challenging task for students of international communication.

Consequently, Helsinki means both progress from cold-war confrontations to peaceful cooperation *and* changes in the strategy of ideological struggle. The new equation brings into better (if still largely implicit) balance the traditional and still continuing opposition between Eastern and Western conceptions of the role of information in international relations.

PHILOSOPHIES IN CONFLICT

The Western approach asserts that human contacts, the "free flow of information and ideas," and other concrete forms of cooperation are *primary functional prerequisites* for peaceful relations and therefore for international security. The Eastern approach insists that forms of cooperation—and particularly informational flows—have the nature of *secondary consequences* of an overall political situation. While Western states say that increased flow automatically advances détente, Eastern states believe that improved security will lead to more relaxation and that one should be selective in choosing the means for cultural and information cooperation.

Accordingly, the equation of security and cooperation is reversed in the two approaches (and the title of the Conference reads correspondingly). One approach views security and peace as "effect" of such "causes" as the free flow of information, while the other places peace and security as primary determinants for the degree and forms of cooperation.

The Western philosophy was crystallized in Finlandia Hall by the Prime Minister of Ireland in these words:

> Peaceful co-operation between nations will grow and develop best if it is made a living reality in the lives of our peoples. . . .*

The Western tendency to make the operative level (including the free flow of information) absolute in international relations and thus to make it the prerequisite for peace and security was neatly manifested by the President of the United States in a sentence directed "to the countries of the East":

> But it is important that you recognize the deep devotion of the American people and their Government to human rights and fundamental freedoms and thus to the pledges that this Conference has made regarding the freer movement of people, ideas and information.*

The Eastern philosophy, on the other hand, was particularly clearly expressed by the First Secretary of the Bulgarian Communist Party and the President of the Country:

> The People's Republic of Bulgaria also attaches great importance to international cooperation in the field of education and culture, of information and human contacts. Opened doors are a symbol of trust and hospitality. Our doors will be open to all people with open hearts, with good and honest intentions, who observe the laws, traditions and customs of their hosts.*

The two philosophies may be expressed in the choice of one word. Dr. Klaus Törnudd, a Finnish expert in international relations, observed (Törnudd, 1975):

*Verbatim record of the meetings of the state of the Conference on Security and Co-Operation in Europe, held at Finlandia Hall, Helsinki, 30 July–1 August 1975.

1. Freer and wider dissemination of information *will* contribute to international understanding.

2. Freer and wider dissemination of information *shall* contribute to international understanding.*

The "will" refers to Western "functionalism" and the "shall" points to the Eastern approach with its tendency to subordinate international cooperation to the more absolute values of peace and security.

An essential component of this philosophical difference is the issue of the *content* of the information flows. The Western approach has a tendency to avoid all considerations regarding the substance of what is being communicated. It is characterized by what Gerbner's 1961 study called the "procedural" (vs. the "substantive") emphasis. It is a principal feature of the Western tradition of freedom of information to speak about *all kinds* of information and thus to bypass any "quality control" as censorship or at least a step toward it. The Eastern approach takes the opposite view: a specification of the kinds of information (and cultural exchanges in general) is understood as an indispensable part of informational exchanges.

"BASKET DIPLOMACY"

The Final Act lists under "Information" a number of measures for (1) "Improvement of the Circulation of, Access to, and Exchange of Information," (2) "Co-operation in the Field of Information," and (3) "Improvement of Working Conditions for Journalists." A careful study of the specific measures will reveal that most of the painstakingly negotiated formulations clearly reflect the Western viewpoint—that of the free flow.

But the "operative" passages should not be studied in isolation. They are an integral part of the whole document in which particular political weight may be placed on the preambles. Thus, the Western outlook is not as pronounced in the preamble to the chapter on information which notes "the need for an ever wider knowledge and understanding of the various aspects of life in other participating States," and acknowledges "the contribution of this process to the growth of confidence between peoples."

Besides reading the practical measures alongside the principles and objectives, one has to understand the broader context of the document and the negotiations which produced it.† The protracted proceedings of the conference

---

*Dr. Törnudd, formerly professor of international politics at the University of Tampere and presently Director of Political Affairs at the Finnish Ministry of Foreign Affairs, was a representative of Finland in the Geneva negotiations during the second stage of CSCE with primary responsibility for the "third basket."

†The agenda of the conference (and the disposition of the Final Act) was provided in the *Final Recommendations* of the Helsinki Consultations, approved by the first stage of the conference held at the level of foreign ministers.

were centered around four problem areas, called "baskets" in the conference jargon, and the Final Act follows the same division. The first (and politically most important) basket deals with "Questions Relating to Security in Europe" including "Declaration on Principles Guiding Relations between Participating States" and "Confidence-Building Measures," such as the prior notification of major military maneuvers.

The second basket pulls together "Co-operation in the Fields of Economics, of Science and Technology and of the Environment." The third basket is entitled "Co-operation in Humanitarian and Other Fields" and it covers "Human Contacts," "Information," "Co-operation and Exchanges in the Field of Culture" and "Co-operation and Exchanges in the Field of Education." The fourth basket deals with the "Follow-up to the Conference," that is, how the process of detente and cooperation in Europe would be continued.

"PACKAGE DEAL"

Each of the baskets includes a variety of elements—political and philosophical principles as well as practical operational measures. They have been carefully designed in relation to each other and intended to form an organic whole. In this respect, the wording in the preamble of the third basket ("Co-operation in Humanitarian and Other Fields," covering four topics including information) is critical. In that preamble the participating states declare:

Convinced that this cooperation should take place in full respect for the principles guiding relations among participating States as set forth in the relevant document. . . .

The "relevant document" is the first basket where, among others, the following sentence is to be found under the first principle, guiding relations between participating states, entitled "Sovereign Equality, Respect for the Rights Inherent in Sovereignty":

They will also respect each other's right freely to choose and develop its political, social, economic and cultural systems as well as its right to determine its laws and regulations.

These are the key elements of a "package deal" made by diplomats in Geneva in the course of the second stage of the conference in Summer 1974. It was agreed that the first principles listed in the first basket will state that each sovereign state has the right to determine its own laws and regulations, while the tenth principle will declare that the rights guaranteed by sovereignty will be exercised in harmony with international law and obligations such as those approved by the conference. The problem of national sovereignty is thus solved by a two-pronged formula which, to a great extent, leaves it to each situation to determine—and each state to interpret—which approach is more relevant: a sovereign state's right of independence or the obligation of an international norm.

This was the diplomatic way of overcoming a fundamental dilemma that accompanied the conference from its first days. The socialist countries were willing to approve an increase in contacts between people and in dissemination of information, and so forth, only on condition that this takes place in accordance with the laws and customs of each country and on the basis of noninterference in internal affairs—a stand which is a logical consequence of their philosophical approach. The Western countries regarded such restrictive conditions as watering down the substance of the third basket and did not approve the Eastern proposals for making such provisions explicit in the preamble to the third basket.

If the operative measures to promote "freer and wider dissemination of information of all kinds," and so forth, are formulations that may be seen as a diplomatic victory for the West, the package deal can be regarded as a balancing construct in the interest of the East. Viewed as a whole—as it should be—the Helsinki document may be interpreted as a definite limitation on the free flow doctrine in international politics. And, what is also significant, a link was established between the principle of free flow and that of national sovereignty.

FREE FLOW RECONSIDERED

Obviously, this is not unrelated to what is happening to the free flow ideology elsewhere in political and diplomatic circles (Nordenstreng and Varis, 1974). The rise and the fall of the orthodox Western doctrine of the free flow of information has been discussed by Schiller (1974). It has been registered, as well, in several resolutions within the United Nations framework. The 18th General Conference of UNESCO, in the fall of 1974, approved a Medium Term Plan for 1977–1982, suggesting that the traditional concept of the free flow of information "needs to be complemented by that of a more balanced and objective flow, both between countries and within and between regions" (UNESCO, 1974).

After thirty years of almost unqualified acceptance in international politics, the free flow in information doctrine is now increasingly on the defensive. Helsinki has not reversed this trend. But, paradoxically, these moves may be almost quixotic, given the quickened technological tempo in the communication sector. The free flow of information was a doctrine originally conceived in terms of visible, tangible information flows—books, magazines, papers, films, TV programs, and news dispatches. Today, though not by any means obsolete or discarded, these older forms must take places beside new message transmission mechanisms, such as direct satellite broadcasting.

The thinking expressed at a U.S. State Department sponsored conference in 1974 reflected the awareness that the sentiment for protecting national cultural sovereignty was spreading rapidly in the international community and that "any international agreement on satellite broadcasting is bound to have some restrictive effect on the international flow of information and ideas." The conference addressed the question: what should the United States do? The answer: move ahead as fast as possible to introduce the technology (in this instance, direct satellite broadcasting) which may have the potential to create its own fait accompli (Laskin, 1974):

> If the United States modifies its position and accepts an international regime under which the consent of the recipient country is required for foreign direct satellite broadcasts, the consequences will be positive. The regime can and should be a mild one. . . . Under a regime of consent, the United States would no longer seem (as it does now for some nations) a superpower seeking to impose American television programming on the rest of the world. In addition, the United States would probably gain the support of other nations that place a high value on the principle of free flow in any further debate with those nations that have and work to preserve closed societies. And finally, and most importantly, a regime of consent would permit the development of international direct satellite broadcasting to move to the stage of practical operations. It is practical operation that must be stressed.

Inherent in this quite sophisticated view is an understanding that technology embraces far more than equipment. There is a growing awareness—not least among U.S. policy makers—that technology as it is designed, installed, and utilized may be an embodiment of the social system which first creates and uses it. Helsinki moved toward a new equation in *conventional areas*. But the more advanced technological forms of information transmission and control are still to be dealt with.

REFERENCES

Gerbner, G. (1961). Press perspectives in world communication: A pilot study. *Journalism Quarterly 38*, 313–322.

Laskin, P. L. (1974). Legal strategies for advancing information flow. *In* "Control of the Direct Broadcast Satellite: Values in Conflict" (Aspen Institute Program on Communication and Society, in association with Office of External Research, Department of State), pp. 59–63. Aspen Institute Program on Communications and Society, Palo Alto, California.

Nordenstreng, K., and Varis, T. (1974). "Television Traffic—A One-Way Street?" UNESCO, Paris. (Reports and Papers on Mass Communication, No. 70.)

Schiller, H. I. (1974). Freedom from the "free flow." *Journal of Communication 24* (No. 1), 110–117.

Törnudd, K. (1975). Contribution to the Colloquium on the Role of Journalists in International Détente. *In* "Journalists and Détente 30 Years After the End of the World War II: Colloquium Proceedings" (T. Varis, ed.), pp. 12–15. Institute of Journalism and Mass Communication, University of Tampere, Finland. (Reports from the Institute of Journalism and Mass Communication, No. 25.)

UNESCO. (1974). "Analysis of Problems and Table of Objectives to be Used as a Basis for Medium-Term Planning, 1977–1982." UNESCO, Paris. (18 C/4.)

13

Reporting from the Third World

Mort Rosenblum

Associated Press

Mort Rosenblum is Chief of Bureau, Associated Press in Paris, and is working on a book on international reporting.

This article, in slightly expanded form, appeared in *Foreign Affairs*, Volume 55, July 1977. It is reprinted by permission from *Foreign Affairs*, July 1977. Copyright 1977 by Council on Foreign Relations, Inc.

I

A popular melody has joined the reggae rhythms in Jamaican nightclubs; it is a song called "The Foreign Press." In rich island dialect, the song accuses correspondents of besmirching Jamaica's good name with false reports throughout the world. It says that, between dispatches, reporters manage to frolic on the beach and in the nightspots, adding: "Why don't they write about that in the foreign press?"

It is no light-hearted calipso spoof. The wife of a prominent Jamaican cabinet minister told an American correspondent, with no trace of mirth: "You (reporters) don't know how you make us suffer with all your lies about communism and violence . . . and if you keep it up, the day will come that you will not be able to come here any more or you'll have your throat cut." Already Jamaica, like scores of developing countries, is loath to grant entry to foreign correspondents.

Leaders in the Third World, with new and growing confidence, are translating into action their frustration with international news coverage. Government criticism of the press is hardly new, but only recently have leaders acted so harshly on such a large scale. Reporters are banned, jailed, and, in some instances, tortured or shot. Dispatches are censored, and news sources are stringently muzzled. International news agency reports are controlled and foreign publications are seized. India, which prided itself on having a free press in the world's largest democracy, expelled five Americans and two British correspondents as part of a series of press restrictions that began in June 1975 and did not end until Prime Minister Indira Gandhi was voted out of office in March 1977. . . .

An Associated Press censorship study for 1976, while giving no overall totals, describes a steady pattern of pressure on correspondents in many parts of the world. New measures have been taken to ban, censor, or intimidate foreign reporters in many countries of the Middle East, Africa, and Southeast Asia, as well as in several countries of Latin America.

This trend is the tip of a political ice floe that shows every sign of resisting efforts to melt it. It reflects not merely a lack of mutual understanding but rather fundamental conflicts among differing concepts of a government's role in society and of a people's right to be informed. While Western newsmen generally act on the assumption that a free press is vital to a well-governed nation, many Third World leaders maintain that the greater goal of national development requires them to subordinate the ideal of free expression. Development of their countries requires unity, they say, and the press focuses on divisions. The Soviet philosophy of a controlled press supports their position and thus complicates efforts to seek common ground.

Third World concern appears to have focused on two principal complaints, articulated in conference after conference:

1. The Western press gives inadequate and superficial attention to the realities of developing countries, often infusing coverage with cultural bias. The traditional emphasis on the dramatic, the emotional and the amusing—the "coups and earthquakes" syndrome—is seen not only as unbalanced but also as detrimental to the development process.

2. The Western monopoly on the distribution of news—whereby even stories written about one Third World country for distribution in another are reported and transmitted by international news agencies based in New York, London, and Paris—amounts to neocolonialism and cultural domination.

There is certainly some justification for these complaints. Yet it is also true, as Western newsmen argue, that the methods by which many Third World governments now seek redress cause serious distortions in the news. In addition, current efforts to form alternative Third World press agencies could further interfere with the free flow of accurate news. On both sides, storms of rhetoric have confused the picture. Some of the most vehement detractors of Western reporting are themselves responsible for the imbalances they decry. And some Western news executives who protest the loudest commit the most blatant misrepresentations of Third World attitudes. Many on both sides, purposely or unwittingly, do not recognize how the problems of one are closely related to those of the other. Although it will not eliminate the real differences in interest, an increased and sincere attempt to achieve cooperation rather than conflict could help to lessen cultural misperceptions which serve neither the Western press nor the Third World.

II

In understanding the problems of Western coverage of the Third World, it is important to recognize that the international newsgathering system has severe limitations. What is commonly referred to as the world flow of information is more a series of trickles and spurts. News is moved across borders by surprisingly thin networks of correspondents for various types of news organizations with widely disparate purposes. Some correspondents, such as those working for television and most newspapers, report back to media in their own countries, and they approach the news from the viewpoint of specific readers and viewers. Others report to agencies which distribute their dispatches regionally or globally, or to internationally circulated magazines, and they attempt to achieve a more universal outlook, including details of interest to readers from many countries.

By far the largest distributors of information are the four Western-based global news agencies, which provide separate reports for their home markets and for various regions in the rest of the world. . . . All four major news agencies have a stated goal of objectivity, which is harmonious with their practical considerations. Thousands of newspapers and broadcasters with positions ranging from the radical Left to the extreme Right receive each of the four services. Neighboring countries with centuries of enmity all rely on them for world news. For example, their subscribers include government-controlled Arab media and conservative Israeli dailies. Each subscriber demands immediate rectification if it feels a story has been distorted. . . .

While a number of Western papers, magazines, and broadcast organizations also maintain correspondents abroad, the total is steadily dropping. Including salary, expenses, and communications, the costs of maintaining a single reporter overseas for a year can be well over $100,000. Provisions of the Tax Reform Act of 1976 lowering the income tax exemptions for U.S. citizens living abroad have increased the costs: *The Chicago Daily News,* which for years had kept a permanent staff of resident and roving correspondents overseas, disbanded its foreign service at the end of 1976, attributing its action at least in part to the new law.

Accurate statistics on reporters abroad are not available, but a good indication of the decrease is found in comparing the Overseas Press Club (of New York) directory of correspondents for 1975 with that of previous years. It listed 429 full-time American correspondents abroad compared to 563 in 1969. Foreign national employees of U.S. media were listed at 247 compared to 366 in 1969. (Of the 1975 total, 54% were based in 19 European countries.) Even those totals are misleadingly high, since they include writers for specialized publications and some expatriates who retain accreditation from small newspapers for prestige purposes. Some areas are almost completely written off. The AP and UPI each has a single full-time correspondent, based in Nairobi, to cover all of black Africa north of Rhodesia; roving correspondents based elsewhere add to the news reports. Their stringers in other African capitals send little, and most are closely watched by their governments. Only a few news organizations keep correspondents in East or West Africa. . . .

Whatever the talents of the men and women involved, a press corps of this size can only sample the news. Even *The New York Times*, with 33 of its own full-time correspondents and a wide range of news agencies to draw on, runs only about 14,000 words a day from all over the world. That is much more than the half-dozen foreign stories carried in most newspapers, but it involves careful selection and editing.

As a general rule, newspaper reporters, particularly the European ones, have greater leeway to interpret news events than do news agency correspondents. At the same time, newspaper correspondents normally have more space in which to discuss opposing sides of a sensitive issue. Both, however, are under great pressure to rush around covering major political events and disaster stories, whereas stories on development trends and social changes are regularly subject to delay. Because newspapers have only so much space and broadcasters have only so much air time, editors feel they must select what their audiences want, or they will lose the readers and viewers who keep them in business. News judgment rests on the potential impact and interest of stories rather than on any sense of international fair play. Even in the newspapers of most Third World countries, news items are predominantly from industrialized countries of the West and East, and stories from other developing countries often conflict.

Sometimes the process itself causes imbalances. Correspondents knew the military was planning to overthrow Isabel Perón in Argentina six months before the actual coup; the date was revised repeatedly. Many were afraid to leave Argentina to cover less dramatic stories for fear of missing the coup and finding the border closed. One newsmagazine reporter postponed a trip to Brazil a half-dozen times. "My boss thinks he's got the village idiot down here," he told friends. "But if I take off and the coup happens while I'm on the plane, I'll be looking for a job."

The smaller countries are squeezed into rapid trips during lulls between major stories in the larger countries. One Latin American scholar comments wryly: "I'm always amazed to see how news breaks in South America along the direct lines of the Braniff route.'' An assistant foreign editor of a major newspaper makes a similar point: ''I am disturbed by the hit-and-miss technique which we must use . . . almost at the correspondent's whim. A reporter finally gets to a place and reports things as new. . . . I'm always reminded of the stars—the light left some years ago and we're just getting around to seeing it. It's misleading and I don't know what to do about it.''

Because reporters tend to travel in packs, circumstances can focus far more attention on a particular event than it might ordinarily receive. Riots in Jamaica happened to coincide with a major International Monetary Fund meeting there in early 1975, so scores of foreign reporters were on hand to report them in chilling detail. Had there been no visiting correspondents, the local Jamaican stringers might not have seen fit to write, and the disturbance might have been a tree falling unheard in a forest.

The situation is similar, or worse, in Africa and Asia. A crisis in southern Africa (or a war in Vietnam) draws correspondents in droves, while the rest of the continent is neglected. Today, wide areas in both are rarely visited; for example, the small island nations of the Pacific and Indian Oceans are all but completely forgotten.

A series of other difficulties and limitations affect foreign reporting. News organizations tend to send young inexperienced reporters to the Third World, transferring them to larger bureaus in industrialized countries as they gain seasoning. Correspondents frequently cannot speak the language of the country they are covering, and translators, if available, are rarely adequate. Unfamiliarity with baffling local customs and thought processes can be dangerously misleading. Under such circumstances, even the best have difficulty, and some reporters working abroad are simply not capable of untangling complicated situations and presenting them clearly to faraway readers. Correspondents are seldom specialists, and a reporter may write about politics, table tennis, budget deficits, and traffic accidents in the same afternoon.

Inadvertent mistakes are also made in editing, rewriting, translating, and transmitting. Last year a young Chilean trainee at UPI was practicing on a teletype machine in Bogotá, and he made up an urgent story that President Alfonso López Michelsen had been assassinated. Through a technical error, the message went to New York and was relayed on the news wire in English and Spanish. The Spanish news agency, EFE, which has an accord with UPI to use its dispatches, relayed the story under its own logotype, without checking it. Although the story was eliminated quickly and UPI officials immediately apologized and explained what had happened, the President charged that he was a victim of an international plot.

Local stringers are generally poorly paid and have little motivation to provide more than a perfunctory relay of local newspaper reports. Because they may also be government employees, they are sometimes subject to extreme pressures, which often means one-sided or distorted dispatches. In addition,

the scarcity of space in print or on the air provides a constant goad to reporters to portray the stories they are covering in the most dramatic light possible. This is particularly true with newsmagazines and television networks.
Generally, foreign correspondents are responsible, with a keen sense of professional ethics, but there have been cases where some have exaggerated and
even invented facts in order to lend strength to their dispatches.

Space limitations have another distorting effect. Correspondents often must
use such shorthand terms as "right-wing dictatorship" and "pro-Peking"
without further explanation, raising more questions then they answer. To the
informed, and to many readers in the countries from which they are reporting,
such meaningless labels and glib generalities may be seen as superficial and
even insulting.

Finally, however hard a correspondent may try to exercise balance and objectivity, he is the prisoner of his own value system in judging a situation.
Narinder Aggarwala, an Indian journalist working with the United Nations,
made this point in the January issue of *The Interdependent*, published by the
United Nations Association:

> When Third World leaders criticize the Western press for biased and distorted reporting,
> they are not, generally speaking, questioning the factual accuracy of Western news agen-
> cies or their correspondents. What they feel chagrined about is the lack of a Third World
> perspective, as well as an appreciation of Third World information needs, in the news
> disseminated by the Western agencies.

III

The efforts of many Third World governments to inject their perspectives into
Western press coverage have in most cases compounded the problem. Many
of them treat the Western press as a monolithic and hostile entity which, if
properly controlled or cajoled, can be induced to act in a certain way. This
philosophy normally leads to frustration and increased bitterness. The sectors
of the press hostile to these regimes at the outset simply grow more hostile,
and have more to criticize, when controls are imposed. And the sympathetic
sectors are either prevented from saying anything—or are converted to hostility because of the measures taken.

Methods used to pressure correspondents vary widely. John Saar of *The
Washington Post* made a trip to South Korea without difficulty, but no one
would talk to him, at any level, because the *Post* had broken the story about
questionable Korean lobbying in the United States. India cut the telephone
and teleprinter lines of several foreign agencies in New Delhi but allowed
them to use their neighbors' communications to send their material. Sometimes reporters are chided gently by low-level officials; sometimes they are
obliquely threatened with death.

One common practice has been to expel a freelance reporter with no major backing as an example to regular staff correspondents. However, after several countries recently expelled correspondents of major news organizations with only lukewarm response, there appeared to be a growing awareness that it is not so difficult to push around the foreign press. Organizations are often reluctant to ask the State Department to join in protesting expulsions because they want to keep themselves separate from government. In some cases, news executives want to keep peace with the government that expelled their correspondent, to make it easier to send a new one. Others, from inertia or lack of a guiding policy, just let the incident go.

The easiest way for a country to control coverage, of course, is simply to deny access. Ronald Koven, foreign editor of *The Washington Post*, negotiated for almost a year to get correspondent David Ottaway into Somalia. "We have the feeling that the Third World is closing down on us, little by little, almost on a monthly basis," Koven said in one of a series of personal interviews I conducted on this subject. "Visas for countries at peace with the United States are sometimes very difficult to get." The *Post*'s widely respected Africa staff is a good example of the problem. Ottaway, along with other reporters, was expelled from Ethiopia, where he had gone when barred from Kenya. Like others, he had serious difficulty obtaining visas to a number of countries. The *Post*'s Robin Wright avoids Angola because she was accused of links with the mercenaries, but few reporters get into Angola anyway. Koven says he does not send reporters to Uganda, even if permitted, for fear of their safety. (The problem is not limited to black Africa. It took years for Jim Hoagland of the *Post* to be allowed back into South Africa after doing his series from there, which won the 1971 Pulitzer Prize.)

When newsmen cannot get into a country, they must write about it from the outside, often relying on questionable dissident sources with little chance to balance their reports with remarks from authorized spokesmen, and the result is likely to cause even more bitterness from the leaders of that country.

The general condition of misunderstanding can increase particular difficulties. *The New York Times* was allowed to send a correspondent, John Burns, into Mozambique for a balanced appraisal of the newly independent country. But officials of another branch of government arrested him and held him for several days. As a *Times* editor explained it, the officials had never heard of *The New York Times*; they thought Burns worked for *Time* magazine, with which they had a quarrel. (In fact, newsmagazines usually come under heavier fire than newspapers because they are often circulated in the countries they cover. The tight format, with emphasis on the more dramatic details which are of particular interest to a foreign reader, often upsets Third World authorities.)

As noted, government manipulation often backfires—but not always. For dramatic examples of how different types of manipulation, combined with the traditional limitations of international reporting, can result in grave distortions for the reader, compare the coverage of the 1973 military takeover in Chile and the 1976 coup d'état against Isabel Péron in neighboring Argentina. In both instances, a well-prepared, professional press corps sought to convey realities to American readers. Yet reporting from the two countries was so shaped by differing government strictures that it is still extremely difficult to make judgments about one in the light of the other.

Although there were fundamental political differences between the two coups, the basic facts were the same—a military junta overturned a civilian president amid expectations of some internal and international resistance. In the process, Chile—where the new rulers restricted coverage and exerted tight control over reporters—emerged with a much harsher image than Argentina, where the coup leaders kept good relations with the press but still controlled the flow of information by covering up their involvement rather than placing fetters on reporters.

The coup against Salvador Allende was forceful and bloody, masked by secrecy and launched by surprise. The junta's plan was to restore quickly what officers considered to be a normal balance, eliminating entrenched leftist control, before facing the world. They shut down communications, imposed curfews and controls, and refused entry to reporters—and almost everyone else—for nearly two weeks. The executions and widespread repression were neither admitted nor convincingly denied, so that the atmosphere was perfect for the inevitable rumors which follow any such upheaval. The few correspondents in Santiago at the time managed to send only brief dispatches under a severe after-the-fact censorship that some called the "file now, die later" plan. Meanwhile, scores of correspondents hovered at the borders in Argentina, interviewing everyone in sight who might have an inkling about what was going on. Although many exercised careful judgment and balance, others relayed farfetched rumors of resistance columns and acts of mass genocide.

The true picture was bad enough, but in addition, wildly exaggerated death figures were published around the world. The new government gained an immediate and lasting reputation for butchery: tales of martyrs and archvillains passed into history. By the time the borders opened, and reporters could see for themselves what was happening, most of the world had made up its mind about Chile.

At the same time, Chilean exiles and sympathizers around the world pressed intense campaigns against the military government, and their charges could not easily be refuted by independent newsmen because few were allowed in. As it turned out, much of the human rights reporting from inside Chile—little as there was—was basically solid because the junta allowed two major sources to operate with some freedom: the Church and the courts. High-level Church leaders substantiated individual charges of disappearance, torture, and execution. They made case studies and assembled overall statistics, making both available to newsmen. Also, Chilean courts accepted habeas corpus writs from relatives of missing persons and, because court records were public, reporters could find well-documented direct accounts of alleged abuses.

When the Argentine military decided to act almost three years later, planners studied the Chilean experience carefully. Selected correspondents and local reporters were kept informed on the progress of coup plans to an almost ludicrous degree. Officers assured the press that the transition would be smooth, bloodless, and fast. Privately, however, several generals were more candid. "There'll be killing, all right—you just won't see it. . . ," one told friends. "Bodies will turn up, but they won't be linked to us. We learned that from Chile."

The coup, as promised, went off without a hitch. Communications were not disturbed, and correspondents were not censored. The airport was closed briefly for security reasons, but there had been so much warning that most correspondents were already in anyway. The immediate image of the new government was one of moderation and restraint. That a large number of leftists were abducted, tortured, and executed was something reporters did not learn about until later. And when they did, they could not prove that those responsible were directly linked to the government, however obvious the connection. Correspondents also knew that, although there were no official curbs, they might fall victim to the same mysterious right-wing death squads blamed for the widespread killings of leftists.

Since readers in the United States assumed that correspondents were working freely, and they were not told of massacres by the government, they assumed that the government was indeed moderate. Thus, as in Chile, though with quite a different result, the world swiftly made up its mind about the Argentine junta. By the time desperate relatives told of missing persons, and qualified sources described how bodies were being dumped at sea from helicopters, interest in the story had waned.

In Argentina, the government saw to it that sources were few. Contrary to the Chilean situation, Church officials said little or nothing, and some Church sources admitted intimidation. Court records were closed. Local newspapers were under strict military control. "Sure, I feel guilty, but what could we do?" asked one senior correspondent of a major news agency at the end of 1976. "We say that 12 guerrillas were killed while raiding a police post. That's the police version, and it's all we have. We can't say that's obvious bull even if we think it is. And then when some mother calls up and says, 'How could my son have attacked a police station on Tuesday when police arrested him on Monday night?' what do you do?"

Viewed from a longer perspective, there were strong similarities in the way security forces in the government's pay dealt with suspected left-wing activists in Chile and Argentina. Both used widespread murder, torture, and arbitrary arrest. However, in Argentina, where reporters were allowed to operate as freely as their courage allowed, but with few available sources, no direct link was established to the government. In Chile, where correspondents were barred and then controlled, but where information could be found, a clear-cut policy of government involvement in human rights abuses was reported from the first days of the coup.

"We applied the same skills and energy toward reporting Chile and Argentina," remarks one well-known correspondent for a major U.S. organization, "and Chile came out much worse. It may be Chile's fault, and it may be because the Argentines were clever. But the reader can't be expected to know the background. He is counting on us to tell it straight, no matter what."

IV

In addition to individual efforts on the part of Third World governments to manipulate the Western press, Third World leaders have been planning concerted strategies to increase their control over the flow of information.

An extreme move toward press restrictions was put forward in a Soviet-sponsored draft resolution at the biennial UNESCO conference late last year in Nairobi. The key sentence in the proposed text—"States are responsible for the activities in the international sphere of all mass media under their jurisdiction"—would have endorsed measures taken against correspondents not only for their own actions inside a given country but also for the actions of their organizations elsewhere. Where authorities have been reluctant to expel reporters or to institute press controls for fear of damaging their international reputation, the sanction of an international body like UNESCO would make a significant difference.

At Nairobi, the resolution was tabled by a vote of 78 to 15, with six abstentions, after active campaigning by Western officials and news executives. But the Soviet Union is expected to continue pushing the issue, and there are varying forms of support from a wide sector of the nonaligned nations. Indeed, while debate was focused on this article, the conference passed without comment several measures that constitute a UNESCO blessing for increased state control of media and the movement of news.

At an April meeting in Florence, convened to further the Nairobi discussions, exchanges were sometimes heated and bitter. UNESCO's Assistant Director-General, Jacques Rigaud, identified a major point of contention: "Decolonization must be carried to its conclusion in the minds of men. It is uncomfortable to have to admit that supposedly universal values sometimes conceal a hard core of self-interest." He added later that values that had "for so long given a certain part of the world a clear conscience look different and are different if one is oppressed or well-endowed, developed or developing, or in danger of never developing."

The new feeling was evident in recent remarks by President Ferdinand

Marcos of the Philippines, where until recent years the press was extraordinarily free. Marcos told the Philippine Broadcasters Association that there was freedom of speech and freedom of the press in the Philippines just as there was in the Western countries. "The only difference is . . . our policy requires that the media wholly participate in the government . . . as committed agents of the government . . . for development."

The Indonesian press director, Soekarno, was more specific in an interview with *The Washington Post* in March: "These critical reports you've all been making lately hamper our speed of development. They draw the attention of the people away from development to other issues which creates frustration. . . . if they (Western reporters) employ the Western tradition of hitting issues face-on, they will not achieve their mission (of creating better government). They must follow the slower, more indirect Indonesian way, or else our government will ban foreign journalists and will ignore their reports." Indonesian Attorney General Ali Said earlier told local editors to stop printing Western news reports on the country. "Let them go to hell," he said.

Leonard Sussman of Freedom House in New York has labeled this concept "developmental journalism." Its thesis is that control of news is not only defensible but essential. Information itself and the means to transmit it are tools of development. Since governments must direct all resources toward the principal goal of development, any reporting that is critical or disruptive might hamper their progress. Governments, it is maintained, must focus attention on their achievements and protect their developing economies from the exposure of weaknesses; critical press coverage might dampen their people's spirits and lessen their chances for world sympathy.

Proponents of a more positive type of developmental journalism say that it is necessary for countries to share useful experiences and ideas that are not now adequately covered. Some liken this kind of journalism to the sort of reporting found in feature sections of Western papers, where readers in Dallas can learn how troublesome community problems were solved in Seattle or Miami. A low-cost housing program in Singapore could be a valuable model for dozens of other nations.

In order to share this sort of information, and to eliminate what many consider to be a Western bias in the information now available, a large number of Third World countries support expanding their own news facilities. The most significant steps in this direction were taken in mid-1976 with a ministerial meeting of 58 nonaligned nations in New Delhi, followed by a summit in Colombo. The summit approved a resolution establishing a Third World news pool as a mechanism to centralize and distribute news items from developing countries around the world.

The then Indian Prime Minister Indira Gandhi set the tone for the meetings, saying:

> The media of the powerful countries want to depict the governments of their erstwhile colonies as inept and corrupt and their people as yearning for the good old days. Leaders

who uphold their national interests and resist the blandishments of multinational corporations and agencies are denigrated and their images falsified in every conceivable way. . . . We want to hear Africans on events in Africa. You should similarly be able to get an Indian explanation of events in India.

The pool is already functioning, to a certain extent, with main relay points in Yugoslavia and India. (The new Indian government is taking a less militant stance, but there are other active supporters.) Under its constitution, any nonaligned nation can volunteer to collect and disseminate news from and to other countries provided it pays all reception and relay costs and does not interfere with the content of the incoming dispatches. Tanjug of Yugoslavia has been doing this on its own since January 1975, using four 38,000-watt transmitters outside of Belgrade that were reported to be part of a $13-million expansion program. Similarly, any nation can transmit its news for relay, and can receive relayed news, provided it pays all of its own costs. The framers of the pool arrangement encouraged countries to form national news agencies, if they had not already done so, to facilitate the exchange of news.

The Nairobi UNESCO conference later in 1976 endorsed the pool idea as part of a compromise agreement to defeat the Soviet proposal. It was also agreed that $130,000 would be spent to study means of efficient pool operation. Apart from the plan approved at Colombo, a number of countries are working toward regional pools, such as a Pan African news agency advocated by Zaïre.

At each international conference when news pools are discussed, numerous speakers repeatedly declare that their aim is not to supplant the major global agencies but rather to supplement them. According to this widely held moderate position, Western correspondents would not be affected by the changes developing countries advocate. However, an African ambassador to UNESCO bluntly expressed a more radical view: "We don't want Western journalists in our countries. They should take their news from us." The difference is crucial.

V

Western responses to Third World complaints and controls range from defensive antagonism to efforts at expanding cooperation. While there is some sympathy for the benign type of comparative developmental journalism, the more radical variant is rejected out of hand by most Western journalists.

"In part the attacks (on the Western press) are justified because attention to events is spasmodic and inadequate," observes Harvey Stockwin, a veteran correspondent for the *Far Eastern Economic Review*. "But they stem in large part from the fact that the Western press is the only one telling leaders what they don't want to hear." Western hostility to Third World positions revolves around that basic point: many leaders use such devices as news pools and developmental journalism as a convenient means to muzzle criticism and hide their own shortcomings.

Actual practice has shown this to be a justifiable concern. Where countries have refused access to correspondents but have provided a steady stream of government-vetted information by radio and by national news agencies, coverage has tended to be relatively uncritical and, by lack of balance, misleadingly favorable. This is particularly true in countries where there is not sufficient interest for reporters to seek out exiled opponents or neutral travelers to provide the needed balance.

Since there is some form of government control, subsidy, or guidance in almost every national news agency of the Third World, it would hardly be reasonable to expect completely balanced reporting on a voluntary basis. No government anywhere enjoys energetic probing by the press. Doubtless, Ron Ziegler would have been delighted to have had the final word when pronouncing the Watergate break-in a "third-rate burglary." Simple human nature makes it very difficult for any person to provide an accurate picture of himself. As a retired UPI executive, Roger Tatarian, noted (in a conference paper for the Edward R. Murrow Center at the Fletcher School of Law and Diplomacy), according to Mrs. Gandhi's definition, the Third World would have had to rely on a national agency controlled by Idi Amin Dada for facts about the Israeli Entebbe raid.

At the UNESCO conference, Western newsmen were vehement in their opposition to the Soviet proposal. George Beebe of *The Miami Herald*, chairman of the World Press Freedom Committee, told reporters in Nairobi that such curbs as the Soviet proposal would be "tragic." He said: "It is essential that we keep communication lines open in this rapidly changing world."

After the April conference in Florence, Beebe took a harder stance in a column for the *Herald*. He wrote: "The UNESCO colloquium . . . convinced delegates from the West that we are fast losing the global war in the field of communications. What was billed as a conference on the 'Free and Balanced Flow of Information,' largely was a series of attacks on the U.S. news agencies and the Western media. This was led by the communists and leftists who exert a great influence on UNESCO." Beebe then added: "There were few newspapermen of stature from over the world. Instead there was a surplus of government officials, news agency representatives and several young radicals . . . . It was the consensus of the Western delegates that the most appropriate word for summarizing the future media outlook is 'frightening'."

Some contend that obstructing the flow of information violates the Universal Declaration of Human Rights.

Speaking for their Western readership, the newsmen make the point that if developed nations are to work cooperatively with developing nations in a new international economic order, they cannot do so in ignorance. As Philip M. Foisie of *The Washington Post* puts it: "We feel it is very important that the American reader and voter is informed by professionals about what is going on in other countries. As one example, if American voters are to spend tax dollars, they have a right to know what is going on.''

While most admit inadequacies in their reportage, Western journalists also defend the job they are able to do under the circumstances. Executives emphatically deny any intentional bias or any form of conspiracy against anyone. Gerald Long, managing director of Reuters, noted in an interview that complaints often are made as a result of mistaken information about how news organizations work. He gave the example of an unnamed American ambassador in Africa who once charged that Reuters was guilty of worse distortion than TASS in reporting news from the United States because it transmitted only stories about racial strife. The ambassador was seeing only those few dispatches selected for publication by the local newspapers, a fraction of the complete Reuters report from the United States.

On the general subject, Long commented:

> We are sometimes accused of not doing what we have not set out to do. How can you give a complete picture of India, in, say, 3,000 words a day? No, we're not and we can't. . . . We must operate on the principle of news as exception. Reuters tries to give a fair picture, a rounded picture, but we can only send a limited amount, and we must be selective.

With regard to cultural bias, Westerners also point out that most agencies employ nationals to write about their own countries, working in their own languages from the point of view of their own culture. Although most of what Uruguayans read about neighboring Argentina is from the global agencies, for example, the dispatches are almost all written originally in Spanish by Argentines with the idea in mind that they would be read largely by other Latin Americans.

The idea that a Third World news pool might solve some of these problems has been greeted by Western newsmen with a mixture of wariness, sympathy, and skepticism. Most global news agency executives say they have no objection to a Third World pool if the idea is only to supplement the existing reports and not to hamper correspondents' work or to close off markets. Stanley M. Swinton, Vice President and Director of World Services for the AP, phrased his personal view this way:

> My basic theory is the more news the better so long as news from one source is not permitted to squeeze out news from international agencies in a twisted Gresham's Law way. . . . For the international news agencies, it is self-defeating to declare war on the Third World's efforts to intramurally distribute more information.

And according to a disinterested observer, Dr. Jacques Freymond, the Swiss Director of the Geneva Institute for Graduate Studies and former Vice President of the International Committee of the Red Cross:

> This is a normal process of evolution of the Third World. We have been too ethnocentric in our reporting of things. Just as in early France all roads led to the capital in spoke and hub patterns with no connecting links, so it is with the patterns of reporting from these countries. If we resist their doing this (forming a pool), we will force them into an

either/or situation; we will force the opposite of what we would want. At the same time, we should try to maintain our world agencies to offer the presence of a pluralistic solution.

Some agencies have offered advice and equipment to new nonaligned agencies, and some retired executives have said they might be available as consultants. In private, however, Western experts generally agree that internal ideological differences, political rivalries and technical difficulties make it unlikely that any wide-based Third World pool would be functioning effectively soon. In fact, a number of eminent Third World jouranlists express similar skepticism.

For many, the limited response to Tanjug's efforts has shown that even sympathetic government-controlled papers do not want unwieldy streams of government press releases from other Third World countries unless there is some actual news value. Tanjug relays several hours of pool material daily, but little is used. And if the dispatches touch on the sort of sensitive political and economic issues that are of interest beyond national borders, they are often incomplete and unreliable. Also, many Third World leaders are reluctant to exchange domination by the international agencies for domination by a Third World agency. Already a rivalry has developed between Tanjug and Samachar of India for leadership in the pool, and this is widely seen as evidence that some larger Third World countries want to use the pool as a means to exert their own political influence.

"In a river, there are big fish and small fish, and the small fish must beware," observes Elebe Ma Ekonzo, director general of the Zaïre Press Agency and former ambassador to Belgium. Elebe prefers smaller regional groupings such as the Pan African agency, but even that, he said in an interview, could take years to organize because of the divisive factors at work.

VI

Obviously, there are no simple solutions to the basic conflicts underlying the Western and Third World approaches to the role of the press. Extremists on both sides must realize that some positions are virtually irreconcilable, and if they are concerned with an improvement they must seek some form of constructive compromise. This is complicated by the character of opposing forces. "Third World" is a convenient term, but it describes little. It covers scores of countries, each with its own national interests and policies. Similarly, there is no common position among news organizations of a single country, much less among all Western countries. Individual editors may become more sensitive, but they are not likely to subscribe to any overall code. With this in mind, there are specific areas where progress might be made.

—Both sides should drop politicized hyperbole and take a reasoned look at realities. At the working level, many of the goals passionately espoused at international meetings were realized long ago. Some are preposterously expensive and impractical. Disinterested experts could compile basic data showing how national and international agencies are already exchanging news, how correspondents operate and what they write, what the news media in developed and developing countries actually use, and what technical and organizational difficulties need to be overcome for further cooperation. A country-by-country survey could detail working conditions of correspondents and the flow of information, including visa restrictions and censorship rules. International discussion should include professional journalists as well as—or instead of—ideology-minded civil servants. Criticisms should be specific, citing particularly objectionable dispatches rather than merely putting forth general ideological condemnations.

—On the basis of realistic information, proponents of the various viewpoints should discuss means of accord and cooperation in private meetings. Such working level sessions as the Tunis conference in November 1976 between European and Arab agencies can provide the means for exchanging criticism and suggestions while preventing frustrations from turning into hostility. There are already scores of joint accords among large and small agencies to share their reporting, and these could be built into a more complete and workable international network.

—A significant Western contribution could be made in several areas. A number of leading American publishers and broadcasters have organized the World Press Freedom Development Committee—which plans to take in news executives from elsewhere in the world—to encourage constructive cooperation. The initial proposal is to raise $1 million for several programs, including training seminars to acquaint Third World journalists with Western methods, visits by foreign journalists to American professional meetings, and trips by Western experts to provide technical assistance. The Committee can also help send Third World journalists to Western universities. There are other possibilities. Although no agency or news organization has funds for widescale training, governments could contribute jointly to an organization that could administer transnational training programs. Cross-cultural training, it should be noted, has limitations and dangers. Sometimes journalists may be frustrated in trying to apply the techniques of a free press in countries where there is government control of information. But a higher level of competence across borders can contribute significantly to future understanding.

—Finally, Third World authorities must be persuaded to see for themselves that their interests are enhanced more by cooperating with the Western press than by fighting it. Editors and officials should use every opportunity to demonstrate that Western reporting practices do not automatically mean hostility and conspiracy. And, in cases where pressure is applied, they should protest vigorously at every possible level. News organizations can use more imagination to find alternative sources of information when borders are closed. If Third World leaders can be shown that access to news will be defended—and that all countries will be covered whether or not reporters are allowed to enter— they are likely to be more reluctant to attempt to manage news. Although much can be gained by improving Western reporting and paying more attention to Third World viewpoints, Western editors must defend the right to report.

These measures are at least a beginning. Practical cooperation and Western defense of free-flowing information may not resolve the basic conflict, but they will go a long way toward ensuring that Americans, Argentines, and Angolans alike will be more accurately informed about what is happening in their world.

14
Nonalignment and Cultural Imperialism

Tran van Dinh

Temple University

Tran van Dinh is Professor in the Pan-African Studies Department, Temple University, Philadelphia. He has published extensively on Vietnam and Southeast Asia. Tran van Dinh is a former diplomat and was a delegate to the Bandung Conference (1955). He was in Colombo, Sri Lanka, during the 1976 5th Summit Meeting of Heads of State or Government of Non-Aligned Countries. He is coauthor of *From Bandung to Colombo: Conferences of the Non-Aligned Countries, 1955–1975*, published in 1976.

This chapter is a slightly abbreviated reprinting of an article that first appeared in *The Black Scholar*, December 1976, and is published by permission of *The Black Scholar*.

I

The roots of nonalignment can be traced back to the 1955 Asian-African Conference in Bandung, Indonesia. (For an historical analysis and a bibliography and documents on nonalignment, see Singham and Tran van Dinh, 1976.) Its antecedents however "are found in the first stirrings of national sentiments among Asians and Africans at the turn of the century, and in the ideals of Pan-Africanism, Pan-Asianism, and Pan-Arabism, which these sentiments produced" (Kimche, 1973, p. 1). These sentiments at first led to a reexamination of indigenous values and cultures. They were given later a political content and impetus by the 1904 Japanese military victory over Czarist Russia, the triumph of the 1917 Bolshevik Revolution and especially by V. I. Lenin's theories on the National Question and Imperialism. (For documents on the National Question and Imperialism, see Possony, 1966.)

Independence movements sprang up both in the colonies and among colonized subjects living in the metropoles, and "though isolated from one another, they developed virtually identical objectives, namely, the search for a new Asian or African personality, and closely linked with it, freedom from colonial domination. This dichotomy of aims runs like a thread through virtually all the nationalist movements of Asia and Africa'' (Kimche, 1973, p. 2). Intellectuals from Asia and Africa (in particular those sympathetic to socialist ideas: W. E. B. Du Bois, Ho Chi Minh, Felix Houphouet-Boigny, Aimé Césaire, Jomo Kenyatta, Kwame Nkrumah, Jawaharlal Nehru, Krishna Menon) met in metropolitan capitals such as Paris and London. In February 1927, many of them attended in Brussels (Belgium) the Congress of Oppressed Nationalities organized by the Association of Oppressed Peoples which had been founded as the ''Anti-Imperialist League'' in Moscow in 1924.* The Brussels Conference was recoganized as a forerunner of the 1955 Bandung Meeting by President Ahmad Sukarno in his opening address.

This brief historical account serves to demonstrate that the sense of cultural identity, of solidarity, existed among Asian and African (including black) revolutionaries in the early twentieth century. To them, cultural imperialism was part and parcel of imperialism and whenever they attacked the latter, they also attacked the former. Richard Wright (1956), an expatriate Paris-based black writer who participated as a journalist in the 1955 Bandung Conference; explained the unity of the 29 participating Asian and African nations:

> Only brown, black and yellow men who had long been made agonizingly self-conscious, under the rigors of colonial rule, of their race and their religion could have felt the need for such a meeting. There was something extra-political, extra-social, almost extra-human about it; it smacked of tidal waves, of natural forces. And the call for the meeting had not been sounded in terms of ideology. The agenda and the subject matter had been written for centuries in the blood and bones of the participants. The conditions under which these men had lived had become their tradition, their culture, their raison d-être. . . . (p. 14)

Richard Wright was not the only Afro-American present at Bandung. Adam Clayton Powell was there too. And although Richard Wright thought that the black congressman from Harlem's ''activities were not my style,'' he admitted that ''Powell's appearance at Bandung was that he felt the call, felt its meaning . . .'' (Wright, 1956, p. 178). This meaning, this call was clear in the Final Comminiqué of the Bandung Conference. Chapter B on Cultural Cooperation, point 2, reads:

> The Asian-African Conference took note of the fact that the existence of colonialism in many parts of Asia and Africa, in whatever form it may be, not only prevents cultural cooperation but also suppressed the national cultures of the peoples. Some colonial powers have denied their dependent peoples basic rights in the sphere of education and culture,

---

*Ho Chi Minh's political activities at that period were typical. In 1920, at the age of 30, and then a founding member of the French Communist Party, he formed the League of Colonial Peoples in Paris and published the journal *Le Paria*. He visited the U.S., wrote about the lynching of blacks and the Ku Klux Klan, and in 1927 attended the Brussels Conference before going to Thailand. (See, Ho Chi Minh, 1970.)

which hampers the development of their personality and also prevents cultural intercourse with other Asian and African peoples. In particular, the Conference condemned racialism as a means of cultural suppression . . . (Singham and Tran van Dinh, 1976, p. 8).

II

Since Bandung, and amidst the ebullient hopes and the creative fervor generated by successive and successful anti-imperialist wars of national liberation exploding in the three continents of Asia, Africa and Latin-America as well as the black struggle in the United States, revolutionary leaders and thinkers in the "Third World"* have scientifically studied the relationship between culture and revolution, between tradition and revolution. One of the most articulate and most progressive among them was Amilcar Cabral. In an address delivered on the acceptance of an Honorary Degree of Doctor of Philosophy at Lincoln University, Pennsylvania, on October 15, 1972 he argued:

Certainly, imperialist domination calls forth cultural oppression and attempts, either directly or indirectly to do away with the most important element of the culture of the subject people. But the people are only able to create and develop the liberation movement because they keep their culture alive despite the continual and organized repression of their cultural life and because they continue to resist culturally, even when their political and military resistance is destroyed. And it is cultural resistance which at a given moment can take on new forms—political, economic, army—to fight foreign domination . . . (Cabral, 1972).

Amilcar Cabral brought the "masses line" into his analysis. He also injected in his thoughts the "classes line":

But, the return to the source is not and cannot in itself be an act of struggle against foreign domination, colonialist or racist. And it no longer necessarily means a return to traditions. It is a denial by the petite bourgeoisie of the country of the pretended supremacy of the culture of the dominant power over that of the dominated people with which it must identify itself. The return to the sources is therefore not a voluntary step but the only possible reply to the demand of concrete, historically determined and enforced by the inescapable contradictions between the colonized society and the colonial power, between the masses of the people exploited and the foreign exploitive classes—a contradiction in the light of which each social structure or indigenous class must define its position. When the return to the source goes beyond the individual and is expressed in groups or movements, the contradiction is transformed into struggle, secret or overt, and is a prelude to the preindependence movement or of the struggle for liberation from the foreign yoke. So, the return to the source is of no historical importance unless it brings not only real involve-

---

*I put "Third World" in quotes, because I do not agree with the division of the world into 1st, 2nd, 3rd, and 4th categories. Rather, I concur with Shrimati Indira Gandhi, Prime Minister of India, when she said, in her inaugural address to the Ministerial Conference of Non-Aligned Countries on the Press Agencies Pool (New Delhi, July 1976): "There is a tendency to divide the world into different categories and the expression 'Third World' is used rather indiscriminately and applied to nonaligned and developing countries. Personally I stand firmly by the concept of One World. . . ." (Document: Embassy of India, Washington, D.C.)

ment in the struggle for independence but also complete and absolute identification with the hopes of the mass of the people who contest not only the foreign culture but also the foreign domination as a whole . . . (Cabral, 1972).

Amilcar Cabral's "masses line" and "classes line" contribution to the analysis of the relationship between culture and revolution saved the legitimate offensive by the "Third World" against cultural imperialism into falling into cultural chauvinism which is divisive, reactionary and which our enemies expected it to happen.

III

By the middle of the 1960s, the escalating Vietnam War, the barbarities inflicted on the peoples of Indochina by the massive American military power and the cruel "pacification program," the rapid "Americanization" of cities—with the accompanying problems of drug, prostitution, crimes—forced the progressive elements in the academic community in the West, in particular in the U.S., to look into certain unexamined aspects of imperialism, such as Mass Communications and their international role. A pioneer in the field is Professor Herbert I. Schiller of the University of California, San Diego. His *Mass Communications and American Empire* (Schiller, 1969) "documents the facts—drawing on industrial and governmental sources—about the 'emerging imperial network of American economics and finance' and how it utilizes the communications media for its defense and entrenchment . . . and for its expansion" (Shayon, 1969).

Mass Communications and American Empire was followed by *The Mind Managers* (Schiller, 1973), which shows how the consciousness of almost every American is programmed and how the manipulation of information and imagery is effectively done in the U.S. His most recent book, *Communication and Cultural Domination* (Schiller, 1976), describes the process of cultural domination and offers some general observations on possible means of resisting it. These works basically expose the imperial nature of the U.S. doctrine of "the free flow of information." This apparently noble doctrine rises with the imperial ascendancy of the United States and was promoted with great conviction and zeal by the father of the Cold War: John Foster Dulles.* Schiller's works are necessary to understand why the nonaligned countries are now starting the much delayed offensive against cultural imperialism.†

---

*He proclaimed: "If I were to be granted one point of foreign policy and no other, I would make it the free flow of information" (Schiller, 1976, p. 24).

†There are other scholars who are engaged in study similar to Schiller and in analyzing the "commodity" character and the material content of information, among them: Dallas W. Smythe (Simon Fraser University, Canada); George Gerbner (Dean of the Annenberg School of Communications, University of Pennsylvania); Kaarle Nordenstreng and Tapio Varis of the Institute of Journalism and Mass Communications, University of Tampere, Finland.

Nonalignment—which is deeply rooted in anti-colonialism, anti-imperialism, in peace and equality and in consistent support of national liberation movements—has since its official birth gradually but solidly moved to the front line in its fight for a new economic order and a new information order without which there is neither real freedom nor lasting peace.

IV

The 1961 Nonaligned Summit held in Belgrade, with the participation of twenty-five countries, reaffirmed the principle that "all nations have the right of unity, self-determination, and independence by virtue of which right they can determine their political status and freely pursue their economic, social and *cultural* (italics mine) development without intimidation or hindrance" (Singham and Tran van Dinh, 1976, p. 12). The 1964 Cairo Summit (42 countries) recognized that "culture helps to widen the mind and enrich life, that all human cultures have their special values and can contribute to the general progress, that many cultures were suppressed and cultural relations interrupted under colonial domination; that international understanding and progress require a revival and rehabilitation of these cultures, a free expression of their identity and national character and a deeper mutual appreciation of their values as to enrich the common cultural heritage of man" (Singham and Tran van Dinh, 1976, p. 34). The 1970 Lusaka Summit (53 nations) reiterated the same principles (Singham and Tran van Dinh, 1976, p. 50).

During the same period (1950s–1960s) various meetings of the Afro-Asian People's Solidarity brought out in practical proposals the Bandung's principles. For example, the Afro-Asian People's Solidarity Conference in Cairo (December 26, 1957–January 1, 1958), in its Resolution on Cultural Exchange and Cooperation, "maintains that the existence of colonialism in many parts of Asia and Africa hinders cultural cooperation and suppresses national culture," condemns racialism as a means of cultural suppression, and urges "the African and Asian nations to preserve their cultural heritage, both national and popular." It recommends "the revision of textbooks used in Afro-Asian schools with a view to removing incorrect information due to imperialist influences," the "inclusion of Afro-Asian studies in school syllabuses of member countries with special emphasis on their common problems," the "establishment of an international university for Afro-Asian studies" (Afro-Asian Peoples' Solidarity Conference, 1958, pp. 257–63).

But one has to wait until the Fourth Nonaligned Summit held in 1973 in Algiers (75 member nations) to see developed a more scientific analysis of cultural imperialism and a more specific strategy to resist it. Under the topic Preservation and Development, the Conference stated that "it is an established fact that the activities of imperialism are not confined solely to the political and economic fields, but also cover the cultural and social fields," and stressed "the need to reaffirm national cultural identity and eliminate the harmful consequences of the colonial era." In Chapter XIII of the Action Program for Economic Cooperation, the Conference recommended a "concerted action in the fields of mass communications." The Conference urged "the Secretary General of the United Nations to establish a special Chair of Nonalignment at the proposed United Nations University so as to facilitate research on the historical evolution and the present and future role of nonalignment in the changing world order" (Singham and Tran van Dinh, 1976, pp. 161, 199). The Algier's decisions were concretized by a number of follow-up meetings.

In May 1975, representatives of 14 nonaligned countries met in Belgrade (Yugoslavia) to prepare the agenda for a Nonaligned Symposium on Information to be held in Tunis (Tunisia) in March 1976. The symposium organization committee composed of six countries—Mexico, Tunisia, Sri Lanka, Cuba, Yugoslavia—agreed that the topics to be discussed at the Tunis meeting should cover:

1. The promotion of mass information media between nonaligned countries. (This has been partially done already since January 1975 by the Pool of News Agencies of Nonaligned Countries in Belgrade.)*

2. The role to be played by the information organs in encouraging cultural interaction between nonaligned countries.

3. The role to be played by the information organs in reinforcing economic and social cooperation between nonaligned countries (Tunis, Secretary of State for Information, 1976).

The proposed Agenda was submitted to the Fifth Ministerial (Foreign Ministers) Conference held in Lima (Peru), August 25–30, 1975.

In Resolution VI, on "Cooperation In the Field of Diffusion of Information and Mass Communications Media," the Lima Conference (81 countries) agreed on the following:

1. The Conference notes with satisfaction the results achieved in promoting cooperation among nonaligned countries in the field of mass communication, including the commencement of a pool of news agencies of nonaligned countries which started operating in January 1975. A meeting of representatives of governments and press agencies of nonaligned countries should be convened to draw up a draft Constitution for the Non-Aligned Press Agencies Pool, which would include elements such as its organizational, structural and operational arrangements and financial participation for consideration and adoption by the Summit at Colombo. The participants accepted with satisfaction the offer of the Government of India to host this meeting at New Delhi in 1976.

2. In order to further stimulate the encouraging results already obtained, Tunisia is appointed as coordinating country in this area. The Conference supports the convening of the symposium on mass media in Tunis in 1976.

---

*The Pool is coordinated by the Yugoslav Tanjug News Agency. During 1975, the Pool has worked out 26 cooperative agreements with 26 official news agencies from nonaligned countries.

3. These coordinating countries shall also implement the means of concerted action in question of mass communications and cultural exchanges in
the framework of the Algiers Programme of Action in particular:

—to revise the cable tariffs for the press and to facilitate more economical
and faster intercommunications.

—to cooperate in the reorganization of communications channels which are
still dependent or which constitute a colonial inheritance and obstruct direct
and rapid communications among nonaligned countries.

—to exchange and disseminate information on mutual national achievements
through newspapers, radio, television and news communication media.

—to share experiences in connection with information media by organizing
reciprocal visits of delegations of experts in information media, exchange
radio and television programmes, films and books, organize cultural exhibits
and artistic festivals.

—to adopt urgent measures to accelerate the process of collective acquisition
of communications satellites and to prepare a code of conduct which regulated
their utilization.

—to programme a joint action before the Secretary-General of the United Nations so that a special chair on the Policy of Nonalignment within the proposed United Nations University might be created and, in the same manner, to
foster similar studies in the universities and institutions of the nonaligned
countries'' (Singham and Tran van Dinh, 1976, p. 181).

V

Armed with specifics in Resolution VI of the Lima Ministerial Meeting, delegates from 38 member states and 13 observers (states and organizations) met
in Tunis (Tunisia) on March 26–30 for the Symposium on Information of
the Non-Aligned countries. The participants remarked ''that the nonaligned
countries are at the moment suffering from a sickness provoked by the domination of their mass communication media by the developed countries having
the monopoly over most of the world's communication media through which
much of the news is transmitted and the activities of nonaligned countries
made public'' (Tunis, Secretary of State for Information, 1976.)

They noted that ''although the cultures and civilisations of nonaligned countries are fundamental parts of the patrimony of whole of humanity, they have
been for a long time targets for distortion and deformation by colonising
States. These states persist in imposing their pattern of civilization and so ac-
centuate the monopoly of mass communication media culture and leisure.
Some of our peoples are still carried in a current of admiration of which they
are captive and which draws them under the yoke of a pattern of civilization
not conforming to their national patrimony and unconnected with our real requirements'' (Tunis, Secretary of State for Information, 1976). The particip-

ants particularly analyzed the role of press transnationals "in systematically distorting the facts about nonaligned countries by the use of the press for retaliation and political penetration.''* They pointed out that "the press is a commodity for these transnationals" and "in its processing and transmission intervene considerations which tend to perpetuate a system of domination in which the authentic interests of the developing countries are consistently ignored or misinterpreted" (Tunis, Secretary of State for Information, 1976). The Tunis Nonaligned Symposium on Information clearly showed that its participants had fully grasped the essentials of the problems they faced. This helped them to work out practical proposals for "The Ministerial Conference of Non-Aligned Countries on The Press Agencies Pool," held in New Delhi (India) July 8–13, 1976.

The importance of the New Delhi conference was demonstrated by the fact that the Meeting of the Coordinating Bureau (the only semipermanent institution of the nonaligned countries), at the level of Foreign Ministers, held in Algiers in May–June 1976 regarded it as "a significant step forward in cooperation among nonaligned countries in the field of information" and called for "the participation of all nonaligned countries in ensuring successful outcome." The call was heard and 59 member states and 7 observers (states and organizations, including the United Nations) sent their information ministers (or equivalent) for the first highest level meeting on Information by nonaligned countries. In her inaugural address, Shrimati Indira Gandhi, Prime Minister of India, clearly and candidly defined the problem:

> In spite of political sovereignty, most of us who have emerged from a colonial or semi-colonial past continue to have a rather unequal cultural and economic relationship with our respective former overlords. They often remain the main source of industrial equipment and technological guidance. The European language we speak itself becomes a conditioning element. Inadequacy of indigenous educational materials made us dependent on the books of these dominant countries, especially at the university stage. We imbibe their prejudices. Even our image of ourselves, not to speak of the view of other countries, tends to conform to theirs. The self-deprecation and inferiority complex of some people of former colonies makes them easy prey to infiltration through forms of academic colonialism. This also contributes to the brain drain.
>
> I am not saying that we should not learn English or French. Nor am I for any narrow linguistic chauvinism which would only divide us. We must learn international languages to communicate and widen our horizon. But rather than unguardedly accepting versions put out by news agencies and publishing houses of the western countries, we should get to know one another directly and keep in touch to have firsthand acquaintance with our respective views.

---

*The participants must have had in mind the case of Chile, where a combination of economic strangulation and mass communication manipulations succeeded in otherthrowing the government of President Allende in 1973. For example, the "CIA covertly channeled $1.5 million to El Mercurio, the largest daily paper in Chile, to insure anti-Allende coverage, to keep the paper solvent. El Mercurio was published . . . by Augustine Edwards, a close friend of Donald M. Kendall, President of Pepsi Cola'' (and an intimate of former President Nixon). (See The New York Times, December 5, 1975; see also Schiller, 1976, pp. 98–99, and Fagan, 1974.)

She illustrated what she said by India's own experience:

In 1972 we had severe drought. We have to marshal all our administrative resources and
our organizational capacities to feed and provide work to millions of people. We did not
allow any one to die. But newspapers and news agencies ignored this heroic achievement,
looking only for disaster stories!

Having perhaps Allende's overthrow in mind, she continued:

The media of the powerful countries want to depict the governments of their erstwhile
colonies as inept and corrupt and their people as yearning for the good old days. This
cannot be attributed entirely to the common human failing of nostalgia. To a large extent
there is a deliberate purpose. Leaders who uphold their national interests and resist the
blandishments of multi-national corporations and agencies, are denigrated and their image
falsified in every conceivable way.*

VI

Shrimati Indira Gandhi's address set the tone for the participants' deliberations
along a well-conceived Agenda, which included:

A report on the progress and functioning of the pool by Yugoslavia.

A report on the International Symposium on the Ways to Develop Information between Nonaligned Countries by Tunisia: Consideration of further
cooperation among nonaligned countries in the field of information.

Constitution of the Nonaligned Press Agencies Pool, including its organizational, structural, operational and financial arrangements.

Consideration of cable tariffs and improvement of mutual communication
facilities.

Adoption of the decisions and recommendations of the Conference.

In my experiences, most conferences fail not solely because of the lack of
goodwill by its participants but mostly because of the lack of theoretical unity
and leadership. The theoretical unity and the leadership were provided in this
conference by its chairman: Shri Vidya Charan Shukla, Minister of Information & Broadcasting, Government of India. His opening speech was a brilliant
analysis of the nature and character of the mass communications in our present world, a precise description of the potential strength and obvious weaknesses of the existing state of information order among nonaligned countries.
It shows his deep knowledge of the nonaligned countries "enemies" in the

---

*Official documents made available to me by M. R. Sivaramakrishnan, Press Counselor, Em-
bassy of India, Washington, D.C. Unless otherwise stated, quotes on the New Delhi Conference
are from the same documents. I quote the Prime Minister of India at length because what she said
was a warning to countries which are not yet aware of the "destabilization" process à la Chile, a
process which threatens the security of a number of countries in the nonaligned movement. The
5th Summit Meeting in Colombo in August 1976 has also paid attention to this matter: Chapter
XVIII: Interference in the Internal Affairs of States, point 144 of the Political Declaration.

field of information, and his ability to provide practical remedies. I just cite only one point, point 7 of his speech, which should be read in its entirety:

Indeed, the growth of most of the international news agencies appears fully linked with the political and economic power which the former colonial countries have tried to wield over the rest of the world. The theme of "free" flow of information, which was chanted in chorus, was aimed to enable all countries in name but only the powerful in reality, to pump their information into all regions of the world without let or hindrance. Nonaligned countries till today have been able to do almost nothing to protect their national interests against such onslaughts, since no safeguards are possible without (a) some degree of development of their own national media and (b) a state of cooperation amongst themselves. In fact the idea of "free" flow of information fits insidiously into the package of other kinds of "freedom" still championed by the adherents of 19th century liberalism. It is painful to recall that many of us have to reckon with such an elitist neocolonialism within our own countries. Such a linkup is typical of the ways through which former colonial powers still wish to maintain their material and intellectual hold and is parallel to a similar linkup witnessed in the economic field where internal elements of vested interests make common cause with external elements in the name of freedom of trade and business. This is yet another area which reveals the deep political implications of the problem of communication media and thus deserves the notice of the higher level of leadership in every country.

Recommendations made by the New Delhi Information Ministerial Conference, in particular, the drafted Constitution of the Press Agencies Pool, were endorsed by the Fifth Summit Meeting of Heads of State or Government of Non-Aligned Countries held in Colombo, Sri Lanka, 16–19 August 1976. (Resolution NAC/CONF.5/S/RES 16).

Reflecting the developments of the nonaligned movement, and its expanding "Third World" membership, the United Nations Educational, Scientific and Cultural Organization (UNESCO), which in the past defended the "free flow of information doctrine" has now replaced it in its research, documentation and policy programs with the concept of the "balanced flow of information." In July 1976, UNESCO sponsored a nine-day conference in San Jose, Costa Rica for 21 Latin-American countries to draw up communications policies for the region. The recommendations of this conference generally followed those of the nonaligned countries.* In late September 1976, Mr. Amadous M'bow, UNESCO Director-General, accused the international news agencies of seeking to emphasize the negative side of news from developing nations and declared that "one of the greatest forms of inequality in the contemporary world is that involving information."†

---

*See also *The New York Times* August 2, 1976. The recommendations of the San Jose Conference were presented to the UNESCO General Conference in Nairobi in October, 1976.

†Agence France Presse, quoted in *India News*, published by the Information Service, Embassy of India, Washington, D.C., October 1, 1976. It is noted that the question of the imbalance of information was persistently pursued by India in the nonaligned meetings as well as at UNESCO conferences.

VII

Since its genesis, the nonalignment movement has been continually criticized and even ridiculed by major western mass media. (Singham and Tran van Dinh, 1976, pp. 195–196; see also Bunnel, 1964.) These attacks which often smacked of a racist attitude, dismissed the movement as simply a "tool of communism." However when UNESCO changed its communication concept from the "free flow of information" to that of "balanced flow of information," when the nonaligned countries developed (at Algiers in 1973 and Colombo in 1976) a coherent offensive against cultural imperialism, then the attacks became vicious, virulent and well orchestrated.* Typical of these was an editorial in *The Washington Post* of July 30, 1976, denouncing the UNESCO-sponsored San Jose Meeting. The *Post* accused UNESCO of trying to convert news "into a national commodity which it is any government's right to exclusively control." To *The Post*, "to convert all news to propaganda in the name of combating "cultural imperialism" is simply to follow the Russian example . . ." Old wine in new bottles! *The Post* chose to ignore the findings of the U.S. Congress on the role of the CIA in the manipulation of the foreign press. For example, the House Committee "found that at least 29 percent of CIA's covert actions over the years were for media and propaganda projects. This figure translates into secret CIA expenditures in the billions of dollars aimed at making other countries toe the covert American propaganda line" (Marks, 1976; see also U.S. Senate, 1976).

The question that must be raised is: Why do the powerful multinationals (or transnationals) of the information industry feel so threatened? The answer is not hard to find. "Third World" countries, in general, and nonaligned countries, in particular, have brought up to the international forum for the first time, a fundamental problem closely related to neocolonialism in one hand and to the new economic order on the other. Even *The Washington Post* editorial of July 30, 1976 admitted that "this newspaper (*The Post*) which offers its news product for foreign sale, has an undeniable self-interest in nourishing an international climate in which the commercial opportunities for Western media are maintained." This admission amounts to an information interpretation of the imperial Gun-Boat, Open-Door diplomacies of the yesteryears and the 1970s B-52 diplomacy. Above all, powerful as they are, the multinationals of the informational industry know that the nonaligned countries have the Just Cause† on their side. But holders of the Just Cause can be

---

*See, *The New York Times* July 1, 19, and 22, and August 20, 1976; *Columbia Journalism Review* March–April, 1976; *Newsweek* September 6, 1976; *Sunday Telegraph* (London) reproduced in *Times of Ceylon Sunday Illustrated* August 8, 1976.

†For an understanding of the Just Cause as seen by the Vietnamese, see (Tran van Dinh, 1974).

defeated if they follow an ill-defined or reactionary direction (ideology), confused strategy and spontaneous tactics.

VIII

Broadly speaking, and in the communications field, the nonaligned countries are potentially very strong but are weak at the present time. Only by long and hard struggle can their weaknesses be eliminated. This is to say that the war against cultural imperialism cannot be won but by a protracted, nonviolent (only ideas will be killed) guerilla warfare. With all my humility and in full realization of the lethal power of the nonaligned countries' enemies, I offer these suggestions:

1. Clearly identify friends, allies, and enemies. Apparently, this seems not to be a very difficult task. In reality, it is the hardest: the enemies are within and without. The nonaligned movement's New Information Order's friends are of course, mostly among the nonaligned nations. In addition, they can count on the cooperation of black scholars in the U.S. Tony Brown, a black scholar on communications has stated (Congress of African Peoples, Atlanta, 1970, 1972) that the communications media in the United States

> have enslaved the Africanoid peoples on this continent much more effectively than the police, the army or any form of force currently available to the vested interests groups that own the United States. The psychological phenomenon of repetition compulsion has created among our people a vicious cycle of self-hate. Its manifestations are subtle yet damaging to our sense of worth without which freedom is impossible.

Mr. Brown's statement can be applied to many countries in the Third World. Nonaligned countries' allies are progressive writers, artists, thinkers, teachers, mass communications researchers, in the industrialized countries, particularly in the United States. The nonaligned's enemies are the multinationals (or transnationals) of the information (or consciousness) industry and their subsidiaries within the "Third World." Such an identification will result in a broad and solid united front, the essential condition for a protracted guerilla warfare.

2. Define the general direction (ideology): The main characteristics of this direction have been generally provided in various resolutions by Nonaligned Summit Meetings, in particular the 1973 Algiers and the 1976 Colombo Conferences. It can be found in the "masses line" and the "classes line" articulated by Amilcar Cabral (1972), in the "promotion of the growth of an organic culture . . . without a rejection per se of what is foreign" (Goonatilake, 1976), in the realization that "culture divorced from politics is forever and always a delusion" (Strickland, 1974). The principal slogans for that direction would be:

—Tradition and Revolution: tradition to mean historic continuity and revolution to mean the transformation of national and information structures along the "masses line" and the "classes line." (See Nguyen-Khac-Vien, 1974, and Tran von Dinh, 1975.)

—Self-reliance (national) and internationalism.

3. Develop proper strategies: the general strategy has been formalized in various Nonaligned Summit Conferences. Its details could be modified with the changing world situation, but it is imperative not to lose sight of the dialectical relationship between technology and ideology, between maximum and minimum programs.

4. Devise precise mechanisms (tactics) to:

—implement the Constitution of the Press Agencies Pool, approved by the 5th Colombo Summit Meeting of the Nonaligned Countries, as well as other relevant resolutions. In the course of the implementation, criticism and self-criticism in a spirit of comradeship should be practiced. Member nations of the nonalignment movement should not hesitate to raise most pertinent questions such as how some national information agencies are used to promote policies totally contrary to the spirit and the letter of nonalignment.

—begin at regional and national level a systematic and scientific study, based on the "masses line" and the "classes line" of the popular "traditional" communication media, such as oral literature, folklore, theater . . . in short to develop an unconventional (or guerilla) communication.* Such a study can be used also to analyze conventional (modern) communication (Tran van Dinh, 1976b).

—start an inventory, for exchange among nonaligned countries, programs which are being implemented separately in some countries, programs which in fact translated the basic concepts of nonaligned new information order (Lent, 1974).

The materialization of the last two points can be achieved by the urgent establishment of a special chair of nonalignment at the United Nations University and the development of similar studies at national universities and research centers in "Third World" countries. These proposals have been approved by both the 1973 Algiers and the 1976 Colombo Summits of Nonaligned Countries:

—make a survey of literature in the industrialized countries, which describes the imperialist designs of the information industry's multinationals. Translate the basic books into as many as possible languages of nonaligned countries. Prepare in national languages simplified booklets on mass communications.

—adopt the principles of centralization in theories, decentralization (or demo-

---

*I have myself begun this type of study (see Tran van Dinh, 1976a).

cratization) in practices. Reassess and reanalyze communications projects and programs on both national and regional levels.

—advise nonaligned countries on the use, misuse, effects, dangers of television. It is wise for countries which have not adopted TV as a mass communication medium not to do it until all conditions for a good use of TV are fulfilled.

REFERENCES

Afro-Asian Peoples' Solidarity Conference. (1958). "Afro-Asian Peoples' Solidarity Conference, Cairo, December 26, 1957–January 1, 1958." Foreign Languages Publishing House, Moscow.

Bunnel, F. P. (1964). "American Reactions to Indonesia's Role in the Belgrade Conference." Southeastern Asia Program, Cornell University, Ithaca, New York.

Cabral, A. (1972). (From a speech given at Lincoln University, Pennsylvania, October 15, 1972.)

Congress of African Peoples, Atlanta, 1970. (1972). "African Congress; A Documentary of the First Modern Pan-African Congress." William Morrow, New York.

Fagen, P. (1974). The media in Allende's Chile. *Journal of Communication 24* (Winter), 59–70.

Goonatilake, S. (1976). Culture: Decolonisation. *Ceylon Daily News* Aug. 16.

Ho-chi-Minh. (1970). "Ho Chi Minh: Selected Articles and Speeches." (J. Woddis, ed.). International Publishers, New York.

Kimche, E. (1973). "The Afro-Asian Movement: Ideology and Foreign Policy in the Third World." Israel University Presses, Jerusalem.

Lent, J. A. (1974). "Mass Media in the Developing World: Four Conundrums." (Paper presented at International Scientific Conference. "The Contribution of the Mass Media to the Development of Consciousness in a Changing World," Leipzig, German Democratic Republic, September 1974.)

Marks, J. (1976). Media in the Third World. *Washington Post* August 27.

Nguyen-khac-Vien. (1974). "Tradition and Revolution in Vietnam." Indochina Resource Center, Berkeley, California.

Possony, T., ed. (1966). "The Lenin Reader." Henry Regnery, Chicago, Illinois.

Schiller, H. I. (1969). "Mass Communications and American Empire." A. M. Kelley, New York.

Schiller, H. I. (1973). "The Mind Managers." Beacon Press, Boston, Massachusetts.

Schiller, H. I. (1976). "Communication and Cultural Domination." International Arts and Sciences Press, White Plains, New York.

Shayon, R. L. (1969). Sounding the alarm. *Saturday Review*, Aug. 16, p. 38.

Singham, A. W., and Tran van Dinh. (1976). "From Bandung to Columbo: Conferences of the Non-Aligned Countries, 1955–1975." Third Press Review, New York.

Strickland, W. (1974). Identity and Black struggle: Personal reflections. *In* "Education and Black Struggle: Notes from the Colonized World" (Institute of the Black World, ed.), pp. 137–143. Harvard Educational Review, Cambridge, Massachusetts. (Harvard Educational Review, Monograph No. 2.)

Tunis. Secretary of State for Information. (1976). (Document by the Tunisian Secretary of State for Information.) Tunis.

Tran van Dinh. (1974). The Vietnam people's army. *The Indochina Chronicle*, Berkeley, California, February 1976.

Tran van Dinh. (1975). Past national struggles and present socialist revolution in Vietnam. *Monthly Review 27* (October), 44–54.

Tran van Dinh. (1976a). A Buddhist–Taoist view of television. *World Buddhism*, April and May, 1976.

Tran van Dinh. (1976b). Ho chi Minh as communicator. *Journal of Communication 26* (Autumn), 142–147.

U.S. Senate. Select Committee to Study Governmental Operations with Respect to Intelligence Activities. (1976). "Final Report," (Book 1, April 26, 1976, pp. 179–203.) Government Printing Office, Washington, D.C.

Wright, R. (1956). "The Color Curtain: A Report on the Bandung Conference." World Publishing, New York.

Author/Subject Index